Reconsidering Cosmopolitanism and Forgiveness

Reframing the Boundaries: Thinking the Political

Series editors: Alison Assiter and Evert van der Zweerde

This series aims to mine the rich resources of philosophers in the 'continental' tradition for their contributions to thinking the political. It fills a gap in the literature by suggesting that the work of a wider range of philosophers than those normally associated with this sphere of work can be of relevance to the political.

Titles in the Series

Kierkegaard and the Matter of Philosophy, Michael O'Neill Burns

Arendt, Levinas and a Politics of Relationality, Anya Topolski

The Risk of Freedom: Ethics, Phenomenology and Politics in Jan Patocka, Francesco Tava, translated by Jane Ledlie

Nietzsche's Death of God and Italian Philosophy, Emilio Carlo Corriero, translated by Vanessa Di Stefano

Lotman's Cultural Semiotics and the Political, Andrey Makarychev and Alexandra Yatsyk

Axel Honneth: Reconceiving Social Philosophy, Dagmar Wilhelm

Creating Society as a Work of Art: Towards an Imaginative Logic of Action in Sartre's "Critique of Dialectical Reason," Austin Hayden Smidt

Ontologies of Sex: Philosophy in Sexual Politics, Zeynep Direk

Reconsidering Cosmopolitanism and Forgiveness: Arendt, Derrida and "Care for the World," Christopher Peys

Reconsidering Cosmopolitanism and Forgiveness

Arendt, Derrida, and "Care for the World"

Christopher Peys

ROWMAN & LITTLEFIELD
Lanham • Boulder • New York • London

Published by Rowman & Littlefield
An imprint of The Rowman & Littlefield Publishing Group, Inc.
4501 Forbes Boulevard, Suite 200, Lanham, Maryland 20706
www.rowman.com

6 Tinworth Street, London SE11 5AL, United Kingdom

Copyright © 2020 by Christopher Peys

All rights reserved. No part of this book may be reproduced in any form or by any electronic or mechanical means, including information storage and retrieval systems, without written permission from the publisher, except by a reviewer who may quote passages in a review.

British Library Cataloguing in Publication Information Available

Library of Congress Cataloging-in-Publication Data

Names: Peys, Christopher, author.
Title: Reconsidering cosmopolitanism and forgiveness : Arendt, Derrida, and "care for the world" / Christopher Peys.
Description: Lanham : Rowman & Littlefield, 2020. | Series: Reframing the boundaries : thinking the political | Includes bibliographical references and index.
Identifiers: LCCN 2020007910 (print) | LCCN 2020007911 (ebook) |
  ISBN 9781786615183 (cloth) | ISBN 9781786615190 (epub)
  ISBN 9781538148297 (pbk)
Subjects: LCSH: Derrida, Jacques. | Political science—Philosophy. | Arendt, Hannah, 1906-1975. | Caring. | Cosmopolitanism. | Forgiveness.
Classification: LCC B2430.D484 P55 2020 (print) | LCC B2430.D484 (ebook) |
  DDC 320.01—dc23
LC record available at https://lccn.loc.gov/2020007910
LC ebook record available at https://lccn.loc.gov/2020007911

Contents

Acknowledgments · vii

Introduction · ix
   "Nobody Cares Any Longer What the World Looks Like" · xiv
   Care and "Caring for the World" · xx
   Book Structure · xxv

1 Derrida: *On Cosmopolitanism and Forgiveness* · 1
   Derrida, Deconstruction, and "Undecidability" · 3
   Derrida: On Forgiveness · 7
   Derrida: On Cosmopolitanism · 16

2 Forgiveness and "Care for the World" · 37
   Vengeance and Forgiveness from an Arendtian Perspective · 41
   Vengeance, Forgiveness, and the *Vita Activa* · 47

3 Caring Cosmopolitanism: Worldly Stories and Narrative Voices · 75
   Care for the Self, Other, or the World? · 80
   Megan Phelps-Roper and a Caring Cosmopolitanism · 95

4 Caring in Time: Negotiating the Gap "between Past and Future" · 107
   Private, Cyclical Time and Public, Rectilinear Time · 112
   "Mind[ing] the Gap" in Time · 118
   Megan Phelps-Roper: Beginning Anew in the Abyss beyond the WBC · 131

Conclusion	143
Bibliography	149
Index	159
Author Information	165

Acknowledgments

I would like to express my profound gratitude, for their invaluable help, advice, guidance, and support at various stages of this project, to my colleagues and friends at the University of St Andrews. In particular, I would like to thank Natasha Saunders, Faye Donnelly, Anthony Lang, and Patrick Hayden. To Patrick, I owe a debt that I fear I cannot pay—his generosity of time, patience, and support throughout the entire process of this book's development cannot be overstated. I would also like to thank Graham Smith, at the University of Leeds, for his support of my work; this book is undoubtedly better as a consequence of his insightful commentary and encouragement. Thanks are also due to Alison Assiter, Evert van der Zweerde, Isobel Cowper-Coles, Frankie Mace, and Scarlet Furness for taking an interest in this book and helping to bring it to fruition at Rowman & Littlefield. The writing of this book would also not have been possible without the loving support of my friends and family. To the Peys clan, the Tates, and the Berrow family, I say thank you and send my love. And finally, I wish to thank my wife, Danielle. She has been a most patient, strong, and inspirational partner throughout every step of this book's production. Without her, I would be truly lost. Dani, *ti yw fy nghariad, fy ngoleuni, yr un sy'n fy nhywys drwy'r dyddiau disgleiriaf a'r nosweithiau tywyllaf.*

Introduction

In February 2017, just weeks after the American Presidential Inauguration brought into office a populist politician with a controversial social media presence, Megan Phelps-Roper stood on a stage in New York City and explained how Twitter allowed her to experience the "power of engaging the Other."[1] In the wake of Donald Trump's rise to power, an ascent characterized by his unconventional use of Twitter and his reliance upon misinformation disseminated through the internet, Phelps-Roper spoke of how this microblogging service played an instrumental role in her decision to dissociate herself from her family's fundamentalist organization: the Westboro Baptist Church (WBC). Describing the drawn-out process of leaving the WBC, an extremist organization that the Southern Poverty Law Center describes as "arguably the most obnoxious and rabid hate group in America,"[2] Phelps-Roper outlined how her encounters with strangers on Twitter helped her to see the world anew and to recognize the inconsistencies in her family's idiosyncratic reading of the Bible; the cruelty in their practice of celebrating human tragedy; and the brutality of picketing funerals.[3] It was within the public domain of Twitter that Phelps-Roper purports to have had discussions which—despite being heated—were characterized by a sense of curiosity and a spirit of care that gave rise to a form of civic friendship with people whom she once believed to be unclean, evil, and damned. That is, Phelps-Roper and her interlocutors on Twitter wove a worldly web of friendship, so to speak, through the repeated practice of acting caringly toward strangers online, putting into practice what might be described as a form of discursive hospitality: a welcoming of the (unknown) Other's voice into the public space provided by this social media platform. Moreover, the care shown to Phelps-Roper came in the form of forgiveness, a response to her past actions that not only allowed her to renew her once-hostile relationship with the world, but also to begin acting politically with people who would once have been the target of her vitriolic rebukes when she was a congregant of the WBC.

When contextualized within a broader framing of global affairs in today's digitally interconnected world, Phelps-Roper's story draws attention to the public significance of being hospitable to and engaging openly with the Other. Seen in this light, her narrative demonstrates how we might go about caring for the bonds of civic friendship that maintain the worldly realm in which the doing of politics can occur: "the political."[4] We find in Phelps-Roper's story a distinctive strain of cosmopolitan hospitality and forgiveness, both of which are practices that I contend are forms of public care capable of repairing, maintaining, and enhancing worldly, political relationships. In this book, I take her account as a reference point in the development of a world-centric, caring theory of political action. Phelps-Roper's experience is remarkable during a period in history when the fragile fabric of the political runs the risk of snapping entirely under the strain imposed upon it by the forces of world-ending alienation. Because Phelps-Roper's past political experiences effectively represent one extreme on the political spectrum in contemporary, global civil society, given that the WBC's radically intolerant ideology and belligerent forms of theological-political evangelism situate this group at the far end of the religious right, her narrative provides an opportunity to explore anew the ideas of cosmopolitan hospitality and forgiveness within the context of an example which showcases a form of civic enmity that directly inhibits the doing of democratic politics.

Though I draw upon Phelps-Roper's experience of political life at the fringes of society, and the story of how she disassociated herself from the WBC, my aim is to offer a political theory of the notions of forgiveness and cosmopolitanism. I focus on these two interrelated ideas—which are connected in terms of an underlying conceptual logic inherent to both—because it is my belief that they are forms of practice that can be enacted for the sake of the worldly realm of politics, whether that be the relational spaces of public action occurring in the phenomenological realm and/or those spheres of human affairs found in cyberspace. It is through cosmopolitanism and acts of forgiveness that we can (re)develop more just, inclusive spaces for the doing of politics in our global age.

In this book, I examine the ideas of cosmopolitanism and forgiveness through the prism of "care," a term that is used throughout the remainder of this text explicitly in reference to the work of Hannah Arendt (1906–1975) and—specifically—her notion of "care for the world."[5] As a means of rethinking the practices of forgiveness and cosmopolitanism, reframing them as forms of political action that "care for the world," this book also draws upon the work of Jacques Derrida (1930–2004). In particular, the deconstructive theory for which Derrida is so well known provides a valuable means of revealing the conceptual topography of the aporetic impasses that he contends are concealed within the notions of forgiveness and cosmopolitanism: the very boundaries that simultaneously constrain and constitute the undergirding logic of these two ideas. In today's digitally interconnected but politically polarized world, it is my belief that such boundaries should be tested and renegotiated precisely because it is through such modes of action that rifts within sociopolitical communities can be overcome and the worldly realm of public, political action can be (re)cultivated. But what are the consequences of rethinking such boundaries in terms of "care"? In what ways does this act of conceptual renegotiation reframe the political and alter the ethico-political landscape? How, then, to map out this terrain? Where Derrida's work helps us to identify the pitfalls and paradoxes inherent to the practices of forgiveness and cosmopolitanism, Arendt's corpus supplies the intellectual tools necessary to theorize an approach to the political that emphasizes the worldly significance of maintaining, repairing, and preserving the web of relationships that constitute and condition the public realm.

A twentieth-century thinker whose work is shaped not only by her training in philosophy but also by her lived experience as a Jewish woman exposed to the evils of Nazi totalitarianism, Arendt's theory of "the political" stands as a testament to the dark potentialities capable of being realized when the realm of human affairs falls into a worldless state of disarray and terror. Having been subjected to the harsh realities of being forced to flee the Nazis in 1933, an escape that rendered her stateless until 1951 (when she became a citizen of the United States), Arendt brings to her work an understanding of the vicissitudes and vulnerabilities of being without political rights and of existing as an outsider with no equal access to or standing in the world. Her experiences of totalitarianism and statelessness, coupled with her extensive knowledge of Western philosophic and political thought, provided her a unique perspective on the human condition, informing her fundamental belief in the need to think and act in terms of the "world," which—for her—corresponds to the "space constituted by the many" where "political activity" can be "performed."[6]

A key concept throughout her body of thought,[7] Arendt's notion of "world" is associated with her understanding of how "things"—both tangible and intangible—can be said to make up the public realm of the political. For her, the political—as a space of relations—is a "human artifact," one which is fabricated by "human hands" and that corresponds with the "affairs" that "go on among those who inhabit the man-made world together."[8] The "world" can be understood as a political community's publicly shared, "common home."[9] For Arendt, however, this "space for politics,"[10] or worldly sphere of political affairs, is a thoroughly fragile fabrication and a thingly entity ever in need of care, most especially during periods of history when (violent) conflict and/or pernicious social forces have made the public realm unfit for human habitation. When the public realm of the political is largely bereft of a kind of unifying "common sense" (sense that it is common to all), civic friendship, and—significantly for Arendt—any notable sense of *amor mundi* (or "love of the world"), there is a need to think anew about what it means to act caringly for the sake of the "world": for the "common home" shared by all who come to inhabit this "space for politics." In terms of conceptualizing care as an act that sustains and enhances humankind's "common home," then, it is to Arendt and her theory of the political that I turn in order to orient us toward a world-centric theory of public care. More specifically, I reconsider the acts of forgiving and cosmopolitan theory throughout this book in terms of Arendt's understanding of the human condition, in particular her theorization of political "action" and the notion of "care" which accompanies it. This, paired with a reconfigured, complementary form of cosmopolitan hospitality, derived from Derrida's work, paves the way for my own theory of cosmopolitanism, one which is noninstrumental, worldly, and ultimately cares for the political experience of freedom.

Derrida engages only infrequently with Arendt's body of thought, drawing upon her work in a 1993 essay entitled "History of the Lie: Prolegomena,"[11] as well as in his own reflections on cosmopolitanism and forgiveness.[12] Arendt, in turn, does not discuss Derrida's work at all. This is unsurprising given that he was at the beginning of his academic career, and largely unconcerned with matters of politics in the latter years of Arendt's life. This being said, the limited academic exchange between Derrida and Arendt pales into insignificance when taking into consideration the possibilities presented to scholars by a concomitant examination of their respective reflections on the Western canon of philosophic and political thought. There are many reasons to read these two thinkers together, not least because they—as Samir Haddad has pointed out—"share much in their personal and intellectual biographies [. . .] and both constantly worked through an intense engagement with the philosophical tradition [. . .] always referring back to traditional texts with a view to challenging and transforming received interpretations."[13] Not unlike Haddad, as well as numerous other scholars who have placed these two prominent, twentieth-century European thinkers in dialogue with one another,[14] I engage with the work of both Arendt and Derrida because I believe that in doing so, new conceptual pathways for thinking about "the political" are revealed. Although I will not be comparing and contrasting their work, nor will I be placing them in conversation with one another, so to speak, I will instead be reading them alongside one another as a means of reconsidering cosmopolitanism and forgiveness. More specifically, I contend that new understandings of what it means to care for the public realm are unearthed by using Arendt's body of thought to supplement that of Derrida's work.

In a conceptual maneuver unique to this book, I provide an Arendtian-inspired response to the paradoxes that can be identified through a Derridean deconstruction of the notions of cosmopolitanism and forgiveness, in order to understand more fully how liberal, democratic communities might go about caring for the world in times of extreme polarization, alienation, and/or (violent) conflict. I use Arendt and Derrida's work to do exactly as Haddad suggests: to challenge and transform their respective interpretations of the political tradition as a means of arriving at a world-centric theory of public care. Recalibrating Arendt's understanding of the human condition, as well as building upon a Derrida's work on the notions of forgiveness and cosmopolitan hospitality, I present a theory of a "caring forgiveness" and a "caring cosmopolitanism." A caring forgiveness and a caring cosmopolitanism are world-centric theories of political action that provide an alternative means by which to consider how the act of forgiving and of welcoming the (unknown) Other's voice are closely interrelated forms of political practice. Much theorizing has been done on both forgiveness and cosmopolitanism, but little research in the field of political theory, broadly defined, treats these two ideas together, least of all from the perspective of "care."[15] Here, I do so using Arendt's notion of "care for the world" as a means of demonstrating how the faculty of forgiving and practices of cosmopolitan hospitality are two interrelated forms of political action that ultimately care for the powerful experience of human freedom: the power to begin new courses of political action with a plurality of other people in the world.

When deconstructed from a Derridean perspective, the paradoxical conceptual logic inherent to the notions of forgiveness and cosmopolitanism are exposed in such a manner that the ethico-political (im)possibilities of putting into practice each of these two ideas can be examined directly. A deconstructive approach, which Simon Critchley and Richard Kearney describe as a type of "conceptual genealogy"[16] in their joint preface to Derrida's *On Cosmopolitanism and Forgiveness* (2001), uncovers the concealed, aporetic underpinnings of the logic of forgiving and welcoming the (unknown) Other. Finding that the possibility of practicing forgiveness and cosmopolitanism is rooted in the impossibility of experiencing each of these two ideas in "pure," unconditional terms,[17] Derrida highlights that humankind's ability to forgive and act hospitably toward strangers is fundamentally a matter of thinking, as well as acting, at and between the boundaries of human (im)possibility. In an effort to "re-world" these two notions, or to theorize them in terms of what Ella Myers describes as a "worldly ethics,"[18] I investigate the conceptual dynamics revealed by a Derridean deconstruction through Arendt's conceptualization of the human condition and her understanding of the "world." I therefore use her distinctive understanding of "the political" to theorize a worldly, caring theory of democratic *praxis*. This is not to say that Arendt's body of thought allows scholars of global politics to transcend entirely the aporetic impasses identified by Derrida's work, but that an Arendtian-inspired response to the paradoxes associated with a Derridean deconstruction of forgiveness and cosmopolitanism allows these two notions to be reconceptualized as worldly, political forms of public care. Accordingly, in this book, I investigate the preternatural nature of Derrida's conceptualization of forgiveness and cosmopolitanism, doing so in order to frame my own examination of these ideas as two thoroughly human forms of public, political action that "care for the world."

1. "NOBODY CARES ANY LONGER WHAT THE WORLD LOOKS LIKE"

A Kansas-based, reformed Calvinist church, one which was founded by Fred Phelps—Phelps-Roper's grandfather—in 1955, the WBC first gained international notoriety for its extreme religious fundamentalism and far-right, political activism in the early 1990s.[19] Making manifest their "hyper-Calvinist" beliefs through their distinctive, prejudicial brand of public ministry,[20] members of the WBC have—since Fred Phelps first began speaking out against homosexuality in 1991—directed the full force of their evangelical energies on what Phelps-Roper's mother, Shirley Phelps, once described as the "militant sodomite agenda."[21] According to Rebecca Barrett-Fox, whose book—*God Hates: Westboro Baptist Church, American Nationalism, and the Religious Right* (2016)—places the WBC's message within the broader context of the religious far-right in the United States, this church not only preaches that "God hates the nonelect," and thus that the "message of salvation should not be offered to the nonelect,"[22] but also that God is "punishing America for its tolerance of homosexuality."[23] It is in terms of this extreme system of beliefs that the WBC understands life in America: their vociferous attacks on members of the LGBTQ community—as well as against Jews, Muslims, other Christian denominations, American soldiers, and politicians—stemming from their contemptuous approach to the so-called nonelect. The WBC congregation regularly pickets the funerals of soldiers killed in combat, as well as those of gay men who have died from AIDS, using explicit, colorful protest signs which have in the past included statements such as: "Thank God for Dead Soldiers"; "Fags Doom Nations"; "9–11 Gift from God"; "Your Rabbi is a Whore"; and "God Hates the World." Such protests and proclamations are a part of the WBC's daily operations, and Phelps-Roper describes how—at five years old—she "joined" her "family on the picket line for the first time," with her "tiny fists clutching a sign" that she "couldn't read yet: 'Gays are Worthy of Death.'"[24] Guided by their fundamentalist religious beliefs, the WBC exhibits a staunchly dogmatic worldview, one which is not only radically intolerant of persons and peoples who fail to conform to their organization's narrow, prejudicial interpretation of the Bible, but also one that is defined by its rigid "us" versus "them" understanding of societal relations.

This view of the world shapes the entirety of the WBC's ideological framework, and it informs the sense of inimicality that characterizes this small but vocal community of Americans. Discussing the views of her former church in a 2015 interview, Phelps-Roper stated that the WBC fostered an in-group/out-group mindset, one that serves as the frame through which this organization sees the world:

> It [was] so strong—"us" versus "them." There [was] no middle ground. That was something again that was also drummed into us. You are either a Jacob or an Esau [. . .] they were twins in the scriptures, and God loved Jacob and hated Esau. This was before they were even born, God loved Jacob and hated Esau, and so, you're either a Jacob or an Esau, and if you are a Jacob, you want nothing to do with the world. The Book of John talks about [how] friendship with the world is enmity with God. "Love not the world, neither the things that are in the world."[25] So, it was very important, this "us"/"them" [. . .] and that definitely solidified this identity.[26]

A self-proclaimed "Jacob," the WBC views itself as the community of faith chosen by God to enter into the Kingdom of Heaven, and that all those who do not share their perspective are akin to an "Esau": the nonelect progenitor of Israel's early biblical enemy, Edom.[27] In her recent book, *Unfollow: A Journey from Hatred to Hope, Leaving the Westboro Baptist Church* (2019), Phelps-Roper describes her family's conflictual relationship with the world as "the quarrel of the covenant," which is to say, the "never-ending struggle of the good guys against the bad," or the "eternal conflict between the righteous and the wicked."[28] Channeling a thoroughly Schmittian understanding of "the political," whereby the "specific political distinction to which political actions and motives can be reduced is that between friend and enemy,"[29] the WBC's self-identification as a "Jacob" puts them at odds with the other peoples of the world: enemies with whom "friendship" is impossible and the possibilities of cultivating a commonly held, political "middle ground" are limited. Pitted against all who exist beyond the theological confines of their church, then, the members of the WBC bring to life an ideological disdain for the world, as well as the "things" in it, and they embody a distinctly anti-world worldview that alienates them from the people who comprise the broader sociopolitical community within which they live, move, and act.

In this sense, when Phelps-Roper speaks about her life as a "Jacob," as well as the period during which she went about leaving the WBC and becoming an "Esau," it is evident that her personal experience of cultivating a renewed relationship with those persons and peoples whom she once treated with contempt required her to overcome an extreme state of alienation from the "world." Though it is difficult to pinpoint precisely how Phelps-Roper and the members of her former church define their usage of the term "world," a word which can be interpreted in an assortment of different ways depending on the biblical text and translation used, I focus here specifically on how this expression pertains to "the political," thereby employing it in notably Arendtian terms as that which corresponds to the "space for politics." Given the extent to which the Westboro Baptists' ideology and activism maintain a rigid us/them conceptualization of "the political," Phelps-Roper's story of forsaking her family and of starting anew *within* the community of "Edom," therefore, offers an example of what it might mean to (re)cultivate the world shared with the (unknown) Other when sociopolitical tensions and political polarization have engendered seemingly intractable states of civic worldlessness. Phelps-Roper's narrative offers but a single experience of someone who has attempted to renew their relationship with the people of the world and to reconcile herself to those whom she had once worked so hard to rebuke, reject, and remain at odds with as a congregant of the WBC. Her story is nevertheless an intriguing account of how the practices of forgiveness and cosmopolitan hospitality care for the world during times of sociopolitical darkness and when states of worldlessness take shape within civic communities.

While the historical context within which Phelps-Roper lives, moves, and acts differs from that of Arendt's lifetime, there is, within an Arendtian register of thought, a theory of politics that is fundamentally concerned with the maintenance, reparation, and preservation of "the political" during "dark times."[30] For Arendt, these are those periods of human history when the public realm of human affairs has fallen into a worldless state of intractable sociopolitical alienation, violence, and/or terror. The threat to the world posed in dark times is, as she writes, "the growth of worldlessness, the withering away of everything *between* [people], [which] can also be described as the spread of the desert."[31] As in early twentieth-century Germany, the danger that exists in deserted spaces of such vast nothingness is "that there are sandstorms in the desert," which "can whip up a movement of their own."[32] Although the "sandstorms" to which Arendt refers are those of the totalitarian movements she once found herself caught up within, the salience of her observations have broader significance. Equating to a loss of shared experiences had between people, the "growth of worldlessness"—or development of states of "world alienation"[33]—is an ever-present hazard whenever and wherever a plurality of people live and act within sociopolitical communities. Throughout her corpus, Arendt underscores that the worldliness of the public, political realm is precarious, ever in need of care, and perpetually under threat precisely because "dark times"—as she writes—"are not only not new, they are no rarity in history."[34] In this sense, when Arendt tells Günter Gaus—during a 1965 interview for German television—that "nobody cares what the world looks like,"[35] she is expressing her concern for the public realm of "the political," which, in her view, has grown "dark" in the modern age.

In emphasizing that there is a perpetual need to care for worldly spaces within which people can speak and act freely together, Arendt's political theorizing can be interpreted as a call to action that flows from her broader critique of contemporary civil society: that humankind has lost its feeling for, love of, and capacity to act politically within the public realm. That is, Arendt's pointed remark to Gaus stems from her deep-seated concern for public life and the overall mission of her work, which George Kateb suggests "should be recognized as the recovery of the idea of political action, in a culture which [. . .] has lost the practice of it, and in which almost all philosophy is united, if in nothing else, in denying intrinsic value to it."[36] More specifically, Arendt sought to re-invigorate "the political" in an historical age when worldlessness had permeated civil society. While the Westboro Baptists' anti-world worldview offers an example of a radical rejection of worldly affairs, a hyperbolic expression of their fundamentalist belief in what Arendt would describe as the "uncompromising otherworldliness of the Christian faith,"[37] their approach to the world is in alignment with the ways in which people throughout history—scholars and laypersons alike—have tended to privilege the *vita contemplativa* and/or the *vita spiritualis* over the various activities that comprise the *vita activa*. In other words, the Arendtian criticism that humankind has largely neglected to "care for the world" strikes a chord when thinking about the ways in which members of the WBC have devoted themselves entirely to the task of securing—at least according to their faith—their respective places in the Kingdom of Heaven. Arendt's conceptualization of the "world" demands that a renewed attention be paid to the very environment that supports people as public, political beings: the "world" and the "things" of the world that provide the conditions of existence for a thoroughly human life.[38]

Extending Arendt's metaphor of the "desert," the conditions that give rise to the "growth of worldlessness and the withering away of everything between people" are not established during a single summer heatwave. Rather, the "desert" can be said to form through a gradual process of desertification, occurring over an extended period of time—maybe even the *longue durée*—and as a plurality of factors crystallize in such a manner that a state of worldlessness comes to condition the sociopolitical relations within civic communities. Here, it is worth emphasizing that Arendt's account of totalitarianism is not, as she writes in a response to Eric Voegelin's critique of *The Origins of Totalitarianism* (1951), "a history of totalitarianism but an analysis in terms of history [. . .] [it] does not deal with the 'origins' of totalitarianism—as its title unfortunately claims—but gives a historical account of the elements which crystallized into totalitarianism."[39] Rejecting the idea that it is possible to trace totalitarianism's chain of causality to a definitive, singular source, Arendt underscores that the totalitarian "sandstorms" of the twentieth century formed gradually and in the wake of what she describes as the break in the Western tradition: with the severance of the "discursive construct of beliefs and conventions based on the presumption of historical continuity in the transmission of inherited patterns across generations."[40] According to Arendt, the break in the Western tradition—though having been completed in the twentieth century with the catastrophic events of the World War I and World War II—took place incrementally as the authority-claiming systems and structures of belief that had long-maintained order in the West eroded: as processes of secularization intensified following the Protestant Reformation; as mass society took shape with the coming of the Industrial Revolution; and as the power of nation-states overcame established forms of political, legal, and moral order.[41] For her, the significance of this rupture—which saw the three-strand, rope-like line of continuity formed by the "trinity" of religion, authority, and tradition cut completely—cannot be overstated because it meant that it was no longer possible to rely on the ideas, beliefs, and mores of the past in the task of understanding, addressing, and overcoming the problems posed by contemporary life.

It is, arguably, neither inherently good nor bad that the tradition has been cut, though new questions about how to proceed in a life of uncertainty are raised when the stability offered by traditional practices, culture, and faith are lost. That is, while we have—as Arendt observes—"the great chance to look upon the past with eyes undistracted by any tradition,"[42] our positions in the world have been fundamentally destabilized, in the sense that the loss of tradition and traditional systems of authority is "tantamount to the loss of the groundwork of the world."[43] Not unlike the metaphorical "fiddler on the roof," who plays for the sake of tradition, people living in the wake of the break in the tradition must—to borrow the words of Tevye, the protagonist of the 1971 film of the same name—try to "scratch out a pleasant, simple tune without breaking [their] neck."[44] But what happens when there is no longer any roof for the fiddler to stand on, no platform upon which to play his song? What does it mean, in other words, to stand one's ground in a world which is without grounds, doing so—moreover—in a manner that allows one to continue playing a "pleasant, simple tune"?

Adamant that the break in the tradition "does not entail [. . .] the loss of the human capacity for building, preserving, and caring for a world,"[45] Arendt recognizes the possibility of acting caringly for the public realm of "the political." That said, the voided nature of the past has left those wishing to understand and/or practice care publicly wondering what exactly they should be caring for, as well as how they might go about doing so in "dark times." What, in particular, are people doing when they act caringly within and for the sake of the public realm of "the political"? In what ways can acts of public, political care be said to counteract the forms of civic alienation and enmity that give rise to worldlessness, to the withering away and tearing apart of the very fabric that maintains the "space for politics"? How, even, can "care"—a seemingly conservative notion—be understood when, as Arendt writes in the preface of *The Origins of Totalitarianism*, "we can no longer afford to take that which is good in the past and simply call it our heritage"?[46] This is, perhaps, the challenge of our time: to care for the world when it is no longer clear what it means to care; no longer apparent why we should care at all; and no longer possible or desirable to suggest that there is any singular, ideal means of caring for our "common home." It is certainly a complicated task, and it is difficult to know where to begin and how to conceptualize care as a public, political form of practice when "nobody cares any longer what the world looks like" and when the traditional "groundwork of the world" has been pulled from beneath our feet.

In addition to identifying what might be described as a crisis in care, which is a plight related to and not unlike the "crisis of culture" that Arendt first wrote about in the early 1960s, she also provides her readers with a means of beginning to think and act caringly for the sake of world *sans* the support supplied by the "groundwork" of the tradition. She does so by theorizing a means of re-engaging with the past and retrieving those ideas, understandings, and practices that might aid us in our present struggles, in the fight to ward off the forces of civic alienation capable of tearing the world asunder. Not only does the approach outlined by Arendt provide a means of selectively and judiciously drawing from history aspects of the past that might be of benefit in today's world, it is also a means of reaching back in time that is commensurable with Derrida's efforts to read the "text" deconstructively, which—for him—constitutes the Western canon of philosophy and politics. This "text" is, in his view, a sort of inheritance, *le héritage*, or as he explains: "the heritage, too, is a 'text,' in the broad but precise sense I give to this word."[47] It "implies not only a reaffirmation and a double injunction, but at every moment, in a different context, a filtering, a choice, a strategy."[48] The person presented with this decision, the "heir," is "not only someone who receives, he or she is someone who chooses, and who takes the risk of deciding."[49] Though more is said about Derrida's approach to the "text" in the subsequent chapter, where I examine in greater detail his deconstructions of cosmopolitanism and forgiveness, it is in terms of his reading of *le héritage* that it becomes possible to investigate ideas in such a manner that their particular legacies, undergirding logics, and underlying arrangements of power can be revealed, reconsidered, and innovatively reconstrued. This is not to say that Arendt and Derrida agree entirely about how the tradition should be understood; they do not, with the former identifying the break in the tradition as an "accomplished fact,"[50] while the latter sees no such rupture at all. In locating a conceptual common ground between Arendt and Derrida, however, I bring together their respective readings of the Western philosophic and political canon as a means of re-theorizing cosmopolitanism and forgiveness.

Drawing upon a different metaphor, one which serves as a starting point for reconsidering what can be done in a world where anything is possible, Arendt—echoing Walter Benjamin—presents the image of a pearl diver. This is someone who "descends to the bottom of the sea, not to excavate the bottom and bring it to light but to pry loose the rich and the strange, the pearls and the coral in the depths, and to carry them to the surface."[51] Navigating the dark "depths of the past," represented by the sea, the diver must carefully select the thoughts and ideas that have "crystallized" into something valuable: the pearls and pieces of coral that "remain immune to the elements."[52] The diver does so with the "conviction" that although "the living" are "subject to the ruin of time, the process of decay is at the same time a process of crystallization," allowing certain thoughts and ideas to be retrieved and admired while others are left at the bottom of the sea.[53] In my efforts to think anew about the "world" and what it means to care for the worldly realm of "the political," I consider the notions of cosmopolitanism and forgiveness as two "pearls," two treasures worth salvaging from the ravages of the past, presenting them—as in bringing them into the present—as valuable forms of public action.

2. CARE AND "CARING FOR THE WORLD"

It is in the first chapter of this book that I "resuscitate"—to borrow Arendt's Benjaminian-inspired usage of the word—the notions of cosmopolitanism and forgiveness, doing so specifically with the help of Derrida and what might be described as his own deconstructive style of "pearl" diving. In the remainder of this section, however, I briefly consider the notion of "care" itself, an idea and form of practice which holds a privileged place in Arendt's body of thought. As a means of framing this book's Arendtian understanding of public care, it is especially necessary here to conceptualize care within the Continental vein of philosophic and political thought from which both Arendt and Derrida's thinking emerged. Specifically, there is a need to highlight how an Arendtian conceptualization of care and "caring for the world" is formed in contrast to the notion of *Sorge*—German for "care"—found at the core of Martin Heidegger's phenomenology.

Well known for his distinctive approach to the study of Being, and infamous for his affiliations with the Nazi party, as rector of the University of Freiburg between 1933 and 1934, Heidegger is one of the most prominent—though thoroughly controversial—philosophic figures of the twentieth century. While it is difficult to separate his overwhelming influence on Continental thought from the controversy that surrounds him, his impact on both Arendt and Derrida should not be overlooked. It is well documented that Heidegger was once Arendt's teacher, briefly her lover, and someone to whom she turned throughout her life. For her, his work was, in varying degrees, a source of intellectual inspiration and yet, at other times, dangerous and abhorrent in its presentation of certain Nazi tendencies. In spite of this, Arendt's association with Heidegger is often used as a means of attempting to discredit her work.[54] Such harsh critique, verging on condemnation (though unique in the more personal nature of its attack in Arendt's case, owing to their intimate relationship), did not touch her alone. The work of thinkers from across the Humanities has been similarly criticized, culminating in the so-called Heidegger Affair in France during the 1980s. Derrida, too, found himself under scrutiny and deeply embroiled in this controversy, specifically as a result of the ways in which, by his own admission, he had "received a visible inheritance" from Heideggerian philosophy, though he nevertheless "never really ceased posing many [...] very serious, central questions," doing so "always with a radical disquiet, restless and bottomless."[55]

Turning briefly to Heidegger's philosophy of Being (as *Dasein*), then, I wish to highlight here how this twentieth-century thinker conceptualized an understanding of *Sorge* that my Arendtian-inspired, Derridean-informed notion of public, political care ultimately calls into question. Where a Heideggerian understanding of *Sorge* is futural and self-centric, my theory of care is conditioned by natality and is dedicated to the maintenance, preservation, and development of the public realm: the worldly "space for politics" shared with a plurality of other people. While other schools of philosophic thought also place "care" at the center of their conceptual universe, such as—for example—the field of feminist relational moral theorizing known as the Ethics of Care,[56] *Sorge* is central to Heidegger's ontology and his distinctive attempt to answer the question: what is the meaning of Being as such?

Responding to a philosophic question he believed had been forgotten throughout the history of Western metaphysics (roughly since Plato), Heidegger developed—most notably in *Being and Time* (1927)—a phenomenological account of human existence, in which the ontological structure of Being is formed in terms of *Sorge*. Not simply a broad category of interrelated forms of human activity, *Sorge*, as Arendt acknowledges in her commentary of Heidegger's work, is the "basic element" that "underlies all the daily care-taking in the world."[57] Naming the condition after a phenomenon that it facilitates, Heidegger maintains that "care" (as *Sorge*) signifies the "way the present appears to us on the basis of a past that we reimagine according to a future that we intend."[58] That is, as Joshua Broggi observes, *Sorge* is the "threefold structure that allows people to care about anything at all," whereby "'care' is actually the background condition for a variety of cases of caring," even though "there might not be anything especially caring-like about the *care* which makes every-day caring possible."[59] From Heidegger's perspective, then, to care about anything in particular is first to *care* about the general state of one's beingness in the world.

Concerned with the temporal conditions of human life, Heidegger demonstrated that it is in terms of time that the meaning of *Dasein* can be found, since people experience their existence temporally in the pre-ontological mode of *Sorge*. If Being is associated with human temporality, then, for Heidegger, people experience their facticity as beings thrown into the world, and he illustrates how they can be said to realize their unique potential as individuated members of the human community. *Sorge* is a sense of care, or rather, a fundamental awareness of one's own finite existence that informs what it means for a person to be a unique human being. "To be, or not to be," really is "the question," though it is Heidegger's response to this query that I contend problematically emphasizes the lonely, self-reflective experience of freedom that he associates with mortality—"when we have shuffled off this mortal coil."[60]

The distinctive essence of a person, *Dasein*—a word historically derived from *Dass-sein*, or the "that-it-is" of a being[61]—is that which Heidegger associates with the "who"-ness of a person: the meaning of Being is *who* you are. In Arendt's words, the "Who of *Dasein*" is the "Self," with "the term 'Self' we answer the question of the Who of *Dasein*."[62] This is something that is ultimately tied to the notion of mortality and the knowledge that one's own death is certain: "only in death, which will take him from the world, does man have the certainty of being himself."[63] Understood in these terms, the ontological structure of *Dasein* is both temporal and temporalizing in the sense that one's life becomes a meaningful totality through an act of projecting one's self toward that which is entirely one's own: death. Through what Heidegger describes as "being-towards-death," the "who" of a person is revealed. By "being-in-the-world" futurally, aware of and concerned with death, *Dasein* can "find itself [. . .] be 'shown' to itself in its possible authenticity."[64] Though "*Dasein* is already a potentiality-for-Being-its-Self," Heidegger maintains that there is a need to have this "potentiality attested," doing so in such a manner that "when one has an understanding of Being-towards-death—towards death as one's *ownmost* possibility—one's potentiality-for-Being becomes authentic and wholly transparent."[65] By projecting one's self toward death, that is, one can come to view one's life as a complete, unified whole, or as a life that *is now*—as in presently—capable of being understood and made meaningful in terms of a past which is potentially yet to come. *Dasein* is thus "its past, it is its possibility in running ahead to this past [and] in this running ahead [one is] authentically time, [one has] time."[66] It is in terms of this having of time—of being able to experience in the eye of one's mind one's lived existence as a totality—that *Dasein* can be said to concern itself with itself, self-reflectively establishing a sense of concern, or care (*Sorge*), for its Self as a finite being with an ever-diminishing amount of time left on Earth.

It is in the face of the possibility of one's ultimate end—the terminal point at which all people are confronted with the nothingness of the unknown before them—that one comes to *care* about "Being-in-the-world," with the accompanying sense of anxiety, angst, apprehensiveness, concern, etc. associated with having limited time on Earth coming to condition how the meaning of *Dasein* is disclosed to itself. "Who" someone is and how this sense of Self is revealed is thus conditioned by *Sorge*, which is felt in the face of a death that is unavoidable. It is in terms of this "anxiety" that existence is experienced and that time can be made meaningful. Because *Sorge* is ontologically prior to the phenomena and practices of care that it facilitates, Heidegger suggests that the meaning of *Dasein* is to be found in care, whereby the essence of Being can be accessed with the structure of care that informs humankind's entire experience of "Being-in-the-world."

Though Heidegger also theorizes the notion of "Being-with-others," which forms a significant part of his understanding of "being-in-the-world," I must underscore here that his phenomenology is rooted in a mode of being that is fundamentally "for-the-sake-of-itself."[67] This is a conceptualization of care which is self-centric: "*Dasein* exists for the sake of a potentiality-for-Being of itself."[68] According to Arendt, the "nature" of Heidegger's "*Dasein* is not that it simply *is* but, rather, that in its being its primary concern [or care] is its being itself," and thus that "care-taking has a genuinely self-reflective character."[69] This is not to say that the Heideggerian approach is hedonistic or that Heidegger's philosophy provides the conceptual framework for an ethic of egoism. Rather, my point is that *Sorge* is engendered in reference to one's self and one's death. For Arendt, it is this aspect of Heidegger's "death-driven phenomenology"[70]—this self-reflective form of existing "for-the-sake-of" one's "ownmost" potentiality—that she directly challenges when outlining her own understanding of the human condition.

A Heideggerian, futurally focused conceptualization of "being-toward-death" is directly at odds with Arendt's understanding of human existence, which is ontologically rooted in "natality—that is—the fact that [all people] have entered the world through birth."[71] Although the differences between Heidegger and Arendt's work are considered more fully in subsequent chapters, it is important to emphasize here that an Arendtian conceptualization of care is world-centric, and *Dasein* is disclosed in the world among a plurality of people during the doing of political action. Thus, where Heidegger thinks about care in self-reflective terms and in *Dasein*'s relation to death, Arendt conceptualizes care as a worldly form of practice and Being as that which is disclosed publicly when one speaks and acts with one's fellow beings. Commenting on Arendt's doctoral dissertation entitled, *Love and Saint Augustine*, in which Arendt distances herself from Heidegger's phenomenology for the first time, Joanna Scott and Judith Stark highlight how "Arendt proposes an alternative definition of care [. . .] central to its meaning is the possibility of 'reconstituting' relationships through friendship, forgiveness, and social bonding."[72] Building upon this conceptual foundation, I elaborate upon this Arendtian notion of care—arguably a type of "'miracle' possible despite death"[73]—in order to develop my theory of a caring cosmopolitanism and forgiveness. My work draws out the notion of care that Arendt alludes to throughout her corpus: that it is important to "care for the world," as it is in the world that people—as she writes—"show *who* they are, reveal actively their unique personal identity."[74] For Arendt, the answer to the Heideggerian question, "Who is *Dasein*?," is revealed in the "world" and thus there is a need to care for spaces where worldly interactions can occur between people.

Interwoven throughout her body of thought, Arendt's notion of care can be understood in reference to other ideas, such as—for example—the idea of "culture." Indeed, in Arendt's conceptualization of "culture," one can recognize the outlines of an Arendtian understanding of care:

> Culture, word and concept, is Roman in origin. The word "culture" derives from *colere*—to cultivate, to dwell, *to take care, to tend and preserve*—and it relates primarily to the intercourse of man with nature in the sense of cultivating and tending nature until it becomes fit for human habitation.[75]

Arendt's theorization of "culture" provides an insightful commentary upon links between culture and politics, yet I take from this passage only her conceptualization of "care," which she relates to the notion of tending to and preserving the natural world. While her etymological exegesis of the word "culture" is associated with the natural world, or the earthly home that all creatures inhabit, this conceptualization is equally pertinent in terms of the non-natural, fabricated world(s) produced by people: the "space for politics." This is an aspect of Arendt's work that is examined throughout the remainder of this book. It is necessary here, however, to recognize that the "world" can be understood as a type of public dwelling place where a plurality of people can appear and act together, which—if adequately tended to or preserved—can become a public space fit for human habitation: a "common home"[76] for the people of a given sociopolitical community. Whereas a Heideggerian conceptualization suggests that—as Arendt observes about Heidegger's work—the "fundamental fear of death is reflected [in] not-being-at-home in the world,"[77] which is the state of isolation that permits *Dasein* to be fully itself, an Arendtian account of care focuses on tending to and preserving this "common home."

Focused on plurality and natality, Arendt maintains that—in contrast to Heidegger's conceptualization of *Sorge*—care ought to be rooted in a civic-minded form of "love for the world" (*amor mundi*). In other words, where Heidegger's self-reflective, "death-driven" notion of *Sorge* is the "background condition for a variety of cases of caring," Arendt's conceptualization of care—specifically the one that she invokes when writing about "the political"—is rooted in a world-centric form of civic *caritas* that Elisabeth Young-Bruehl suggests is understood as a love that "unites self and others."[78] This is a non-erotic, non-agapic notion of love, one which is associated with the joy of being with and sharing the public realm with other people. These are individuals Arendt describes in terms of an Aristotelian notion of *philia politike*, whereby those with whom we must share the public realm of the political are understood as "civic friends" to be respected as people with equal standing in the "world."[79] Caring for the world is thus not driven by a form of existential "anxiety" but by the love of acting publicly with one's civic friends and of experiencing that which can only be manifested in the political when a plurality of distinct but equal people act in concert: freedom. Differentiating her work from that of Heidegger's, then, Arendt claims that "care" should be practiced not out of concern for one's death but, rather, in the spirit of *amor mundi* and a sense of gratitude for the possibility of freely beginning new courses of public action with other people in the "space for politics." It is in these terms—*amor mundi*, plurality, and natality—that I develop my understanding of a caring forgiveness and cosmopolitanism throughout this book, "resuscitating" and reconsidering two ancient ideas from the perspective that there is a pressing need to think and act politically not simply for the sake of the Self but for the sake of the "world," where all people can experience freedom and consequently where power can be re-engendered.

3. BOOK STRUCTURE

The first chapter of this book examines the ideas of forgiveness and cosmopolitanism as they are found in Derrida's work. He does not conceptualize these two ideas in relation to the notion of "care" nor does he assume an Arendtian conceptualization of "care for the world." With his genealogical practice of deconstruction, however, Derrida cuts to the conceptual core of both the notions of forgiveness and cosmopolitanism, revealing the problems, pitfalls, and paradoxes inherent to the underlying logics of these two ideas. By identifying and isolating the issues and aporetic underpinnings which undergird these two concepts, his work effectively locates the boundaries inherent to the concepts of forgiveness and cosmopolitanism; these are the conceptual limits that this book seeks to rethink politically in terms of Arendt's world-centric understanding of public care.

Against the theoretical backdrop provided by Derrida's deconstruction of forgiveness, the second chapter of this book conceptualizes the act of forgiving as it is found in Arendt's body of thought, in order to begin addressing the paradoxes uncovered by a Derridean approach. Returning to the Arendtian form of "care for the word" which was introduced in the opening pages of this book, this chapter theorizes a world-centric, "caring forgiveness" devoted to the maintenance, reparation, and preservation of the human relationships that comprise the public realm of the political. Whereas chapter one reveals the conceptual boundaries identified by a Derridean deconstruction of forgiveness, this chapter employs Arendt's body of thought to confront the aporetic, binary relationships that give rise to the undecidability of (un)forgivable transgressions, the (un)conditionality of enacting forgiveness, and to demonstrate how a "pure" practice of forgiveness demands a form of power which is simultaneously unconditional and without sovereignty. Although Arendt does not explore forgiveness in terms of a Derridean deconstruction, I contend that it is with her body of thought, and through the prism of public care, that it becomes possible to consider these paradoxes anew, effectively *re*-thinking the unthinkable—at least as it pertains to the act of forgiving.

In the third chapter of this book, cosmopolitanism is considered in terms of an Arendtian conceptualization of care and a Derridean understanding of cosmopolitan hospitality. Appropriating aspects of Arendt's understanding of political action, and Derrida's conceptualization of universal, cosmopolitan hospitality, I construct a world-centric theory of radically welcoming the narrative voice of the (unknown) Other: a caring cosmopolitanism. A caring cosmopolitanism is an ethico-political form of cosmopolitan theory guided by the idea of caring for the worldly space of political action that emerges when a plurality of people speak and act together in the public realm. More specifically, this Arendtian-inspired conception of cosmopolitanism is concerned with the narrative nature of the political interactions that occur in these public spaces. In this sense, cosmopolitan care refers to a form of public practice that cares for the storied realm of political action. This discussion illustrates how caring for the world can be understood in terms of acting hospitably to the (unknown) Other, offering new insights into the ways in which we think about caring for the most human aspect of human beings: an individual's voice.

In the final chapter of this book's effort to read Arendt and Derrida's work together for the purpose of constructing a world-centric theory of public care, I use these two thinkers' respective understandings of temporality to reconsider the paradoxicality of humankind's being-ness in time and to theorize the type of temporal orientation needed to negotiate the ever-transitory, never fully present moment of the "now." Although time and temporality may—on first glance—seem an odd topic on which to conclude a book about the notions of forgiveness and cosmopolitanism, it is my belief that that no investigation into these two forms of practice is more important. It is humankind's being-ness in time that conditions human existence entirely and—ultimately—constrains people's ability to act politically in the world. As a part of this book's attempt to rethink the boundaries of the political in terms of a "caring forgiveness" and "caring cosmopolitanism," then, its fourth chapter uses Arendt and Derrida's unique understandings of human temporality to rethink the (n)ever-present confrontation occurring in the ever-fleeting moment of the "now," where the forces of past and future play perpetually on all people as they attempt to "negotiate" (Derrida) the boundaries of their existence in both time and space.

NOTES

1. Megan Phelps-Roper, "I Grew Up in the Westboro Baptist Church. Here's Why I Left," TED Talks, 2017, https://www.ted.com.

2. "Westboro Baptist Church," *Extremist Files Database* (Southern Poverty Law Center, 2018). https://www.splcenter.org/fighting-hate/extremist-files/group/westboro-baptist-church.

3. Phelps-Roper, "I Grew Up in the Westboro Baptist Church. Here's Why I Left."

4. Though the nature and notion of "the political" has long been debated by scholars of the philosophy and politics, most especially by those working in the Anglophone world, I invoke this idea throughout this book specifically in reference to Arendt's theory of the political. As is subsequently shown, by "the political," I mean the worldly realm of public "action," or the "space for politics" where freedom can be experienced and power can be (re)engendered between a plurality of persons and peoples in the mode of human togetherness. For readers interested in the concept of "the political," I recommend James Wiley's recent book, *Politics and the Concept of the Political: The Political Imagination* (New York: Routledge, 2016).

5. Hannah Arendt, *The Human Condition* (Chicago: The University of Chicago Press, 1958), 254; Hannah Arendt, *Men in Dark Times* (New York: Harcourt, Brace & World, Inc., 1968), 14.

6. Hannah Arendt, "The Crisis in Culture: Its Social and Its Political Significance," in *Between Past and Future: Eight Exercises in Political Thought* (New York: Penguin Books, 2006), 214.

7. Siobhan Kattago, "Hannah Arendt on the World," in *Hannah Arendt: Key Concepts*, ed. Patrick Hayden (Durham, UK: Acumen Publishing, 2014), 52–65.

8. Arendt, *The Human Condition*, 52.

9. Hannah Arendt, "On the Nature of Totalitarianism: An Essay in Understanding," in *Essays in Understanding, 1930–1954: Formation, Exile, and Totalitarianism*, ed. Jerome Kohn (New York: Schocken Books, 1994), 358.

10. Hannah Arendt, "'What Remains? The Language Remains': A Conversation with Günter Gaus," in *Essays in Understanding, 1930–1954: Formation, Exile, and Totalitarianism*, ed. Jerome Kohn (New York: Schocken Books, 1994), 17.

11. See: Jacques Derrida, *Without Alibi*, ed. and trans. Peggy Kamuf (Stanford, CA: Stanford University Press, 2002), 28–70. "History of the Lie" was originally a lecture given by Derrida in 1993, as part of a lecture series at The New School of Social Research. The particular lecture series was devoted to Arendt's thinking about "the political."

12. See, in particular: Jacques Derrida, *On Cosmopolitanism and Forgiveness*, eds. Simon Critchley and Richard Kearney, trans. Mark Dooley and Michael Hughes (London: Routledge, 2001); Jacques Derrida, "To Forgive: The Unforgivable and the Imprescriptable," in *Questioning God*, eds. John D. Caputo, Mark Dooley, and Michael J. Scanlon (Bloomington, IN: Indiana University Press, 2001), 21–51.

13. Samir Haddad, "Arendt, Derrida, and the Inheritance of Forgiveness," *Philosophy Today* 51, no. 4 (2007): 416.

14. For example, see: Bonnie Honig, "Declarations of Independence: Arendt and Derrida on the Problem of Founding a Republic," *The American Political Science Review* 85, no. 1 (1991): 97–113; Marguerite La Caze, *Wonder and Generosity: Their Role in Ethics and Politics* (Albany, NY: State University of New York Press, 2013); Marguerite La Caze, "It's Easier to Lie If You Believe It Yourself: Derrida, Arendt, and the Modern Lie," *Law, Culture and the Humanities* 13, no. 2 (2017): 193–210; James R. Martel, "Can There Be Politics Without Sovereignty? Arendt, Derrida and the Question of Sovereign Inevitability," *Law, Culture and the Humanities* 6, no. 2 (2010): 153–66; Cláudia Perrone-Moisés, "Forgiveness and Crimes against Humanity: A Dialogue between Hannah Arendt and Jacques Derrida," *HannahArendt.Net: Journal for Political Thinking* 2, no. 1 (2006); Andrew Schaap, "The Proto-Politics of Reconciliation: Lefort and the Aporia of Forgiveness in Arendt and Derrida," *Australian Journal of Political Science* 41, no. 4 (2006): 615–30.

15. A notable exception to this claim can be found in the work of Siobhan Kattago. Underlining the political pertinence of an Arendtian notion of "care for the world" to practices of forgiveness and cosmopolitanism, Kattago gestures toward the line of thought that I have pursued throughout this book. In passing, she highlights how "Arendt's use of the phrase *amor mundi*, or 'love of the world,' includes care, concern, and responsibility" and that it "shares much with Kant's cosmopolitanism and sense of hospitality in *Perpetual Peace*," offering a "political reading of the Christian precept of love of one's neighbor writ large." [Siobhan Kattago, "Why the World Matters: Hannah Arendt's Philosophy of New Beginnings," *The European Legacy* 18, no. 2 (2013): 175; Kattago, "Hannah Arendt on the World."]

16. Simon Critchley and Richard Kearney, "Preface," in *On Cosmopolitanism and Forgiveness*, eds. Simon Critchley and Richard Kearney, trans. Mark Dooley and Michael Hughes (London: Routledge, 2001), viii.

17. Ernesto Verdeja, *Unchopping a Tree: Reconciliation in the Aftermath of Political Violence* (Philadelphia: Temple University Press, 2009), 24.

18. Ella Myers, *Worldly Ethics: Democratic Politics and Care for the World* (London: Duke University Press, 2013). I return to Myers's work in chapter three, as part of my theorization of a "caring cosmopolitanism."

19. The Westboro Baptist Church is a "TULIP" Baptist Church. The acronym TULIP stands for "*T*otal Depravity; *U*nconditional Election; *L*imited Atonement; *I*rresistible Grace; *P*erseverance of the Saints." [Megan Phelps-Roper, *Unfollow: A Journey from Hatred to Hope, Leaving the Westboro Baptist Church* (London: Riverrun, 2019), 42.]

20. Rebecca Barrett-Fox, *God Hates: Westboro Baptist Church, American Nationalism, and the Religious Right* (Lawrence, KS: University Press of Kansas, 2016), 50. As Barrett-Fox notes, the WBC's hyperbolic doctrines have notable and direct associations with the ideas espoused by British theologian, John Gill (1697–1771).

21. "Westboro Baptist Church," *ADL* Report, https://www.adl.org/resources/profiles/westboro-baptist-church.

22. Barrett-Fox, *God Hates*, 197, n. 20.

23. Ibid., 5.

24. Phelps-Roper, "I Grew up in the Westboro Baptist Church. Here's Why I Left."

25. This reference is to 1 John 2:15-17, from the 1611 King James Bible: "Love not the world, neither the things that are in the world. If any man love the world, the love of the Father is not in him." Though the WBC maintains that the King James Bible is the only legitimate book of scripture, the references to biblical texts found throughout the remainder of this book are from the New International Version (NIV).

26. Sam Harris, "Leaving the Church: A Conversation with Megan Phelps-Roper," *Making Sense*, July 3, 2015, https://samharris.org/podcasts/leaving-the-church/.

27. It is in the book of Genesis that we find the story of Esau and Jacob, the fraternal twins of Isaac and Rebekah.

28. Phelps-Roper, *Unfollow*, 8.

29. Carl Schmitt, *The Concept of the Political*, trans. George Schwab (London: The University of Chicago Press, 2007), 26.

30. Arendt, *Men in Dark Times*. This is a phrase she appropriates from Bertolt Brecht's poem, "To Posterity," or "To Those Who Follow in Our Wake" (1939). Bertolt Brecht, *Bertolt Brecht: Plays, Poetry and Prose*, eds. John Willett and Ralph Manheim (London: Eyre Methuen, 1976), 318–20.

31. Hannah Arendt, *The Promise of Politics* (New York: Schocken Books, 2005), 201. Original emphasis.

32. Ibid., 201–2.

33. Arendt, *The Human Condition*, 248–56.

34. Arendt, *Men in Dark Times*, ix.

35. Arendt, "'What Remains? The Language Remains,'" 20.

36. George Kateb, "Freedom and Worldliness in the Thought of Hannah Arendt," *Political Theory* 5, no. 2 (1977): 143.

37. Arendt, *The Human Condition*, 251.

38. Ibid., 22.

39. Hannah Arendt, "A Reply to Eric Voegelin," in *Essays in Understanding, 1930–1954: Formation, Exile, and Totalitarianism*, ed. Jerome Kohn (New York: Schocken Books, 1994), 403.

40. Douglas B. Klusmeyer, "Hannah Arendt on Authority and Tradition," in *Hannah Arendt: Key Concepts*, ed. Patrick Hayden (Durham, UK: Acumen Publishing, 2014), 138.

41. Hannah Arendt, *Between Past and Future* (New York: Penguin Books, 2006), 26–27.

42. Ibid., 28.

43. Ibid., 95.

44. Norman Jewison, *Fiddler on the Roof* (United States: United Artists, 1971).

45. Arendt, *Between Past and Future*, 95.

46. Hannah Arendt, *The Origins of Totalitarianism* (London: Harvest Book, 1968), ix.

47. Jacques Derrida and Elizabeth Roudinesco, *For What Tomorrow . . . (A Dialogue)*, trans. Jeff Fort (Stanford, CA: Stanford University Press, 2004), 8.

48. Ibid.

49. Ibid.

50. Arendt, *Between Past and Future*, 26.

51. Hannah Arendt, "Introduction: Walter Benjamin, 1892–1940," in *Illuminations: Essays and Reflections*, ed. Hannah Arendt, trans. Harry Zorn (New York: Schocken Books, 1968), 54.

52. Ibid.

53. Ibid.

54. In terms of such attempts, we need only to recall the so-called Hannah Arendt scandal that sprang up after the publication of Elżbieta Ettinger's book, *Hannah Arendt/Martin Heidegger* (New Haven, CT: Yale University Press, 1995), and the ways in which its controversial claims were embraced by scholars critical of Arendt's work (such as Richard Wolin). Though I am unable here to rehash the details of this "scandal," which was not really a scandal at all (given the findings of Elisabeth Young-Bruehl's biography of Arendt), other scholars have written extensively about both the personal and scholastic relationship between Heidegger and Arendt. See, in particular: Dana R. Villa, *Arendt and Heidegger: The Fate of the Political* (Princeton: Princeton University Press, 1996); Dana R. Villa, *Politics, Philosophy, Terror: Essays on the Thought of Hannah Arendt* (Princeton: Princeton University Press, 1999), 61–86.

55. Derrida and Roudinesco, *For What Tomorrow . . . (A Dialogue)*, 13.

56. Because this book shares an interest in the notion of "care" with the approach to moral theory known as the Ethics of Care, or Care Ethics, it is inevitable that there is conceptual crossover between my work and that of scholars like Carol Gilligan, Nel Noddings, Virginia Held, Sara Ruddick, Eva Feder Kittay, and Joan Tronto. Where care ethicists—to speak in (very) broad terms—develop their moral universe in terms of the dynamics of giving and receiving care, as well as the ways in which relations of dependency have historically been constructed along gendered lines, I understand the notion of "care" in decidedly Arendtian terms. In this sense, rather than find my feet in this body of feminist relational theory, I have situated myself in the Continental

tradition of philosophic and political thought, doing so specifically in relation to the notion of *Sorge* developed by Heidegger; as has been discussed, I have built my theory of care in contrast to the Heideggerian approach. This being said, in terms of my investigation of "caring for the world," I would be remiss in failing to recognize how Tronto's work has nevertheless colored my thinking about "care" as a public, political form of worldly practice. Her definition of "care," in particular, has helped give structure to aspects of my own understanding: "[C]aring [should] be viewed as a *species activity that includes everything that we do to maintain, continue, and repair our 'world' so that we can live in it as well as possible.* That world includes our bodies, our selves, and our environment, all of which we seek to interweave in a complex, life-sustaining web." [Berenice Fisher and Joan Tronto, "Toward a Feminist Theory of Caring," in *Circles of Care: Work and Identity in Women's Lives*, eds. Emily K. Abel and Margaret K. Nelson (New York: State University of New York Press, 1990), 40; Joan Tronto, *Moral Boundaries: A Political Argument for an Ethic of Care* (London: Routledge, 1993), 103. Original emphasis.]

57. Hannah Arendt, "What Is Existential Philosophy?" in *Essays in Understanding, 1930–1954: Formation, Exile, and Totalitarianism*, ed. Jerome Kohn (New York: Schocken Books, 1994), 179.

58. Joshua D. Broggi, *Sacred Language, Sacred World: The Unity of Scriptural and Philosophical Hermeneutics* (London: Bloomsbury, 2016), 31.

59. Ibid. Original emphasis.

60. William Shakespeare, "The Tragedy of Hamlet, Prince of Denmark," in *The New Oxford Shakespeare: The Complete Works, Modern Critical Edition*, ed. Gary Taylor et al. (Oxford: Oxford University Press, 2016), 2040.

61. Martin Heidegger, *Heidegger: Basic Writings*, ed. David Farrell Krell (London: Routledge, 2011), 3.

62. Arendt, "What Is Existential Philosophy?" 179. Here, Arendt references Heidegger: "The question of the '*who*' of *Dasein* has been answered with the expression of 'Self.'" [Martin Heidegger, *Being and Time*, trans. John Macquarrie and Edward Robinson (Oxford: Blackwell Publishing, 1962), 312.]

63. Arendt, "What Is Existential Philosophy?" 179.

64. Heidegger, *Being and Time*, 313.

65. Ibid., 313 and 354.

66. Martin Heidegger, *The Concept of Time*, trans. William McNeill (Oxford: Blackwell Publishing, 1992), 20E–21E.

67. Heidegger, *Being and Time*, 416. Original emphasis.

68. Ibid. Original emphasis.

69. Arendt, "What Is Existential Philosophy?" 179.

70. Joanna Vecchiarelli Scott and Judith Chelius Stark, "Rediscovering Hannah Arendt," in *Love and Saint Augustine*, eds. Joanna Vecchiarelli Scott and Judith Chelius Stark (Chicago: University of Chicago Press, 1996), 124.

71. Hannah Arendt, *Love and Saint Augustine*, eds. Joanna Vecchiarelli Scott and Judith Chelius Stark (London: The University of Chicago Press, 1996), 51.

72. Scott and Stark, "Rediscovering Hannah Arendt," 181. See also: Kattago, "Why the World Matters," 172.

73. Scott and Stark, "Rediscovering Hannah Arendt," 181.

74. Arendt, *The Human Condition*, 179. Emphasis added.
75. Arendt, "The Crisis in Culture," 208. Emphasis added.
76. Arendt, "On the Nature of Totalitarianism," 358.
77. Arendt, "What Is Existential Philosophy?" 179.
78. Elisabeth Young-Bruehl, *Hannah Arendt: For Love of the World* (New Haven, CT: Yale University Press, 2004), 327.
79. Arendt, *The Human Condition*, 243.

Chapter 1

Derrida

On Cosmopolitanism and Forgiveness

In *On Cosmopolitanism and Forgiveness* (2001), a text that was published as part of Simon Critchley and Richard Kearney's co-edited book series, "Thinking in Action," Derrida critiques global political affairs through his deconstructions of the notions of forgiveness and cosmopolitanism.[1] The text is comprised of two distinct sections, the first is based on an address given to the International Parliament of Writers in Strasbourg (1996)—a speech entitled, *Cosmopolites de tous les pays, encore un effort!*—and the second is based on answers Derrida gave in an interview on the subject of forgiveness for the French journal *Le Monde des débats* (December 1999). Presenting deconstructions of two ideas with conceptual roots deep in *le héritage*, which is to say, the Western tradition, Derrida responds—with his distinctive philosophic approach—to events and phenomenon taking place around the globe.

In the first part of his book, Derrida critically evaluates the legacy of cosmopolitan thought, doing so not simply as an exercise in abstract theorizing, but in the mode of a pointed criticism of the rising anti-immigrant sensibility in France during the 1980s and 1990s.[2] The second part of the book presents his deconstruction of the notion of forgiveness, in a manner congruent with his examination of cosmopolitanism, calling into question instances of political (re)conciliatory action that were, increasingly, a prominent part of global public life. Because it was "not only individuals, but also entire communities, professional corporations, the representatives of ecclesiastical hierarchies, sovereigns, and heads of state" who were now asking for "forgiveness," Derrida saw fit to deconstruct the concept of forgiveness as a means of critically considering its association with the cases of repentance, confession, and apology that were "multiplying" on the "geopolitical scene" during the final years of the twentieth century.[3] More than a form of detached, apolitical analysis, the deconstructivist approach practiced by Derrida in *On Cosmopolitanism and Forgiveness* reveals the conceptual underpinnings supporting these two notions in a manner that allows him to engage actively—or to intervene philosophically—in global political affairs.

What precisely, however, does Derrida mean when he speaks and writes about "deconstruction"? And in what ways, specifically, does this form of philosophic thought allow him to take action, and to intervene ethically and politically in the realm of human affairs? At first glance, we might wonder whether—given the similarities between Derrida's notion of deconstruction and Heidegger's practice of reading the history of Western metaphysics destructively (as in *Destruktion*)—a deconstructivist approach is incommensurable with a care-centric mode of thought, especially one which prioritizes the conservation and *re*-construction of the world within which we live, move, and act politically. Furthermore, in concluding that the purpose of deconstruction is not simply to destroy ideas, concepts, themes, and so on in what ways does it facilitate more positive, regenerative action? How does a Derridean deconstruction of cosmopolitanism and forgiveness contribute to the (re)creation of what might be considered a better—arguably more just—world through its thoroughly critical, destructive mode of engaging with the basic structures, concepts, and beliefs that inform, constitute, and condition the human experience of being in the world? It is in seeking answers to these questions that I begin my reflections on cosmopolitanism and forgiveness, doing so not because there is a need to rethink the practice of deconstruction in and of itself, but because a Derridean deconstructivist approach reveals the conceptual logic undergirding each of these notions: informing the Derridean experience of justice that I reconsider in terms of the "world."

Divided into three sections, I first provide an overview of Derrida's deconstructive approach, before turning to his deconstructions of forgiveness and cosmopolitanism specifically. Accordingly, section one highlights how deconstruction is a genealogical form of criticism animated by a hyperbolic sense of justice. The second and third sections of this chapter investigate the conceptual logics inherent to the notions of forgiveness and cosmopolitanism, respectively, with Derrida's deconstructions facilitating an exposition of the binary oppositions that undergird each of these ideas. These are the aporetic binaries that inform the underlying conceptual dynamics which I theorize throughout the remainder of this book—Arendt's body of thought serving as a compass with which to navigate the ethico-political terrain uncovered by deconstruction. Responding to the series of aporias disclosed by Derrida's deconstructivist account of cosmopolitanism and forgiveness, I fashion a theory of political action shaped by Arendt's notion of "care for the world."

1. DERRIDA, DECONSTRUCTION, AND "UNDECIDABILITY"

Rejecting the existence of a rigid divide between theory and practice,[4] Derrida's philosophic project of deconstruction—a form of thinking in action—"aspires to change things and to intervene [. . .] in what one calls the *cité*, the *polis*, and more generally the world."[5] Not unlike the philosophy of *praxis* outlined within Marxist thought, according to which philosophic interventions do not simply interpret the world but seek to change it, deconstruction can be understood as a type of "performative interpretation" that puts thinking into action in a manner that demands, as Marx writes, "a ruthless criticism of everything existing."[6] As a form of "ruthless criticism," deconstruction puts into practice a characteristically active mode of critical philosophic inquiry, one which is animated by a hyperbolic sense of justice. It is, as Critchley and Kearney observe, a "concrete intervention in contexts that is governed by an undeconstructable concern for justice."[7] Though it has long been acknowledged—both by Derrida himself and by scholars of his work—that defining deconstruction poses certain intrinsic challenges, perhaps even proving to be impossible because of the ways in which the word "deconstruction" itself "acquires its value only from its inscription in a chain of possible substitutions,"[8] Critchley and Kearney's description of the Derridean approach provides a sturdy foundation upon which to develop our thinking about this form of "ruthless criticism" in two primary ways.

First, to frame how Derrida understands the complex web of meaning that supports and structures all of human existence, Critchley and Kearney underscore that deconstruction is an "intervention in *contexts*." This notion of "context" is significant for a Derridean conceptualization of human existence because he understands the world as "text," which—as he writes in *Limited Inc* (1988)—is "limited neither to the graphic, nor to the book, nor even to discourse, and even less to the semantic, representation, symbolic, ideal, or ideological sphere."[9] What he describes as "text" implies all "structures called 'real,' 'economic,' 'historical,' socio-institutional, in short: all possible referents."[10] Including "all possible referents," and thus referring to the entire semiological system of signs and their correlates, the "text" is the linguistic system of writing—more specifically what he describes as *"archi-écriture"* (or arche-writing)—that encapsulates all of human affairs. This conceptualization of textuality and (arche-)writing—with its ontological claim that the present is shaped by a play of *"différance,"* according to which "language, or any code, any system of referral in general, is constituted 'historically' as a weave of differences"[11]—gives rise to the now infamous notion that *"il n'y a pas de hors-texte."*[12] Though the suggestion that "there is nothing outside the text"—or, alternatively translated, that "there is no outside-text"—has garnered much criticism from thinkers such as Michel Foucault and John Searle, it is—for Derrida—but another means of saying that "there is nothing outside context."[13] The etymological root, derived from the Latin "con," meaning "together" or "with," and "*texere*," to "weave, to make, to fabricate," gives us a definition in the *Oxford English Dictionary* of the "continuous text or composition with parts duly connected"; or the "whole structure of a connected passage regarded in its bearing upon any of the parts which constitute it; the parts which immediately precede or follow any particular passage of 'text' and determine its meaning." Conjuring the image of a fabric, this is an understanding of "textuality" that Derrida develops from Edmund Husserl's work, considering an object of enquiry not only as an object in and of itself but as part of a broader fabric of (non)discursive forces.[14] To deconstruct an aspect of the "text" is, thus, effectively to unravel the entirety of this textile, purposefully cutting into and through its various constituent parts, layers, seams, etc. in order to inspect forensically the very fibers of its being.

Derrida's deconstructive intervention is therefore a cutting into "context," doing so in such a manner that he moves into the "text"—as Critchley and Kearney observe—"via an analysis that is at once historical, contextual, and thematic, to bring out the logic of the concept."[15] This movement, or "conceptual genealogy,"[16] is what I present here in Benjaminian terms, seeking to understand how the "pearl" that the metaphorical "pearl diver" has retrieved and—"resuscitated" in Arendt's own Benjaminian language—has come to be formed at the bottom of the ocean in the first place.[17] When thinking about cosmopolitanism and forgiveness as "pearls," for instance, it is not only interesting to contemplate the genealogical narratives of these notions, but also to consider the broader systems of meaning that inform how such "pearls" presently appear and exist to us as valuable entities. To think deconstructively is thus to begin to understand that the very possibility of the existence of "pearls" is dependent on the seeming impossibility of an irritant—usually a parasite and not the proverbial grain of sand—becoming enveloped by nacre and "crystallized" into a thing of luster and value. In the words of Nicholas Royle, deconstruction is "the experience of the impossible; what remains to be thought; a logic of destabilization always already on the move in 'things themselves'; [. . .] a theoretical and practical parasitism or virology; what is happening today in what is called society, politics, diplomacy, economics, historical reality, and so on: the opening of the future itself."[18] This experience of thinking the impossible—or of the possibility of something like a pearl becoming possible in terms of its impossibility—is deconstruction, which is the very "performative interpretation" that realizes this conceptual dynamic and allows us to understand the broader context of this entity's existence in today's world. Thus, when Critchley and Kearney write about how deconstruction is a "concrete intervention in contexts," they are describing a foray into an all-encompassing "text" through a study of particular "things"—or "pearls"—whose history and meaningfulness have been shaped by the interplay of the (non)discursive, (non-)present forces that inform their worldly existence.

In addition to the ways in which deconstruction is an "intervention in contexts," Critchley and Kearney—as part of their introductory remarks to *On Cosmopolitanism and Forgiveness*—also note that this form of "ruthless criticism" is "governed by an undeconstructable concern for justice." Though this is a conceptualization of justice which has notable affinities to the hyperethical thought of Emmanuel Levinas, it is foremost necessary to note that the possibility of acting justly can only be said to take place during instances of sheer "undecidability." For Derrida, "undecidability" is associated with the paralyzing experience of not knowing what to do when we are forced to think and act in the face of the impossible, when no rules or formulas can be applied to address a well-defined "problem": this is an "experience" which is "heterogenous, foreign to the order of the calculable and the rule, [but] is still obliged [. . .] to give itself up to the impossible decision."[19] Such an experience is characteristic of the aporetic dynamics of (im)possibility ever at play in notions like cosmopolitanism and forgiveness. Having written extensively on the notion of a "problem," Derrida puts this word "in tension with" the Greek word, "aporia."[20] Where a "problem" is a "prosthesis that we put forth in order to represent, replace, shelter, or dissimulate ourselves, or so as to hide something unavowable," an "aporia" is a matter of "not knowing where to go," an experience of impossibility that "separates us in the very place where *it would no longer be possible to constitute a problem.*"[21] The characteristic experience of the aporia is the "non-passage," of not knowing what to do, and it is "the point where the very project or problematic task becomes impossible and where we are all exposed, absolutely without protection, without problem [. . .] that is to say [. . .] incapable of sheltering ourselves behind what could still protect the interiority of a secret."[22] Thus, to think deconstructively about notions—for instance, cosmopolitanism and forgiveness—is to attend directly to the undecidable relations of (im)possibility that structure particular ideas, words, concepts, themes, and so on; these are the conceptual dynamics that gave rise to the "mad" experience of the aporia—a type of "madness of the impossible"—that engenders the ethical demand to think and act more justly in the world.[23]

We may be justified, perhaps, in wondering how the experience of undecidability is a matter of "justice." We might ask how, for instance, Derrida's understanding of the experience of the impossible possibility gives rise to the sense of responsibility that leads him to believe that "deconstruction is justice"?[24] How does a Derridean approach to deconstruction act for the sake of justice? Though these questions take root in various places throughout

Derrida's corpus, his responses to them are fundamentally shaped by his reading of Levinas's work (notably in his essay "Force of Law: The 'Mystical Foundation of Authority'"[25]), with a Levinasian notion of ethicality directly informing the sense of responsibility that powers Derridean deconstruction. Critchley, too, in *Ethics-Politics-Subjectivity: Essays on Derrida, Levinas and Contemporary French Thought* (1999), investigates the relationship between the work of Derrida and Levinas:

> Derrida paradoxically defines justice as an experience of that which we are not able to experience, which is qualified as "the mystical," "the impossible," or "aporia" [. . .] justice in an "experience" of the undecidable. However, and this is crucial, such an undecidable experience of justice does not arise in some intellectual intuition or theoretical deduction, rather it always arises in relation to a particular entity, to the singularity of the other [. . .] that is to say, justice arises in the particular and non-subsumptive relation to the Other, as a response to suffering that demands an infinite responsibility.[26]

Here, Critchley highlights Derrida's theoretical indebtedness to Levinas, a thinker known for his idiosyncratic notion of alterity and his understandings of ethics as first philosophy. Critchley draws our attention to the ways in which a Derridean understanding of undecidability—in its "relation to a particular entity, to the singularity of the other"—is shaped by a Levinasian notion of otherness, whereby—for Levinas—the "face" of the Other is that which "governs me, whose infinity I cannot thematize and whose hostage I remain."[27] This is an ethically charged conceptualization of alterity, one which Critchley suggests generates a "pre-reflective sentient disposition towards the Other's suffering that [forms] a basis for ethics and responsibility."[28] This is an ethic that Derrida carries into his approach to deconstruction; specifically, it is an Other-oriented sense of ethics that forms the beating heart of his notion of justice.

Differing from the sense of justice associated with the law (as *droit*), the justice of Derridean deconstruction aligns with Levinas's notion of *la droiture de l'accueil fait au visage*,[29] or—as translated by Derrida—"the equitable honoring of faces."[30] Though Derrida's translation of this excerpt is sometimes contested,[31] this is a conceptualization of justice animated by an infinite responsibility to the (unknown) Other, a form of concern for a singular being who is always—though this figure might not be present in the world—owed respect and an equity of treatment. This is an obligation to the *ipseity* of the Other—someone whose appearance Derrida describes in Levinasian terms as the "arrival" of "God"[32]—that he associates with our movement toward and through the aporetic experience engendered during moments of undecidability, which is to say, an injunction to extend as far as humanly possible our care, concern, love, and so on to all whom appear before us. Informed by this infinite, unceasing demand to act responsibly in the "face" of the (unknown) Other, deconstruction is thus—arguably—a characteristically Other-centric form of philosophic action. A type of Other-oriented mode of thought, deconstruction, is performed for the sake of the Other and a more just treatment of them. I use the word "them" here because the "Other" is both a singular being, and yet, not representative of a singular person at all, but rather the multitude of all humanity. Not unlike the notion of "dying to the self" found in the Christian tradition of faith, which demands a relinquishment of a self-centric existence and the putting into practice of a radical sense of beingness toward the infinite (God); a Levinasian understanding of acting responsibly toward the (unknown) Other is a call of and for a justice which is ultimately unfathomable, without limits, and free from any worldly conditions.

But what are the political implications of such a radically Other-oriented ethics? How can this transcendental notion of justice, as it relates to deconstruction, cultivate new spaces and forms of democratic action? That is, in what ways—if at all possible—does this extreme form of ethics conserve and enhance "the political"? With these questions in mind, I turn my attention to Derrida's deconstructions of forgiveness and cosmopolitanism, proceeding on the conceptual grounds that his approach offers a "concrete intervention in contexts" that is "governed" by a radical "concern for justice." I go forward with the belief that Derrida's approach—because of the ways in which it operates, as Critchley observes, in a "quasi-transcendental register"[33]—arguably neglects to account adequately for the political necessity of thinking and acting caringly for that which is shared with the "Other": the "world."

2. DERRIDA: ON FORGIVENESS

Corresponding with Derrida's turn to more thoroughly ethical and political topics in the 1990s, his examination of forgiveness offers a "concrete" philosophic intervention during a period when humanity saw "the proliferation of scenes of repentances or of asking 'forgiveness.'"[34] Against this backdrop, he saw it necessary to critique how forgiveness—a decidedly Judeo-Christian notion—was being practiced and instrumentalized by individuals and groups from all across the (international) political spectrum, as well as individuals and nongovernmental actors from across (global) civil society. Acting into this "context," which must be understood here in a double sense, as both the so-called real world where human affairs are taking place, and the all-encompassing "text" within which all meanings are ascribed, Derrida's reflections on forgiveness offer a deconstructive critique—a "conceptual genealogy"— of a notion with conceptual roots extending deep into the Western tradition of thought: investigating how this idea has been understood and practiced throughout human history.

Contending that there is not "anything secular in our time,"[35] Derrida argues that the contemporary world exists within a state of "*globalatinisation* [which] takes into account the effect of Roman Catholicism [that] today overdetermines all language of law, of politics, and even the interpretation of what is called the 'return of the religious.'"[36] Underscoring the hegemonic influence that religion has had on human existence in the West, Derrida suggests that forgiveness is an idea that is inseparable from its foundations in Christian teachings. In this way, his thinking is in line with that of Arendt when she writes:

> The discoverer of the role of forgiveness in the realm of human affairs was Jesus of Nazareth. The fact that he made this discovery in a religious context and articulated it in religious language is no reason to take it any less seriously in a strictly secular sense.[37]

Derrida, who maintains that even the notion of "the secular" is a religious one,[38] consequently affirms Arendt's understanding that the religious foundations of the concept of forgiveness are significant, but do not prevent its being theorized/practiced in secular contexts. Although the tendency in the contemporary (international) political arena—both scholastically and practically—is to separate the secular from the non-secular, attempting to ground the doing of politics in nonreligious terms, this is not entirely possible when considering forgiveness, as the influence of Judeo-Christian precepts to the practice of this particular notion are undeniable. Secular scholars who study, and practitioners who do politics, therefore ought not be thwarted by the rootedness of forgiveness in Christian theology, though they must take into account how this "pearl" has been "crystallized" in terms of the ethics outlined within this tradition of faith.

A. Unconditional Forgiveness and Conditional "Forgiveness"

Derrida identifies two strands of forgiveness within the Christian tradition: the supernatural, unconditional and the human, conditional forms of this notion. In writing of the former, he highlights the "radical"[39] character of forgiveness that is articulated repeatedly throughout the New Testament: the infinite, unmitigated form of forgiving related to the unconditional imperative to love one's neighbor (*agape*). Like the unqualified, unquantifiable conception of love found in—for instance—Jesus's Parable of the Prodigal Son,[40] an unconditional form of forgiveness is associated with what Derrida calls a "hyperbolic ethics," which is an ethics that "tends to push the exigency to the limit and beyond the limit of the possible."[41] A hyperbolic ethics is an "ethics beyond ethics," for it "carries itself beyond laws, norms or any obligation."[42] This pure form of forgiveness, if there is such a thing at all, is found in the realm of the hyperbolic, and it demands "the *unconditional*, gracious, infinite, aneconomic forgiveness granted *to the guilty as guilty*, without counterpart, even to those who do not repent or ask forgiveness."[43] From this perspective, forgiveness is not characterized by pragmatism, proportionality, or the execution of a set of well-defined procedures. Rather, it possesses a certain unfathomable, unbounded, and unconditional quality that can only be understood, if it is even possible to understand at all, as a hyperbolic notion without quantifiable limits or conditional requirements.

By contrast, "conditional" forgiveness refers to that which is considered and commonly practiced within the human realm. For example, conditional forgiveness is associated with the semantics and the logic that informs the confession-forgiveness dynamic, as found in the Catholic confessional booth. In this space, a sinner confesses, repents, and apologizes for their sins as a means of asking for forgiveness from a priest, who—as a representative of God—has the power to absolve these indiscretions in return for a penance. For Derrida, this so-called forgiveness, which can be granted only after a wrongdoer satisfies certain conditions, cannot be understood as "forgiveness" at all. This is a point that he demonstrates in three primary ways.

First, a Derridean conception of "pure" forgiveness can take place only between two singularities—the wronged and the wrongdoer—and, thus, "as soon as a third party intervenes, one can speak of amnesty, reconciliation, reparation, etc., but certainly not of pure forgiveness."[44] Therefore, the presence and intervention of a party other than the victim and the perpetrator—such as a priest, judge, or state legislator—eliminates forgiveness from this interaction. Within such spaces, one can only speak of reconciliation, restorative justice, retributive justice, or amnesty, but not forgiveness.

Second, Derrida contends that conditional forgiveness, as found in the confessional booth, can be construed as a form of reconciliation, justice, or even something else entirely, precisely because it is the product of a specific type of transaction. Because this process may demand truth-telling, call for an apology, require repentance, include a promise not to re-commit the wrong and/or, ultimately, may depend upon a penance in order for "forgiveness" to be granted, this act is characterized by a formulaic process and a certain negotiation between parties, which—Derrida argues—erodes the purity of forgiveness. Although he recognizes the utility of such a conditional process of reparation—especially as it pertains to the political realm and the pursuit of national reconciliation in the wake of sociopolitical conflict—he takes issue with the conditional logic of the exchange. He argues that a "pure" forgiveness cannot be qualified by certain terms and conditions.

Without delving too deeply into Derrida's understanding of gifts and the relational process of gift giving, it is necessary at this point to highlight how an unconditional forgiveness is a gift truly given. That is, as he writes, "forgiveness must be a gracious gift, without exchange and without condition."[45] Originally reflecting upon the idea of forgiveness in his native language of French, and therefore, on the French word *pardon*,[46] Derrida underscores how the French root word, *don* (ultimately from the Latin, *donum*, meaning "gift"), refers to the giving or donating of a gift; this is a point he uses as a means of illustrating the link between the notions of forgiveness and gifts. The logics of both these two concepts are aporetic in nature, for they are each characterized by the paradoxicality of the unconditional and the conditional, whereby a "pure" forgiveness and a "pure" gift must be "good,"[47] or—alternatively stated—be given without conditions and be free of a sovereignty that could establish a hierarchical relation of power between the donor and donee of this gift. According to Derrida, gifts purely and truly given are a type of "goodness," or a "giving goodness," whose "source remains inaccessible [to both parties]."[48] Stemming from a so-called goodness that is only accessible in terms of the "hyperbolic," gifts—and thus forgiveness—must be given entirely without condition, which is to say, their being given must defy the logic of reciprocity. Describing a gift, Derrida states:

> It must not circulate, it must not be exchanged, it must not in any case be exhausted, as a gift, by the process of exchange, by the movement of circulation of the circle in the form of return to the point of departure. If the figure of the circle is essential to economics, the gift must remain *aneconomic*.[49]

There can be no exchange or transactionality with regard to "pure" (for) giving, for the "goodness" of such a deed exceeds the conceptual bounds imposed by any logical and semantic conditions. Although Arendt does not theorize forgiveness in such transcendental, hyper-ethical terms, it is significant that she too emphasizes that acts of forgiveness are "aneconomic," since it is an action that interrupts vicious cycles of violence and counterviolence. The "gift," to foreshadow my subsequent discussion, is the new beginning that the act of forgiving instigates in both time and space.

Closely related to his observations about the gift-like nature of unconditional forgiveness is Derrida's third criticism of conditional "forgiveness": its teleological character, whereby forgiving is a means of achieving some end goal. Arguing that a "pure" forgiveness must not seek any predetermined end, Derrida is critical of how—for instance—the active pursuit of a reconciled relationship between actors, and/or a national healing, directly challenges the "infinite" quality of a "pure," unconditional forgiveness. Because forgiveness—in its "pure" form—is unending, unfathomable, and thought to exceed human capability, it cannot serve as a means to an end. Again, Arendt similarly suggests that forgiveness cannot be considered or understood in utilitarian, instrumental terms because it is directly related to her theory of freedom, which is explored in chapters 2 and 4. In an effort to illustrate how forgiveness must be non-teleological and non-utilitarian, Derrida writes:

> The language of forgiveness, at the service of determined finalities, [is] anything but pure [. . .] each time forgiveness is at the service of a finality, be it noble and spiritual (atonement or redemption, reconciliation, salvation), each time that it aims to re-establish a normality (social, national, political, psychological) by a work of mourning, by some therapy or ecology of memory, then the "forgiveness" is not pure—nor is its concept.[50]

Summarizing this point, Ernesto Verdeja suggests that as "forgiveness becomes instrumentalized, it is drained of its transformative power and simply becomes a tool in a larger political and social project."[51] Unconditional forgiveness must therefore remain a "moral action in its own right," and it must "eschew any *telos* of reconciliation."[52] It must not aim at, according to Derrida, a "finalized" forgiveness, since such a predetermined "forgiveness" is not forgiveness at all, as it is a "political strategy or a psycho-therapeutic economy."[53] Unconditional forgiveness, then, is non-instrumental and serves no end, while the predetermined purpose-driven nature of a conditional "forgiveness" is related to an "economy of reparation" that facilitates the production of some end state.[54]

Although Derrida calls into question the logistics, transactional character, and *telos* of a conditional "forgiveness," he highlights that this conception is indissociable from the supernatural, unconditional understanding of it. Conditional forgiveness, which conforms to some type of predetermined, transactional process between parties, is fundamentally irreducible but nevertheless linked to the infinite, unfathomable understanding of unconditional forgiveness. Derrida argues that because unconditional forgiveness forms the essence of conditional forgiveness and because it is impossible to conceptualize pure forgiveness in human terms, the two forms of forgiveness cannot be dissociated from one another. As he states:

> The unconditional and the conditional are, certainly, absolutely heterogeneous, and this forever, on either side of a limit, but they are also indissociable. There is in the movement, in the motion of unconditional forgiveness, an inner exigency of becoming-effective, manifest, determined, and, in determining itself, bending to conditionality.[55]

Derrida argues that without its unconditional form, forgiveness is not a comprehensible concept. However, he also contends that because the actualization of a preternatural, "pure" forgiveness must assume a semantic—and therefore human—form (whether it be in the form of a spoken/written language, actions shared between parties, or some other exchange of meaning), the unconditional is inseparable from the conditional. It is impossible to think of, understand, grant or, ultimately, experience forgiveness without appealing simultaneously to both the "pure" and "impure" conceptions of this notion, even though it is only the "pure," transcendental understanding of this idea—if such a thing exists at all—that can be truly understood as the unconditional "gift" of which he speaks.

B. Forgiveness and the Unforgivable

In addition to the aporetic relationship between the heterogeneous indissociability of the conditional and the unconditional, Derrida uncovers a second aporia that intersects with this initial paradox: that true forgiveness only forgives the unforgivable. In this regard, Derrida takes issue with the positions adopted by Arendt and thinkers like Vladimir Jankélévitch (1903–1985), both of whom focus on the atrocities committed during the Holocaust and both of whom affirm that the imprescriptibility of crimes committed inhibits the forgivability of such offenses. Jankélévitch famously claims that the act of "pardoning died in the death camps."[56] He describes the atrocities of the Holocaust as "metaphysical crimes," and he asserts that the "ontological wickedness" of the Nazis exceeded the scope of legal prescription precisely because their efforts aimed at the eradication of the "human essence or, if you will, the "hominity" of human beings in general."[57] Like Jankélévitch, Arendt observes that when the concentration camps became "laboratories where changes in human nature [were] tested," and when totalitarian regimes carried out the seemingly impossible task of rendering masses of people superfluous, the Nazis "discovered without knowing that there are crimes which men can neither punish nor forgive."[58] She claims that "when the impossible was made possible it became the unpunishable, unforgivable absolute evil."[59] Accordingly, Arendt writes:

> Men are unable to forgive what they cannot punish and that they are unable to punish what has turned out to be unforgivable [. . .] we can neither punish nor forgive such offenses and that they therefore transcend the realm of human affairs.[60]

While Arendt's position evolved over time, as the people of the world began to develop a political and legal language, or means of talking about and responding to genocidal atrocities, the crimes of the Holocaust were, initially, impossible to forgive because they defied the possibility of human understanding and, ultimately, humankind's power to levy punishments. For both Arendt and Jankélévitch, then, the crimes against humanity committed under the reign of totalitarian governments originally marked a boundary between what is forgivable and what is unforgivable: delineating between the realm of human affairs and the realm of the preternatural.

Suggesting that the possibility of punishment cannot serve as the indicator of what is forgivable, Derrida takes issue with both Arendt and Jankélévitch's positions. Derrida argues that the unforgivable character of a crime is that which, paradoxically, makes it possible to forgive. It is the unfathomable nature of unpunishable crimes that may be capable of being forgiven. In this sense, forgiveness only becomes possible at the point of the unforgivable, which—for both Arendt and Jankélévitch—are imprescriptible wrongs that exceed the bounds of human punishment. As Derrida summarizes:

> Is [the unforgivable] not, in truth, the only thing to forgive? [. . .] If one is only prepared to forgive what appears forgivable, what the Church calls "venial sins," then the very idea of forgiveness would disappear. If there is something to forgive it would be what in religious language is called mortal sin, the worst, the unforgivable crime or harm. From which comes the aporia, which can be described in its dry and implacable formality without mercy: forgiveness forgives only the unforgivable [. . .] there is only forgiveness, if there is any, where there is the unforgivable [. . .] forgiveness must announce itself as impossibility itself. It can only be possible in doing the impossible.[61]

Because punishments are practices levied by human institutions within human organizations, it must, by necessity, be possible for people to understand, issue, and administer them. In this sense, the prescriptibility of a crime is the antithesis of human impossibility because punishment—as a legal and/or sociopolitical practice—is inherently possible to enact within the human realm. Punishable crimes are those types of wrongs that cannot be forgiven because forgiveness—where the act of forgiving is true and pure—is infinite, unfathomable, and unconditional. For Derrida, "It is only against the unforgivable, and thus on the scale *without scale*, of a certain inhumanity of the inexpiable, against the monstrosity of radical evil that forgiveness, if there is such a thing, measures itself."[62] Forgiveness, from Derrida's perspective, is therefore possible only in instances where punishment is impossible, for it is only those crimes which are impossible to fathom and punish that are worthy of the infinite, unconditionality of forgiveness. This foundational aspect of his understanding effectively means that forgiveness is fundamentally an otherworldly notion, an idea which I endeavor to re-world as a public, political practice of care.

C. The Power of Forgiveness

In asserting that forgiveness forgives only the unforgivable, Derrida not only demonstrates that forgiving emerges with the impossible, but also uncovers how forgiveness relates to power. In challenging Arendt and Jankélévitch's positions on the nature of unforgivable crimes, Derrida questions the human power to punish—or the human capability to make decisions and administer judgments—which he contends "supposes a power, a force, a sovereignty."[63] Each time forgiveness is effectively exercised, it supposes some sovereign power: the ability of a single party to demonstrate their power over others by way of a judgment that bestows a verdict upon a person or group of persons.[64] This display of power, understood in a Weberian sense of one party assuming power over another, is not characteristic of "pure" forgiveness because unconditional forgiving is related to a "hyperbolic ethic" that transcends the trappings of human "laws, norms, and obligations," as well as the coercive dynamics of power that develop when individuals and groups have the ability to determine the fate of others. As a form of domination, "power over" is an aspect of human exchange that erodes the purity of forgiveness by introducing "sovereignty" into the transactional process of judgment.

This issue of "sovereignty" is significant for Derrida's analysis of forgiveness because the dynamic of one party holding power over another can transform forgiving into a "poison" or a "weapon."[65] Referring to his understanding of gifts and the act of gift giving, Derrida asserts that forgiveness is associated with a cycle of giving—arguing that giving is also a form of taking. Because he contends that to give is to set in motion a process of exchange, whereby the act of gifting someone something also invites a reciprocal action, whether it be a simple verbal expression of gratitude or a more grandiose gesture, he argues that there is a violent economy associated with the giving of gifts. Regarding this as a vicious cycle, Derrida posits that true gifts do not foster relations of exchange, when he writes that if there is a gift, "the *given* of the gift, [. . .] must not come back to the giving, [. . .] it must not circulate, [. . .] it must not in any case be exhausted, as a gift, by the process of exchange."[66] Gift giving must not instigate a reciprocal reaction, because gifts—if they are gifts truly and purely given—must not create an imbalance of power, whereby the recipient of a gift becomes indebted to the donating party. This debt, because it necessitates taking from the donee, is a form of harm. Gift giving becomes, according to Derrida, harmful the moment "the gift puts the other in debt, with the result that giving amounts to hurting, to doing harm."[67] Derrida is consequently critical of how gifts can be used as a means for donors—as debtholders—to maintain, express, and extend their power over others. He is adamant that a "theory of the gift" must be "powerless by its very essence."[68] But such a statement evokes yet another paradox: that gifts must be given by a party empowered enough to give a gift but without acting upon or generating any new anatomies of power. Forgiveness, as a type of gift, must come from a place of power, while—at the same time—remaining powerless. Derrida writes: "What I try to think as the 'purity' of a forgiveness worthy of its name, would be a forgiveness without power: *unconditional but without sovereignty.*"[69] Such a pernicious, hierarchical relation of power is one that I contend can be mitigated by the state of equality characteristic of public, political interactions occurring between civically equal friends in the "world."

D. Confronting the Aporias of Forgiveness

Although the intersection of aporias that structure the logic of forgiveness transforms this notion into a "mad" pursuit, a sort of "madness of the impossible," Derridean deconstruction demands an experience of the aporetic nature of forgiving because it is through the paralysis induced by these paradoxes that one can begin to take responsibility for one's decisions and actions. In other words, it is in the face of such aporias that deconstruction not only destroys ideas, words, concepts, themes, and so on—intervening in a particular "context"—but also acts as a form of criticism which is animated by an "undeconstructable concern for justice." By revealing the unsolvable paradoxes of the conditional and unconditional, the forgivability of the unforgivable, and the powerful powerlessness that structure the logic of this notion, Derrida shows how the notion of forgiveness does not pose any "problems." Rather, this idea is one which is inherently aporetic. Thus, to consider forgiveness, and to practice it, is to express a willingness to "go through pain and aporia,"[70] which is to experience the sheer "madness" of a moment that is characterized by its "undecidability." It is consequently necessary to confront fearlessly the experience of (im)possibility that the aporetic logic of this notion begets, doing so in such a manner that we retain a radical openness to the "face" of the (unknown) Other and thus seek to act ever more justly toward the stranger who appears before us.

Despite the fact that Derrida asserts that the paradoxicality of forgiveness cannot be escaped, he nevertheless encourages his readers to confront the aporetic logic of this idea by locating a compromise between the extremes of the aporias inherent to the act of forgiving. To appeal both to the conditional and unconditional strands of forgiveness is a process that Derrida describes as a "negotiation"[71] between two opposing polarities. Although I consider Derrida's notion of negotiation in terms of Arendt's Kantian conceptualization of the imagination in chapter 4, it is important to underscore here that a Derridean understanding of negotiating requires us to think in a "to-and-fro" manner, "between two positions, two poles, two choices [. . .] always [going] from one to the other [. . .] [without] establishing oneself anywhere."[72] Derrida directly links this back-and-forth, leisure-less mental activity to his notion of responsibility when he states:

> We have to negotiate between the unconditional and conditional. They cannot be dissociated, although we know they are absolutely heterogeneous and incommensurable. It is because these incommensurable poles are indissociable that we have to take responsibility, a difficult responsibility, to negotiate the best response in an impossible situation.[73]

In this sense, experiencing forgiveness is necessarily a negotiation between the pure and impure, between the human and superhuman, and between the possible and the impossible. Because there is no formula that can be used to overcome the aporetic character of the conceptual relationships that structure the logic of forgiveness, Derrida suggests that it is only possible to confront the paradox of forgiveness by appealing simultaneously to both the conditional and the unconditional, privileging—to the greatest extent possible—the hyperbolic ethical demand of that which is infinite and unfathomable.

Departing from this understanding of how to act responsibly in the face of the aporetic, the subsequent chapters of this book present a series of what may be considered conceptual "negotiations," theorizing both a form of forgiveness and cosmopolitanism that addresses the paradoxical issues inherent to these two ideas. I attempt to confront the aporias that Derrida's analysis reveals in order to theorize a political forgiveness that overcomes—as far as is theoretically possible—the paradoxes and pitfalls identified by a deconstruction of the faculty of forgiving. To do so, I use Arendt's work to theorize forgiveness as a form of "caring for the world." I demonstrate that in caring for worldly, public spaces—which are constituted by the relationships that are formed between actors in the political realm—forgiveness protects freedom and "power." It is by thinking in terms of an Arendtian notion of power, and the experience of freedom which accompanies it, that we can pass through the aporetic impasse revealed by a Derridean deconstruction. A care-based conceptualization of forgiveness, as a political practice performed in public spaces and during moments which are thoroughly conditioned, is an approach that allows for the experience of a certain miraculousness associated with the seemingly preternatural power of this idea/practice.

3. DERRIDA: ON COSMOPOLITANISM

In the final section of this chapter, I focus on Derrida's deconstruction of cosmopolitanism, examining his understanding of cosmopolitanism by investigating three key aspects of his work, all of which frame my theorization of cosmopolitan theory in the latter half of this book. I cast light upon his understanding of (un)conditional hospitality, his argument for "cities of refuge," and his perspective on *mondialisation*. Derrida's deconstruction of cosmopolitanism serves as an ideal departure point from which to begin constructing my own theory of this idea: a "caring cosmopolitanism" inspired by an Arendtian conception of "the political" and a Derridean understanding of radically welcoming the (unknown) Other.

Derrida's examination of cosmopolitan theory, like his discussion of the notion of forgiveness, uncovers the logical structure of cosmopolitanism that has been fundamentally shaped by Christian doctrine. In particular, he shows that cosmopolitanism is a notion that developed in terms of a Christianization of Stoic philosophy, before evolving as part of Kant's conception of universal hospitality, which Derrida understood to be at the conceptual core of its contemporary manifestations. To provide an overview of his genealogical movement into the historical "text" that constitutes *le héritage*, Derrida writes:

> We could identify the cosmopolitan (*cosmopolitique*) tradition common to a certain Greek stoicism and a Pauline Christianity, of which the inheritors were the figures of the Enlightenment, and to which Kant will doubtlessly have given the most rigorous philosophical formulation in his famous *Definitive Article in View of Perpetual Peace*: "The law of cosmopolitanism must be restricted to the conditions of universal hospitality."[74]

Kant's account of hospitality holds special significance in the history of political thought, though it was the Apostle Paul, whose "language continues to structure and condition the modern concepts of the rights of man or crimes against humanity,"[75] and who transmuted a certain Ciceronian conception of cosmopolitanism.[76] Derrida aims to disentangle this notion from its religious roots in order to construct a secular, humanist form of cosmopolitan theory. According to Hent de Vries, Derrida "turns to religion" as a means of "trivializ[ing]" the role of the religious by "stripping" religion of its "ontological and axiological privilege."[77] In line with Heidegger's approach to *Destruktion*, which calls for a "shaking off the ontological tradition" and "staking out the positive possibilities of that tradition," Derrida focuses upon the Christian character of cosmopolitanism because he seeks to emancipate cosmopolitan theory from the very tradition that propelled it through history. As with his conceptualization of forgiveness, the hyperbolic character of cosmopolitan hospitality formed from Christian teachings privileges the unconditional over the conditional: this is a relationship I seek to re-balance and re-world with the help of Arendt's body of thought.

A. Cosmopolitanism and the Unconditionality of Hospitality

Throughout Paul the Apostle's writings in the New Testament, there is a discernable transmutation of Greco-Roman ideas about natural law, hospitality, and the cosmos into a Christian message, which effectively allows Christian ideals to be considered in political terms.[78] Derrida highlights the political nature of Saint Paul's work by demonstrating how his writings Christianized the Stoic conception of the "world" by reconceiving it as a *"fraternal community of human beings, of fellow creatures, brothers, sons of God, and neighbors to one another."*[79] In drawing such a conclusion, Derrida refers to the writings of the Apostle Paul in Ephesians 2:11-22. These verses describe how the Jews and Gentiles, two peoples once alienated from one another by differing ritual practices, became reconciled through Christ: "In Christ Jesus you who once were far away have been brought near by the blood of Christ [. . .] [He] has made the two groups one and has destroyed the barrier, the dividing wall of hostility."[80] Here, it is not so much the story of reconciliation between Jew and Gentile which is of interest to Derrida; rather, it is the language and logic shaping a Christian conception of cosmopolitanism. Derrida subsequently leads us to what are perhaps the most significant verses in this entire passage, Ephesians 2:19-22, in which the language closely mirrors a Stoic conception of cosmopolitanism:

> You are no longer foreigners and strangers, but fellow citizens with God's people and also members of his household, built on the foundation of the apostles and prophets, with Christ Jesus himself as the chief cornerstone. In him the whole building is joined together and rises to become a holy temple in the Lord. And in him you too are being built together to become a dwelling in which God lives by his Spirit.

Presented here in terms of God's home, the "dwelling place in which [He] lives," the Apostle Paul weaves together the themes of hospitality and world citizenship in a manner that fuses a Judeo-Christian conception of the "divine" with ancient understandings of citizens and non-citizens, insiders, and outsiders. For Derrida, this passage "revive[s], radicalize[s], and literally 'politicize[s]' the primary injunctions of all the Abrahamic religions," since "foreigners" and "strangers"—two closely related but different terms for noncitizens—become "members" or "fellow citizens" in a political community of faith.[81] The Apostle Paul does not speak of Gentiles becoming Jews; instead, he contends that the purpose of the coming, as well as the death, of the Messiah was "to create [in Christ] one new humanity."[82] This religious and political reconfiguration, which effectively founds a world *polis* through the elimination of hostility toward strangers, and the corresponding expressions of inhospitality produced by this hostility, ultimately universalizes the welcome that had previously been reserved for the Israelites, the chosen people of God, free to enter the "strong city."[83] As they were no longer foreigners to each other, the Jews and the Gentiles became equal citizens in the new community born of this Christian conception of humanity, with all human beings welcomed as fellow members in God's house. In short, Derrida demonstrates how Paul the Apostle, by establishing a *cosmopolis* in Christ, theorized an unbounded, universal conception of hospitality upon Jesus's unconditional love for all of humanity.

By highlighting the religious underpinnings of cosmopolitanism, through a methodological process which De Vries terms "reverse implication," Derrida "folds the transcendental [. . .] back into the empirical and the historical."[84] A Derridean approach uncovers the infinite unfathomability of an "unconditional welcome" and suggests that unconditional hospitality is irreducible and cannot be limited by psychologisms, sociologisms, biologisms, or any other naturalistic reductionism that pervades the realist interpretation of the world and ourselves.[85] Understood as an enigmatic act of welcome, one which theoretically asks us to exceed the limits of our own comprehension, a Derridean notion of hospitality is in alignment with Levinas's conception of responsibility: having a radical obligation to welcome the infinite alterity of the "face" of the Other. Derrida's hospitality therefore mirrors Levinas's sense that approaching the face of the Other is to welcome a figure who represents all of humanity. This welcoming is what Levinas calls a "metaphysical event of transcendence,"[86] for, in the act of coming face-to-face with an Other, one confronts the infinite, a notion whose *ideatum* surpasses its own idea.[87] In this paradigm, the appearance of the Other is akin to experiencing the kind of "love" that Victor Hugo famously describes in his novel about compassion, social injustice, and redemption, *Les Misérables* (1862). Loving another person is to see the face of God; the universe is contained in one single being, implying that one person represents the infinite, or a dilatation of that being *to* God. In Hugo's words: "*La réduction de l'univers à un seul être, la dilatation d'un seul être jusqu'à Dieu, voilà l'amour.*"[88] As he also suggests, in a manner that reminds us of Derrida's notion of the aporetic experience of justice, if God is behind everything, but everything hides God, then to love another being—an Other who appears before us—is to render that being transparent: "*Dieu est derrière tout, mais tout cache Dieu. Les choses sont noires, les créatures sont opaques. Aimer un être, c'est le rendre transparent* (God is behind everything, but everything hides God. Things are black, creatures are opaque. To love a being, is to render that being transparent)."[89] Recognized as an act of and toward infinitude, hospitality "overflows the thought that thinks it."[90] Like an unconditional form of forgiveness, then, unconditional hospitality is characteristically uncharacterizable: the revelation of God.

The hyperbolic practice of acting hospitably to the Other is a preternatural notion in that it refers to a welcoming of the *unknown* Other: a person who is not simply a foreigner (as a foreigner possesses certain juridical-political rights) but rather an anonymous stranger (someone without any rights), welcomed in spite of their anonymity. As Derrida writes, hospitality is an "intentional experience which proceeds beyond knowledge toward the Other as absolute stranger, as unknown, where I know that I know nothing of him [. . .] [it] is owed to the Other as stranger."[91] As he states elsewhere:

> Absolute hospitality requires that I open up my home [. . .] to the absolute, unknown, anonymous other, and that I *give place* to them, that I let them come, that I let them arrive, and take place in the place I offer them, without asking them either reciprocity (entering into a pact) or even their names.[92]

Here, unconditional hospitality means to give one's home freely to an Other without requiring anything in return, and without knowing, or even wanting to know, this person's name or place of origin. Like forgiveness, which is a gift truly and purely given, hospitality must be an absolute, unconditional welcoming of the Other as a stranger, without stipulations or an expectation of reciprocity.[93] Hospitality, in this way, is again similar to forgiveness because an absolute welcoming of the Other cannot by qualified nor can it be characterized by the circularity of an economic transaction, whereby giving place to the Other also necessitates a taking from them (e.g., money, services, or even their name in return for the hospitality given). In short, unconditional hospitality is to offer a place in one's home freely to all those who knock the door. This is an aspect of Derrida's cosmopolitan theory I retain in my conceptualization of a caring cosmopolitanism, according to which the Other's *story* ought to be welcomed freely into the political world—a "common home"[94] shared by all people who appear in public to speak and act together—as a narrative "thing" capable of becoming a part of the larger, ever-unfolding story of human history.

B. The Ethics and Politics of Hospitality

It is the unconditional giving of one's place of dwelling over to the Other that structures the logic of unconditional hospitality. The notion of "giving place" is of particular importance to Derrida's conception of hospitality because it links the ethical and the political. Evoking the notion of inclusion and exclusion, or of being an insider or an outsider, hospitality—for Derrida—is synonymous with ethics, "insofar as it has to do with the *ethos*, that is, the residence, one's home, the familiar place of dwelling, inasmuch as it is a manner of being there, the manner in which we relate to ourselves and to others [. . .] *ethics is hospitality*."[95] Derrida argues that hospitality is "always about answering for a dwelling place, for one's identity, one's space, one's limits, for the *ethos* as abode, habituation, house, hearth, family, home."[96] This conceptualization of ethics, understood as a "familiar place of dwelling," mirrors the Apostle Paul's configuration of cosmopolitanism in Ephesians, for both speak in terms of the "home." Arendt, too, is a scholar who thinks along these lines, referring to the public realm of the political as a "common home" within which a plurality of people can appear, move, and act together. Where Arendt's "common home" is understood in more thoroughly secular terms, there is some value in considering hospitality, from a Derridean perspective, as being equated with the house of God: being welcomed into the universal community of faith is to enter the divine household. This is an inherently ethical idea, so much so, in fact, that Derrida wonders if the phrase, "an ethic of hospitality," is not redundant when he asks rhetorically, "is such an expression not tautologous?"[97]

Although the idea that "ethics is hospitality" echoes Levinas's conception of welcoming the Other, a Derridean conceptualization is political where a Levinasian theorization is not, since the idea of "giving place" to the Other raises questions about what it means to belong.[98] Derrida's "ethic of hospitality" is indissociable from politics because "giving place" to the Other introduces the thoroughly political issues of "place" and "belonging" (or being from a place) into the dynamics of hospitality. Associated with the idea of how people live within delimited sociopolitical communities, to be from a place—or to be from a particular home, community, city, state, and so on—presupposes power, or a sovereignty, which is capable of maintaining the lines of demarcation that condition the existing order.[99] Derrida's model, because it revolves around the notion of "giving place," emphasizes the issue of sovereignty since acts of welcoming presuppose that an insider/outsider, foreigner/barbarian, or citizen/noncitizen dichotomy exists, where one person, or group of people, belongs and another does not.[100] Sitting at the theoretical and practical core of (global) politics, the notion of place, and the idea of belonging to a particular place, is one of the basic conditions undergirding the political order throughout recorded history.

While cosmopolitan ideas and understandings have—to varying degrees—permeated this order, the doing of global politics nevertheless continues to revolve around the notion of belonging. Moreover, human existence continues to be conditioned by barriers, boundaries, and borders, all of which are manifested when people act (in)hospitably to other people. Welcoming the Other is therefore an ethical and political act, as hospitality must be, at once, ethically unconditional but also conditioned by the factors that characterize politics. As Derrida writes: "Between an unconditional law or an absolute desire for hospitality on the one hand and, on the other, a law, a politics, a conditioned ethics, there is distinction, radical heterogeneity, but also indissociability."[101] His work on the notion of hospitality therefore stresses the paradoxicality of an (un)conditional welcoming of the Other, a point which he unpacks more fully with reference to Immanuel Kant's influential treatise on cosmopolitanism, *Perpetual Peace* (1795).

C. "Cities of Refuge" and *Cosmopolitics*

The short tractate, *Perpetual Peace*, is a defining text in the history of international political thought, having had a lasting impact on both international law and global politics. Kant is an Enlightenment thinker whose formulation of cosmopolitan law is of particular interest to Derrida, because it is a "Law of World Citizenship" that is "Limited to Conditions of Universal Hospitality."[102] This is a paradoxical notion of "world citizenship," a *limited* form of *universally* welcoming the (unknown) Other, which Derrida locates at the center of cosmopolitan thought as an ethical idea that cannot be detached from the conditions imposed by the realities of (international) law and (global) politics. The ethical imperative for a universal hospitality is distinct from—but nevertheless linked to—politics, which dictates that hospitality can never be unconditional. As Derrida observes, a Kantian law of cosmopolitanism "encompasses universal hospitality *without* limit," but it is the borders of the nation, state, public, and political spaces that prevent the Earth from being "unconditionally accessible to all."[103] The social, political, and legal realities of living in a delimited, conditional world mean that hospitality—though ethically universal and therefore unlimited—must be restricted by the limitations of the international political realm.[104]

The empirical realities of world politics, which restrict how and to what extent the Other can be welcomed, led Kant to limit the scope of what it means to welcome others in two primary ways. This is summarized by Derrida: "First of all [Kant] excluded hospitality as a *right of residence (Gastrecht)*," limiting it to "the *right of visitation (Besuchsrecht)*," and, second, he "assigns to it conditions which make it dependent on state sovereignty."[105] Invoking the sentiment of an unconditional hospitality, Kant presents a limited form of welcome that is subject to the rules, regulations, and rights of the Westphalian state system. A Kantian model is consequently state-centric and extends hospitality only to those persons being welcomed as temporary guests. Underscoring the paradoxicality of Kant's formulation of hospitality, Derrida acknowledges that the idea of welcoming the Other remains "obscure" and that humanity must not "imagine [itself] to have mastered" the idea of cosmopolitanism.[106] In an effort to expand Kant's "law of world citizenship," and thus to further "master" the notion of cosmopolitan hospitality, Derrida calls for "cities of refuge," as a means of elaborating upon the Kantian "spirit"[107] and for the writing of a "new world contract" that focuses on cities, rather than states.[108]

For Derrida, this "new world contract" is akin to a "new charter of hospitality," which represents a "new ethic," or a "new cosmo*politics* of the cities of refuge."[109] Here, the term "cosmopolitics" refers to a politics of the cosmos, with "cosmos" referring to the universe and "politics"—stemming from the Greek word, *polis*, meaning "city." A Derridean cosmopolitanism, as it relates to an ethic of the cosmos, is thus an ethico-political theory of and for cities, which ought to be a place of refuge for all people. This shifts the burden of responsibility for welcoming the Other from states to cities, broadening the scope of who may seek asylum, as Derrida writes:

> Whether it be the foreigner in general, the immigrant, the exiled, the deported, the stateless or the displaced person [. . .] we would ask these new cities of refuge to reorient the politics of the state. We would ask them to transform and reform the modalities of membership by which the city (*cité*) belongs to the state.[110]

Calling for an abandonment of the state-centric model of Kant, Derrida outlines a "cosmopolitics" that calls for "cities of refuge" to welcome the stranger "in general." He maintains that cities should be understood as "what one calls structures of welcoming (*les structures de l'accueil*), a welcoming apparatus (*les structures d'accueil*)."[111] The hope is that cities will offer a form of hospitality that is less restrictive and more open to all, thereby maintaining the idea and purity of the unconditional welcome. This is a theoretical conceptualization that I too employ when I theorize a caring cosmopolitanism (chapter 3), and argue that the *polis*—considered in terms of an Arendtian notion of "world"—can be understood as the space of political action. Where Derrida critiques Kant for focusing on the state rather than the microcosm that is the city, I, in turn, re-examine the *polis* in terms of the "world," and—to borrow Hugo's idiosyncratic expression—dilate the city, rendering it even more "transparent," so to speak; in other words, I open this singularity—the city as locality—more fully to the (unknown) Other, which is to say, "God." The possibility of "giving place" to a plurality of persons in the "world" is therefore magnified.

The notion of cities as "structures of welcoming" introduces an additional complexity inherent to Derrida's thought, which has led scholars such as Puspa Damai, for example, to conclude that the city can be understood in Levinasian terms.[112] As a "self" in and of itself, the city—for Damai—is an embodied Other in its own right, whose very existence as a distinct, singular entity is dependent upon the arrival and presence of the "face" of the (unknown) Other.[113] When conceptualized in this manner, the city is a "unicity"[114]—albeit inherently "labyrinthine"[115]—whose very "oneness or *ipseity*"[116] is reliant upon the presence of the Other and/or the expected arrival of the Other.[117] A city, as Damai suggests, is "at once more than one and less than one, insofar as it subsists only by going outside of itself towards the Other."[118] This Levinasian-inspired theory of the city is critical to a Derridean conceptualization of cosmopolitan hospitality because it allows the dynamic of welcoming between the city—an Other in and of itself—and another party to be understood in hyper-ethical terms. According to this distinctly Levinasian conceptualization, one which is presented in explicitly Christian language, hospitable interactions between the city and the Other can be reconfigured in such a way that the "visitation that is the arrival of the Other" is a matter of the arrival of "God."[119] Once again "folding" the "transcendental back into the empirical and historical" (to reuse De Vries's description of a Derridean approach), Derrida describes the coming of the Other in unconditional terms, when he states: "'come,' 'enter,' 'whoever you are and whatever your name, your language, your sex, your species may be, be you human, animal, or divine.'"[120] The interaction between the city and the Other is thus a matter of the ever-present potential arrival of the unknown. This is the arrival of someone or something who/that Derrida describes in terms of the "messianic," or the appearance of "God" at the gates of the city.

According to Kearney, in a piece entitled, "Derrida and Messianic Atheism," Derrida "embraces a 'messianicity' beyond the concrete, historical 'messianisms' of the Abrahamic (and other) traditions," and he theorizes a "messianicity" that "involves an endless waiting with no sense of what kind of Other might arrive."[121] Within this conceptual paradigm, universal hospitality is a matter of being unconditionally open to, and awaiting, the appearance of the "divine": the Messiah whose appearance in the world is simultaneously immanent and ever on the horizon, an understanding encapsulated in Mark 13:32-34, where it is written:

> No-one knows about that day or hour, not even the angels in heaven, nor the Son, but only the Father. Be alert and pray! You do not know when that time will come. It's like a man going away: He leaves his house and puts his servants in charge, each with his assigned task, and tells the one at the door to keep watch.

Echoing this understanding, Derrida theorizes messianicity as a radical openness to the Other, according to which, the city ought to be ever alert with its gates open in preparation for the appearance of "God." Such a conceptualization of messianicity corresponds to, as Kearney observes, "an unconditional 'yes' to what is always still to come."[122] For Derrida, then, the city is a Self that needs to be "alert," or, indeed, to proactively "pray" for the messianic arrival since, as is suggested by Levinas, each encounter at the city's gate can be said to engender a "face-to-face" interaction with the infinite.[123]

Derrida's Levinasian-inspired conceptualization alters, fundamentally, the dynamic of power at play during acts of welcoming the Other, as it means that no single party wields supreme power over an Other when coming "face-to-face." Power is not understood in a singular sense, nor is it considered in terms of the "classical conception of sovereignty," whereby—as Damai avers—"sovereignty is defined as an absolute and perpetual power of the [ruler]."[124] Rather, a Derridean conception of hospitality mirrors a Levinasian one, according to which the welcomed Other, whose fate is determined by the actions of the host, can be said to hold power over the party that does the welcoming. This conception of power, as a type of mutual subjectification, is acknowledged when Derrida writes:

> It's *as if* the master, *qua* master, were prisoner of his place and his power, of his *ipseity*, of his subjectivity (his subjectivity is hostage). So it is indeed the master, the one who invites, the inviting host, who becomes the hostage [. . .] And the guest, the invited hostage, becomes the one who invites the one who invites, the master of the host. The guest becomes the host's host. The guest (*hôte*) becomes the host (*hôte*) of the host (*hôte*).[125]

Being held hostage to the Other is distinctly Levinasian, an understanding that informs the logic of hospitality: both sovereignties, the self and the Other, holding one another hostage when they come face-to-face.[126] This sharing of power generates a specific type of responsibility for the Other because one becomes a "self" only in relation to the Other: a self cannot be understood as a self in isolation from someone else.[127] The self/Other paradigm disappears; there can be no *I*, understood as a self, when—as Levinas argues—"it is only in approaching the Other that I attend to myself."[128] The face-to-face interaction can therefore be said to shape the identities of both the Other and the city, since the very existence of each is dependent upon the presence of the other's "face."[129] Relating this to *ethos*, Derrida writes that "being at home with oneself (*l'être-soi chez soi—l'ipseite même*—the other within oneself) supposes a reception or inclusion of the other."[130] A city, as a figure (an Other) who welcomes, and is held hostage by the welcomed, only becomes a home, a familiar place of dwelling, in the presence of the face of the Other. Embodying the figure of the Other, the city relies upon the existence of the stranger to "be at home with [itself]."

If cities are the embodied figures of the Other, then, the city's identity—as the host who welcomes the guest—is constituted by the "face" of the foreigner who asks for hospitality: the city relies upon the stranger in order to establish its identity as a sovereign, a relation which empowers the guest. Moreover, if, as Levinas suggests, to approach the face of the Other is to approach the infinite, then cities—as embodied selves—confront infinity when they welcome strangers. The identity of the *polis*, as a home or familiar place of dwelling, relies upon the arrival of the unknown Other, whose face represents infinitude. In this sense, Derrida's appeal for a new "cosmopolitics"—or an ethic of hospitality for cities—seeks to make way for the arrival of the unfathomable. It is through the act of welcoming the Other that there is "hope, beyond all 'messianism,' of a universalizable culture of singularities, a culture in which the abstract possibility of the impossible translation could nevertheless be announced."[131] Cities, by welcoming the Other, act in a cosmopolitan manner by openly anticipating, and subsequently receiving, the infinite: they unify both the self and the Other in the community of all humankind. This is a common unity of all people, beyond difference—though not *différance*—and sociopolitical divisions.

Cities as "structures of welcome," despite necessarily being rooted in specific geographical places, with their own varied languages, cultures, and histories, become sites of universality when they embrace the infinite of the unknown Other. Such an understanding amounts to a cosmopolitical act of hospitality of and for humanity. This is an important aspect of both a caring forgiveness and a caring cosmopolitanism, since the realm of public action is a worldly common "home" for human beings in so far as the Other is welcomed as a co-practitioner of acting and speaking there. It is within the paradigm of Arendt's body of thought, however, that such a dynamic of welcoming the Other can be better understood, as it is in terms of the "world" that Derrida's "quasi-transcendental" understanding can be both grounded and "dilated."

D. *Mondialisation*

By expanding the scope of who is welcomed into the city, and by reconsidering the city as the site of welcome, Derrida's "cities of refuge" shift the burden of hospitality away from the state. A Derridean theory of cosmopolitanism therefore differs from both the Stoic and the Kantian conceptions of the cosmopolitan ideal, since it is "more in line with what lets singular beings (anyone) 'live together.'"[132] In an effort to build upon these older understandings of cosmopolitanism, Derrida's project of writing a "new world contract" attempts to "cultivate the spirit of this tradition."[133] This being said, his theory, which he sometimes refers to as a "democracy to come," is a city-centric model of cosmopolitanism that has yet to arrive in the world, and one that he suggests becomes possible at the level of impossibility. For Derrida, "The democracy to come [is] the *khôra* of the political."[134] Invoking the thoroughly enigmatic—and notoriously difficult to translate—ancient Greek word "*khôra*," which is a term that "resists any binary or dialectical determination, any inspection of a philosophical *type*, or let us say, more rigorously, of any *ontological* type,"[135] Derrida affirms that a democratic vision of a cosmopolitan "city of refuge" is an "unplaceable place"[136] of welcoming the "messianic": "the infinite" yet to arrive and approach the gates of the *polis*. Reaching beyond the cosmopolitan tradition of Kant, a "democracy to come" is that which Damai playfully describes as a "messianic-*city*" (as opposed to "messianicity").[137] Moreover, a "democracy to come" seeks to limit and share sovereignty, as such cities are inclusive spaces, unconditionally open to the unknown Other, and are conceptualized in intersubjective, non-hierarchical terms. It is therefore through "cities of refuge" that universal hospitality can be experienced, and thus that the "privilege of citizenship [can be extended] in the *world*."[138] The word "world" (in French, *monde*) is emphasized here precisely because Derrida suggests that the "democracy to come," as a cosmopolitan order yet to exist, necessitates that we rethink the notion of "world." This is an observation that Derrida makes, in passing, when he notes that a "democracy to come" requires "another thought and another putting into practice of the concept of the 'political' and concept of 'world'—which is not the same as cosmos."[139] Throughout the remainder of this book, taking Derrida up on his call to reconsider these two concepts, I consequently theorize the notion of "world" in Arendtian terms, examining how two practices of "caring for the world"—what I call a caring forgiveness and caring cosmopolitanism—reframe what it means to think and act politically at a time in history when new forms of world alienation appear to be tearing the public realm asunder.

From a Derridean perspective, the idea of "world" is closely related to the notion of the "global"—so much so that the French word *mondialisation* is often translated into English as "globalization"—yet Derrida prefers to use the word *monde* (in "reference to the world—*monde, Welt, mundus*—which is neither globe nor the cosmos").[140] Not unlike Arendt's notion of "world," that which refers to the human artifact, *mondialisation* is a concept which refers to the human face of globalizing processes. *Mondialisation* is a "worldwide-ization" that "wishes to be a humanization,"[141] and it "gestures toward a history" that "distinguishes it from that of the globe, of the universe, of Earth, of the *cosmos* even (at least of the cosmos in its pre-Christian meaning)."[142] Focusing on how *mondialisation* relates to the idea of humanity, Derrida writes the following about the historical legacy of the notion of "world":

> For the world begins by designating, and tends to remain, in an Abrahamic tradition (Judeo-Christian-Islamic but predominately Christian) a particular space-time, a certain oriented history of human brotherhood, of what in a Pauline language [. . .] one calls *citizens of the world* (*sympolitai*, fellow citizens [*concitoyens*] of the saints in the house of God), brothers, fellow men, neighbors, insofar as they are creatures and sons of God.[143]

Derrida presents the notion of "world" in relation to cosmopolitanism and Christianity, highlighting that world citizenship includes all people as fellow members, or citizens, in the universal community of all humankind, as they dwell in the all-encompassing house of God. Because both the notion of human rights and crimes against humanity presuppose the understanding that there are certain inalienable rights extended to all who possess membership of this universal community, the Pauline conception of "world citizenship" cannot be overlooked. The language and legacy of this Christian ideal inform contemporary conceptions of international law and (world) politics, which—for Derrida—regulates the "process of *mondialisation*, the becoming-world of the world."[144] Seen in this light, *mondialisation* is a process of (re-)configuring the world in Judeo-Christian terms, exporting the linguistic, social, cultural, economic, legal, and political understandings of the West to the entirety of the globe.

While Derrida contends that we must preserve the so-called best aspects of the Western tradition, namely human rights[145] and the spirit of Kant,[146] he warns against what can be perceived as the pernicious side effects of *mondialisation*, among them, the dangers of neoliberalism and linguistic, political, and military hegemonies. He cautions against the "negative recourse, the vengeance of the body proper against an expropriatory and delocalizing tele-technoscience, identified with the globality of the market with military-capitalistic hegemony, with the globalatinisation [*mondialatinisation*] of the European democratic model."[147] Derrida consequently suggests that the cosmopolitan tradition must be scrutinized, since the universalizing character of this religiously charged idea is closely linked to processes that generate stark power imbalances (such as between the global north and global south); eradicate linguistic diversities; impose Western sociopolitical understandings upon non-Western peoples; and further entrench the military-industrial complex. Derrida hopes that a "democracy to come"—a cosmopolitanism fashioned from a new "world contract" and a "new ethic of hospitality"—can counter the negative effects of *mondialisation*, while nevertheless expanding human rights alongside the notion of world citizenship: extending the reach and validity of human rights, ensuring citizenship for all people, and welcoming the (unknown) Other unconditionally.

For me, such a "cosmopolitan vision"—to borrow Ulrich Beck's phrase[148]—is a noble dream for the world, yet, and perhaps ironically, exhibits a distinct form of worldlessness associated with a radically Other-centric ethics. That is, Derrida's prioritization of the Other, which he suggests ought to be welcomed (and forgiven) unconditionally in a "messianic" manner, errs on the side of worldlessness precisely because it focuses too fully on the "infinite," which—in a thoroughly Levinasian formulation—is the "face" of the Other. When thinking in such hyperbolic ethical terms, of the Other's sheer singularity, as the so-called face of God, do we not lose our sense of the "world"? Does the "world" not disappear when we fail to focus our attention directly upon it, which is to say, when we neglect to care directly about and for that which simultaneously connects and separates us from the Other? As the subsequent chapters illustrate by way of an examination of Arendt's body of thought, focusing entirely on the Other inhibits political action, when attention paid to the "face-to-face" interaction eclipses our concern for the worldly web of relationships engendered when a plurality of people speak and act together. While Derrida's "democracy to come" attempts to expound upon the "spirit" of Kant, a Derridean approach does so to the detriment of what Arendt refers to as the "world." Recognizing the fundamental political significance of the "world," and of thinking and acting for the sake of the public realm of "the political," I present a more worldly, "world"-centric theory of politics fashioned from an Arendtian reconceptualization of Derrida's understanding of cosmopolitanism (and forgiveness). I re-world Derrida's theory of cosmopolitan hospitality through Arendt's work.

I argue that in order to properly welcome the Other, it is necessary to act hospitably to the narrative voice of this stranger, foreigner, and outsider. To welcome the Other's narrative voice is to embrace a fellow co-storyteller within the space of the political, where publicly shared words and deeds become the "worldly" artifacts that bring a plurality of people together and allow "power to" emerge. By welcoming the narrative voice of the (unknown) Other, I contend that the unconditionality of Kant's universal welcome is more fully upheld within the conditions imposed by human language, law, and politics. A caring cosmopolitanism attempts to map the aporetic terrain unearthed by a Derridean deconstruction of cosmopolitanism, providing a worldly theory of cosmopolitan hospitality devoted to the unconditional welcoming of the voice of the (unknown) Other, and the accompanying story, as a worldly "thing."

NOTES

1. Derrida, *On Cosmopolitanism and Forgiveness*.
2. The development of this anti-immigrant sensibility in France began taking shape when the *Front National* saw a rise in public popularity in the early 1980s, when an "*immigration zéro*" mentality assumed a more mainstream place in French politics. Derrida's critique, however, was largely directed at both the 1993 passing of the "Pasqua Law," a piece of immigration legislation named after the then *Ministre de l'Intérieur*, Charles Pasqua, and the subsequent proposal of the 1996 "Debré Law," which was a reform bill proposed by Pasqua's successor, Jean-Louis Debré. Enhancing the regulations contained within Pasqua's Law, the Debré bill sought to "close loopholes" in the 1993 legislation, creating a national registry of French citizens and their foreign guests; allowing officials to collect the biometric details of people from outside the European Union who wished to reside in France; developing a system

for denying visas to would-be visitors from developing countries if they could not provide evidence of a place of lodging for the extent of their stay; and providing the police with increased powers to monitor the movements of immigrants in the country. [Shelese Emmons, "The Debre Bill: Immigration Legislation or a National 'Front'?" *Indiana Journal of Global Legal Studies* 5, no. 1 (1997): 358.]

3. Derrida, *On Cosmopolitanism and Forgiveness*, 28.

4. Jacques Derrida, *Theory and Practice*, eds. Geoffrey Bennington and Peggy Kamuf, trans. David Wills (London: The University of Chicago Press, 2019).

5. Jacques Derrida, "Force of Law: The 'Mystical Foundation of Authority,'" in *Deconstruction and the Possibility of Justice*, eds. Drucilla Cornell, Michel Rosenfeld, and David Gray Carlson (London: Routledge, 1992), 8–9.

6. Jacques Derrida, *Specters of Marx: The State of the Debt, the Work of Mourning and the New International*, eds. Bernd Magnus and Stephen Cullenberg, trans. Peggy Kamuf (London: Routledge, 2006), 63; Karl Marx, "Theses on Feuerbach," in *The Marx-Engels Reader*, ed. Robert C. Tucker (London: W.W. Norton & Company, Inc., 1978), 145; Karl Marx, "For a Ruthless Criticism of Everything Existing," in *The Marx-Engels Reader*, ed. Robert C. Tucker (London: W.W. Norton & Company, Inc., 1978), 12–15.

7. Derrida, *On Cosmopolitanism and Forgiveness*, viii.

8. Jacques Derrida, "Letter to a Japanese Friend," in *Derrida and Différance*, eds. David Wood and Robert Bernasconi, trans. Andrew Benjamin (Evanston, IL: Northwestern University Press, 1988), 4.

9. Jacques Derrida, *Limited Inc*, ed. Gerald Graff (Evanston, IL: Northwestern University Press, 1988), 148.

10. Ibid.

11. Jacques Derrida, *Margins of Philosophy*, trans. Alan Bass (Brighton, UK: The Harverster Press, 1982), 12.

12. Jacques Derrida, *De la grammatologie* (Paris: Les Éditions de Minuit, 1967), 227; Jacques Derrida, *Of Grammatology*, trans. Gayatri Chakravorty Spivak (London: The Johns Hopkins University Press, 1997), 163.

13. Derrida, *Limited Inc*, 136.

14. Jacques Derrida, *Speech and Phenomena: And Other Essays on Husserl's Theory of Signs*, trans. David B. Allison and Newton Garver (Evanston, IL: Northwestern University Press, 1973), 109–13.

15. Derrida, *On Cosmopolitanism and Forgiveness*, ix.

16. Ibid., viii.

17. Though Derrida's philosophy is indebted to Benjamin's work in several notable ways, with the former developing a notion of messianicity from the latter's eclectic body of thought, scholars like Fischer and Weber have suggested that a Derridean deconstructivist approach might have been directly influenced by a Benjaminian approach to reading of *le héritage*. [Gerhard Fischer, ed., *With The Sharpened Axe of Reason: Approaches to Walter Benjamin* (Oxford: Berg Publishers, 1996), sec. 1; Samuel Weber, *Benjamin's Abilities* (London: Harvard University Press, 2008), 122–28.]

18. Nicholas Royle, "What Is Deconstruction?" in *Deconstructions: A User's Guide*, ed. Nicholas Royle (London: Palgrave, 2000), 11.

19. Derrida, "Force of Law," 24.
20. Jacques Derrida, *Aporias* (Stanford: Stanford University Press, 1993), 11–12. Original emphasis.
21. Ibid. Original emphasis.
22. Ibid., 12.
23. Derrida, *On Cosmopolitanism and Forgiveness*, 39.
24. Derrida, "Force of Law," 22 and 15.
25. Ibid.
26. Simon Critchley, *Ethics-Politics-Subjectivity: Essays on Derrida, Levinas and Contemporary French Thought* (London: Verso, 1999), 99.
27. Derrida, "Force of Law," 22.
28. Critchley, *Ethics-Politics-Subjectivity*, 98.
29. Emmanuel Levinas, *Totalité et Infini: Essai Sur l'extériorité* (Dordrecht: Martinus Nijhoff Publishers, 1987), 80.
30. Derrida, "Force of Law," 22.
31. Alphonso Lingis, for instance, translates Levinas's notion of "*la droiture de l'accueil fait au visage*" as "the uprightness of the welcome made to the face." See: Emmanuel Levinas, *Totality and Infinity: An Essay on Exteriority*, trans. Alphonso Lingis (London: Martinus Nijhoff Publishers, 1979), 82.
32. Jacques Derrida, "Hostipitality," trans. Barry Stocker and Forbes Morlock, *Angelaki: Journal of the Theoretical Humanities* 5, no. 3 (2000): n. 17, p. 17.
33. Critchley, *Ethics-Politics-Subjectivity*, 99.
34. Derrida, *On Cosmopolitanism and Forgiveness*, 28.
35. Richard Kearney, "On Forgiveness: A Roundtable Discussion with Jacques Derrida," in *Questioning God*, eds. John D. Caputo, Mark Dooley, and Michael J. Scanlon (Bloomington, IN: Indiana University Press, 2001), 67.
36. Derrida, *On Cosmopolitanism and Forgiveness*, 32. Original emphasis.
37. Arendt, *The Human Condition*, 238.
38. Kearney, "On Forgiveness: A Roundtable Discussion with Jacques Derrida," 67.
39. Michael Janover, "The Limits of Forgiveness and the Ends of Politics," *Journal of Intercultural Studies* 26, no. 3 (2005): 228.
40. Luke 15:11-32. Martha Nussbaum similarly points to this biblical story as an example of how an "ethic of unconditional love" can be said to inform a more thoroughly non-retributive, non-resentful form of forgiveness; this is a understanding of the act of forgiving she develops in *Anger and Forgiveness: Resentment, Generosity, Justice* (Oxford: Oxford University Press, 2016).
41. Derrida, "To Forgive: The Unforgivable and the Imprescriptable," 29.
42. Derrida, *On Cosmopolitanism and Forgiveness*, 35–36.
43. Ibid., 34–35. Original emphasis.
44. Ibid., 42.
45. Ibid., 44.
46. Note that in French, "*donner*" is the verb "to give," and "*don*" is a noun meaning "gift."

47. The notion of "good" is a theme that Arendt explores in her work and is briefly considered in the subsequent chapter. Cf. Arendt, *The Human Condition*, 76 and 240.

48. Jacques Derrida, *The Gift of Death* (Chicago: University of Chicago Press, 1995), 41.

49. Jacques Derrida, *Given Time: I. Counterfeit Money*, ed. Peggy Kamuf (Chicago: The University of Chicago Press, 1992), 7. Original emphasis. Chapter 4 highlights how forgiving is undergirded by an aneconomic, linear temporal logic, according to which the practice of forgiving inserts both an end and a new beginning into the changeless flow of time.

50. Derrida, *On Cosmopolitanism and Forgiveness*, 31–32.

51. Ernesto Verdeja, "Derrida and the Impossibility of Forgiveness," *Contemporary Political Theory* 3 (2004): 26.

52. Ibid., 25.

53. Derrida, *On Cosmopolitanism and Forgiveness*, 50.

54. Verdeja, "Derrida and the Impossibility of Forgiveness," 25.

55. Derrida, "To Forgive: The Unforgivable and the Imprescriptable," 45.

56. Vladimir Jankélévitch, "Should We Pardon Them?" *Critical Inquiry* 22, no. 3 (1996): 567.

57. Ibid., 555.

58. Arendt, *The Origins of Totalitarianism*, 458–59.

59. Ibid., 459.

60. Arendt, *The Human Condition*, 241.

61. Derrida, *On Cosmopolitanism and Forgiveness*, 32–33.

62. Derrida, "To Forgive: The Unforgivable and the Imprescriptable," 34. Original emphasis.

63. Derrida, *On Cosmopolitanism and Forgiveness*, 59.

64. Ibid.

65. Derrida, "To Forgive: The Unforgivable and the Imprescriptable," 22.

66. Derrida, *Given Time*, 7. Original emphasis.

67. Ibid., 12.

68. Ibid., 30.

69. Derrida, *On Cosmopolitanism and Forgiveness*, 59. Original emphasis.

70. Kearney, "On Forgiveness: A Roundtable Discussion with Jacques Derrida," 62.

71. Ibid., 58.

72. Jacques Derrida, *Negotiations: Interventions and Interviews, 1971–2001*, ed. Elizabeth Rottenberg (Stanford, CA: Stanford University Press, 2002), 12.

73. Kearney, "On Forgiveness: A Roundtable Discussion with Jacques Derrida," 58.

74. Derrida, *On Cosmopolitanism and Forgiveness*, 18–19.

75. Derrida, *Negotiations*, 375.

76. Derrida, *On Cosmopolitanism and Forgiveness*, 19. For an account of Cicero's stoicism, see Thomas L. Pangle, "Socratic Cosmopolitanism: Cicero's Critique and Transformation of the Stoic Ideal," *Canadian Journal of Political Science* 31, no. 2 (1998): 235–62.

77. Hent De Vries, *Religion and Violence: Philosophical Perspectives from Kant to Derrida* (London: The Johns Hopkins University Press, 2002), 298–99.

78. For a thorough examination of the Apostle Paul's influence on Derrida's work, see Theodore W. Jennings, *Reading Derrida/Thinking Paul: On Justice* (Stanford, CA: Stanford University Press, 2006). Notably, as Derek Heater observes, "it was St Paul, almost in spite of himself, who, more than anyone else, transmitted Stoic beliefs and principles to Christianity." [Derek Heater, *World Citizenship and Government: Cosmopolitan Ideas and the History of Western Political Thought* (London: Palgrave Macmillan, 1996), 23.]

79. Derrida, *Negotiations*, 374–75. Original emphasis.

80. Ephesians 2:13-14.

81. Derrida, *On Cosmopolitanism and Forgiveness*, 19.

82. Ephesians 2:15.

83. See Isaiah 29:1-3: "We have a strong city; God makes salvation its walls and ramparts. Open the gates that the righteous nation may enter, the nation that keeps faith."

84. De Vries, *Religion and Violence*, 299.

85. Ibid.

86. Levinas, *Totality and Infinity*, 254.

87. Ibid., 49. Derrida interprets *Totality and Infinity* as an extensive treatise on hospitality.

88. Victor Hugo, *Les Misérables*, ed. Émile Testard, vol. IV (Paris: Edition Nationale, 1890), 194.

89. Ibid., 195.

90. Levinas, *Totality and Infinity*, 25.

91. Derrida, "Hostipitality," 8.

92. Jacques Derrida, *Of Hospitality: Anne Dufourmantelle Invites Jacques Derrida to Respond* (Stanford, CA: Stanford University Press, 2000), 25. Original emphasis.

93. Ibid., 83.

94. Arendt, "On the Nature of Totalitarianism," 358.

95. Derrida, *On Cosmopolitanism and Forgiveness*, 16–17. Original emphasis.

96. Derrida, *Of Hospitality*, 149–51. Original emphasis.

97. Derrida, *On Cosmopolitanism and Forgiveness*, 16.

98. Derrida describes Levinas's work as an "Ethics of Ethics." [Jacques Derrida, *Writing and Difference*, trans. Alan Bass (London: Routledge, 2001), 138.]

99. In a discussion of "home," both material and intangible, Alison Blunt and Robyn Dowling summarize this point aptly when they write: "Home-spaces and home-making practices are intimately bound together over a range of scales, and are closely shaped by the exercise of power and resistance and by what is imagined as 'foreign' or unhomely." [Alison Blunt and Robyn Dowling, *Home* (London: Routledge, 2006), 188.]

100. In *Totality and Infinity* (1969: 77), Levinas describes the relation of power between the faces of two Others, when he writes, "The face in its nakedness as a face [. . .] joins me to himself for service; he commands me as a Master."

101. Derrida, *Of Hospitality*, 147.

102. Immanuel Kant, *Perpetual Peace*, ed. Lewis White Beck (New York: The Library of Liberal Arts, 1957), 20.

103. Derrida, *On Cosmopolitanism and Forgiveness*, 20–21. Original emphasis.

104. Kant, *Perpetual Peace*, 21.

105. Derrida, *On Cosmopolitanism and Forgiveness*, 21–22. Original emphasis.

106. Ibid., 22.

107. Lasse Thomassen, ed., *The Derrida-Habermas Reader* (Chicago: University of Chicago Press, 2006), 261–62.

108. Derrida, *Negotiations*, 376.

109. Derrida, *On Cosmopolitanism and Forgiveness*, 5. Original emphasis.

110. Ibid., 4. The pronoun "we" used here refers to the International Parliament of Writers, of which Derrida was a founding member and vice president.

111. Jacques Derrida, *Acts of Religion*, ed. Gil Anidjar (London: Routledge, 2002), 361.

112. Puspa Damai, "Messianic-City: Ruins, Refuge and Hospitality in Derrida," *Discourse* 27 (2005): 70.

113. Ibid.

114. Ibid., 69.

115. Jacques Derrida, *Dissemination*, trans. Barbara Johnson (London: The Athlone Press, 1981), 341.

116. Damai, "Messianic-City," 69.

117. Here, it is somewhat significant to recognize that the "self" presented in Derrida's body of thought is a fragmented one. This conceptualization of the self is directly informed by his understanding of language, which stems from his deconstructive approach and his—as Caroline Williams observes—"re-thinking the boundaries of subjectivity, theory and *praxis* as conceived throughout the Western philosophical tradition—an activity which focuses upon language as the ordering force of the world." [Caroline Williams, *Contemporary French Philosophy: Modernity and the Persistence of the Subject* (London: Continuum, 2001), 109.] Given Derrida's language-based, deconstructive reconsideration of the tradition and his qualms about the possibility of an undivided, "solitary mental life" in the temporal moment of the "now," the present period of time that he suggests is always influenced by the imprint(s) left by a prior experience (i.e., a "trace"), Derrida contends that "my own presence to myself has been preceded by language" and that "the text occupies the place before 'me': it regards me, invests me, announces me to myself, keeps watch over my most secret present, surveys my heart's core—which is precisely a city, and a labyrinthine one—as if from the top of a watchtower planted inside me, like [a] 'transparent column' which, having no inside of its own, is driven, being a pure outside, into that which tries to close upon itself." [Derrida, *Speech and Phenomena*, 68; Derrida, *Dissemination*, 340–41.] Thoroughly permeated and shaped by language, the "self" is a maze-like entity that conceals its innermost secrets, a "labyrinthine" "city" over which language stands as a "glass column"—or a "watchtower"—that "traverses, dominates, regulates, and reflects, in its numerous polysemy, the entire set of squares." [Ibid., 341.] Echoing—maybe even drawing directly upon—Wittgenstein, who contends that "our language can be seen as an ancient city" comprised of a "maze

of little streets and squares, of old and new houses, and houses with additions from various periods and this surrounded by a multitude of new boroughs with straight regular streets and uniform houses," Derrida underlines the fragmented, divided nature of the self in a world "preceded by language," which is—itself—a labyrinth-like city comprised of old winding streets, small squares, dark alleyways and a vast array of ever-evolving structures. [Ludwig Wittgenstein, *Philosophical Investigations*, eds. G.E.M. Anscombe, R. Rhees, and G.H. Von Wright, trans. G.E.M. Anscombe, *The Philosophical Quarterly* (Oxford: Basil Blackwell, 1958), para. 18.]

118. Damai, "Messianic-City," 70.
119. Derrida, "Hostipitality," n. 17, p 17.
120. Derrida, *Of Hospitality*, 137–39. Original punctuation.
121. Richard Kearney, "Derrida and Messianic Atheism," in *The Trace of God: Derrida and Religion*, eds. Edward Baring and Peter E. Gordon (New York: Fordham University Press, 2015), 202.
122. Ibid.
123. Derrida, *Acts of Religion*, 56–57.
124. Damai, "Messianic-City," 71.
125. Derrida, *Of Hospitality*, 123–25. Original emphasis.
126. As Levinas states: "I am hostage to the other. I am the hostage of my other. One recognizes the other insofar as one is oneself a hostage. The important thing here is that *I* am the hostage." [Jill Robbins, ed., *Is It Righteous to Be?: Interviews with Emmanuel Levinas* (Stanford, CA: Stanford University Press, 2001), 132–33. Original emphasis.]
127. I later reaffirm this understanding in Arendt's work, which sits in contrast to Heidegger's self-centric phenomenology.
128. Levinas, *Totality and Infinity*, 178.
129. Here, Levinas's indebtedness to Martin Buber's work is evident, as this Levinasian understanding mirrors the Buberian notion of *Ich und Du*—or "I and Thou." This challenges a Heideggerian understanding of *Dasein*.
130. Derrida, *On Cosmopolitanism and Forgiveness*, 17.
131. Derrida, *Acts of Religion*, 56.
132. Giovanna Borradori, *Philosophy in a Time of Terror: Dialogues with Jürgen Habermas and Jacques Derrida* (Chicago: The University of Chicago Press, 2003), 130.
133. Ibid.
134. Jacques Derrida, *Rogues: Two Essays on Reason*, trans. Pascale-Anne Brault and Michael Naas (Stanford, CA: Stanford University Press, 2005), 82. For a more detailed discussion of this concept, see: Jacques Derrida, *Khôra* (Paris: Galilée, 1993); Jacques Derrida, *On the Name* (Stanford, CA: Stanford University Press, 1995).
135. Derrida, *On the Name*, 99–100. Original emphasis.
136. Ibid., 111.
137. Damai, "Messianic-City." Emphasis added.
138. Borradori, *Philosophy in a Time of Terror*, 130. Emphasis added.
139. Ibid., 130–31.

140. Jacques Derrida, "The Future of the Profession or the University without Condition (Thanks to the 'Humanities,' What Could Take Place Tomorrow)," in *Jacques Derrida and the Humanities: A Critical Reader*, ed. Tom Cohen (Cambridge: Cambridge University Press, 2001), 25.
141. Ibid.
142. Derrida, *Negotiations*, 374.
143. Ibid., 374–75.
144. Ibid., 375.
145. Borradori, *Philosophy in a Time of Terror*, 132.
146. Thomassen, *The Derrida-Habermas Reader*, 261–62.
147. Derrida, *Acts of Religion*, 89.
148. Ulrich Beck, *Cosmopolitan Vision* (Oxford: Polity Press, 2006).

Chapter 2

Forgiveness and "Care for the World"

"Had I chosen the love of the world over the love of my family?"[1] This is the question that Megan Phelps-Roper asked herself when she began to have doubts about the deeply held, reprehensible views that her family, members of the WBC, espoused. In fact, her conception of "love for the world" was far from what could be considered, in Arendtian terms, as *amor mundi*, and yet, the "world" loved her. Through her story, we learn that forgiveness is a powerful alternative to revenge. "With each new kindness," she explains, referring to her interactions with newfound friends (many of whom she first encountered on Twitter), "I understood with ever greater clarity the depths of my ignorance about the world."[2] It became obvious to her that the people of the world—whom she had once considered to be the flawed Esau to her (own status as a) perfectly "chosen" Jacob—were not the "demons" she "had been warned about," as they did not "hate" her, in spite of her previous participation in the activities of the WBC, nor did they expect her to hate her family.[3]

Forgiveness can remove people from the vicious logics of endless violence, or cycles of revenge. In her transition away from the WBC, which eventually led to a renewal of her relationship with the world, Phelps-Roper was put into conversation, via Twitter, "with people and ideas that effectively challenged beliefs that had been hammered into [her] since [she] was a child—and that conversation had been far more illuminating than the decades' worth of rage, isolation, and efforts to shame and silence."[4] In her 2017 TED Talk, which has been viewed by over 8.5 million people (as of November 2019), she describes how her public apology[5] led her to experience forgiveness, and to be welcomed into the world:

> In the days just after I left [the WBC in 2012], the instinct to hide was almost paralyzing. [. . .] I wanted to hide from the world I'd rejected for so

long—people who had no reason at all to give me a second chance after a lifetime of antagonism. And yet, unbelievably, they did. The world had access to my past because it was all over the Internet [. . .] but so many [people] embraced me with open arms anyway. I wrote an apology for the harm I'd caused, but I also knew that an apology could never undo any of it. [. . .] People had every reason to doubt my sincerity, but most of them didn't. And—given my history, it was more than I could've hoped for—forgiveness and the benefit of the doubt. It still amazes me.[6]

Because the forgiveness Phelps-Roper experienced is inextricably bound up in the care provided to her, and because of the ways in which forgiveness establishes relationships, the public nature of her apology, and her subsequent actions, as well as those of her "friends," gave rise to a worldly web of relationships, (re)connecting parties on Twitter and, later, in the phenomenological world. Acts of forgiveness, in this instance, are an example of public, political "care for the world." Phelps-Roper acknowledges that "bit by bit," her "shame was being replaced by profound gratitude to Twitter," for providing her with a much-needed public forum and space to engage with other people.[7] Her Twitter friends can be said to have cultivated a new web of relationships, binding together a worldly space of public action. Such practices of forgiveness put an end to the old, pernicious courses of action that Phelps-Roper had previously perpetuated with a "special sort of zeal."[8] With her story, we catch a glimpse of the power of forgiveness. Specifically, we can see how forgiving—as an act that emerges not from a divine source on high but from within the realm of human affairs—has the power to break cycles of vengeance and to cultivate anew what, in Arendtian terms, can be understood as the "'web' of human relationships"[9] that maintains the integrity of the "world": forgiveness cares for that which holds together the "space for politics." This is where the political power of freedom is realized and new courses of action can be instigated in the mode of human togetherness.

Reconsidering forgiveness from an Arendtian perspective, this chapter seeks to understand more fully the ways in which it is a distinctly *non*-"messianic" and *non*-transcendental form of action. This being said, I endeavor to illustrate how forgiveness is a thoroughly human *praxis* that does the miraculous: inserting into the world a new course of action—a new beginning—where and when, previously, no such point existed. Here, then, I examine how—as Nicolas de Warren suggests—"Arendt's thinking assigns to forgiveness a sacralized power of redemption for the human condition without which there can neither be any enduring creativity of plurality nor any love of the world."[10] The "miraculousness" of forgiveness corresponds to the way in which it is a "remedy against irreversibility," that is, a form of action that offers the "possible redemption for the predicament of irreversibility—of being unable to undo what one has done though one did not, and could not, have known he was doing [...] forgiving, serves to undo the deeds of the past, whose 'sins' hang like Damocles' sword over every new generation."[11] How miraculous to conceive of the possibility of an action which can turn back time, effectively reversing the irreversible, and thus removing the sins that pose a threat to power, or the burden of an ever-present past represented by this "sword." Where Derrida suggests that the possibility of forgiveness is a matter of forgiving the unforgivable, a conceptualization which is indicative of how he understands this notion in preternatural, unworldly terms, Arendt maintains that the act of forgiving is directly associated with "action"—the "one miracle-working faculty of man" that is "ontologically rooted" in "the miracle that saves the world, the realm of human affairs, from its normal, 'natural' ruin [...] natality."[12] Action, and by extension forgiveness, is that which corresponds to the promise of a new beginning inherent to all human beings: the potentiality of beginning anew, an "action they are capable of by virtue of being born."[13] Rather than allow the "sword of Damocles" to hang perpetually over "the political," forgiveness is thus the act that brings forth this new beginning, doing so in such a manner that people can act anew and thereby enact the very power that is already present within them.

In this chapter, as part my effort to understand more fully the "miraculousness" of forgiveness, I conceptualize it in terms of Arendt's notion of "care for the world," doing so in a three-part discussion of the three types of activity that comprise the *vita activa*: "labor," "work," and "action." This is a reconsideration of Arendt's tripartite understanding of the human condition that I carry out in terms of my aim of theorizing two incommensurable, but indissociable, responses to wrongdoing: vengeance and forgiveness. In turning to her conceptualization of labor, work, and action, my hope is to provide an overview of these three interrelated activities *and* to understand how forgiveness can be conceived of as a miracle, thereby casting light on how acts of forgiving—unlike practices of revenge—are public forms of practice that care for the (re)development of "power." This is an investigation that explores how vengeance and forgiveness relate to "power," which is—from an Arendtian perspective—not understood as coercion but as humankind's non-coercive capacity to begin new courses of action; such a capacity exists only so long as a plurality of distinct but equal people continue to speak and act together in the public realm. It is in these terms that we can not only understand how forgiveness is an act that, as Phelps-Roper remarks, "amazes," but also a form of practice indicative of how a world-centric, dialogical conceptualization of the political corresponds to what, in Derridean terms, can be referred to as a "power [...] *without sovereignty*."[14] That is, by considering forgiveness as a form of "caring for the world," the problems which Derrida identifies at the conceptual core of this notion dissolve, with the paradox of power he uncovers being transformed by the mediating presence of the "world" that sits in between people, and the end state of reconciliation that erodes the "purity" of forgiveness being presented not as an end but—rather—as a new beginning.

Before unpacking the notions of vengeance and forgiveness in terms of Arendt's conceptualization of the *vita activa*, there is first a need to examine how she considers vengeance to be "the exact opposite" of forgiveness, and how the act of forgiving is an alternative to punishment.[15] This is a line of thought that brings us to a discussion not only of Arendt's account of offenses that are punishable, and thus also forgivable, but also those that are imprescriptible, unforgivable, and which might therefore require us think about the possibility of being thoroughly unable to enact justice. In thinking with Arendt, we might need to entertain the possibility that there is nothing that can be done on Earth to adequately respond to crimes of atrocity. Potentially, that is, we might need to recognize that such acts of evil—as a consequence of their radicality and sheer unfathomability—leave little else for us to do, trusting that—as Arendt observes in her reading of the Gospels—the perpetrators of these crimes "will be taken care of by God in the Last Judgment," which is "not characterized by forgiveness but by just retribution (*apodounai*)."[16] Though Phelps-Roper's actions, for example, as well as those of the WBC more generally, must be understood in different terms than these radically evil crimes, there is a need here—given Arendt's work, as well as that of Derrida—to consider how certain types of offenses challenge humankind's ability to understand and ultimately respond to such acts of atrocity.

Building upon the ways in which Arendt conceptualizes—in *The Human Condition* and *The Origins of Totalitarianism* (1968)—"those offenses which, since Kant, we call 'radical evil,'"[17] the second section of this chapter—by drawing upon an Arendtian notion of "labor" and "work"—demonstrates how vengeance is a violent form of fabrication. Revenge is a coercive, hierarchical notion, undergirded by what is understood as the "power over" conceptualization of power, which—for Arendt—is not a form of power at all, but rather, the conceptual core of violence and the underlying logic that corresponds to the fabricating activity of *homo faber* (man the maker). Notably, for Arendt, it is from the vantage point of *homo faber* that the "miraculousness" of forgiveness can be understood with even greater clarity, not only because this form of *praxis* can "undo the deeds of the past" but also because the faculty of forgiving is an act of "redemption" that is not derived from some outside source; instead, forgiveness is a potentiality contained within the activity of "action" itself.[18] That is, where *homo faber* exists in a "predicament of meaninglessness," and can only be "saved" from their situation when—during "action"—people imbue the fabricated world with meaningful stories (what, in Derridean terms, we might be described as the "text"), forgiveness is a redemptive act that "does not arise out of another and possibly higher faculty, but is one of the potentialities of action itself."[19] Unlike the activities of "labor" and "work," then, "action" contains within it the seeds of its own salvation: forgiveness, a powerful act "ontologically rooted" in natality. Such a notion is "miraculous" because, "from the viewpoint of *homo faber*, it is like a miracle, like the revelation of divinity, that meaning should have a place in this world."[20] Because "action" is inherently laden with meaning, and because this meaningfulness can be safeguarded and "saved," without needing to appeal to a higher power (or form of activity), forgiveness is miraculous: the faculty of forgiving *is* the act which cares for the "world," a remedy whose meaning can be found in the freedom of "action."

Subsequently, the third part of this chapter explores Arendt's understanding of the "world" and the "power to" formulation of power that characterize the political activities that occur in the public realm. Examining more closely the activity of "action," I illustrate how an Arendtian understanding of "power" is non-hierarchical, conditioned by plurality, nonviolent, and that which corresponds to the experience of freedom: the raison d'être of politics.[21] Unlike vengeance—a powerless form of violence—forgiveness is a practice of action; it is both a practice of and for the "power to" act together that is present in the "world." This power—because it is a potentiality that can last only so long as a plurality of people do politics with one another in the public, political realm—is always at the risk of being lost, or of being dissolved by the array of (violent) "world"-ending forces of alienation that exist within sociopolitical communities during times of "darkness." Accordingly, we need to care for power. More specifically, we need to care for freedom, the experience which—in the realm of politics—goes hand-in-hand with power. Forgiveness is a form of public, political care. Because forgiveness is form of practice that cares for the worldly "web of human relationships" that give shape to "the political," we need to forgive the "miraculous" act that brings forth the "miracle" of natality. Thinking and acting in terms of forgiveness can give rise to new courses of action within the political realm. This is a "caring forgiveness."

1. VENGEANCE AND FORGIVENESS FROM AN ARENDTIAN PERSPECTIVE

An in-depth consideration of Arendt's tripartite theory of the *vita activa* provides a starting point from which to better understand how the notions of vengeance and forgiveness are indissociable—though incommensurable—aspects of her broader body of thought. It is in terms of her understanding of "labor," "work," and "action"—the three forms of activity that comprise the *vita activa*—that an Arendtian understanding of "care" can be conceptualized as form of a public, political practice that preserves, repairs, and maintains the "world." Before conceptualizing the notions of vengeance and forgiveness in terms of these activities, however, there is a need not only to examine how forgiveness is the conceptual and practical opposite of vengeance, but also to consider how the act of forgiving offers an alternative to practices of punishment. Furthermore, it is necessary to investigate the way in which Arendt conceptualizes the notions of vengeance, punishment, and forgiveness in relation to what Kant describes as acts of "radical evil": crimes of such magnitude that they defy humankind's ability to comprehend, judge, and adequately respond to such deeds. Where Derrida would argue that it is only in terms of those crimes which are radically evil that we can even begin to speak of forgiveness, Arendt—along with thinkers like Vladimir Jankélévitch—finds forgiveness to be possible only if human beings retain their ability to understand and respond to offenses committed against people and the world. She maintains, therefore, that forgivability is linked with the possibility of punishing human "trespasses," with unforgivability corresponding to those "offenses" that defy the possibility of punishment.

The notions of vengeance and forgiveness, both of which are related to the notion of punishment, are ideas that can be found throughout Arendt's corpus. As part of her sustained interest in understanding evil, totalitarianism, alienation, and—more broadly—the complexities of both the *vita activa* and the *vita contemplativa*, she reflects upon the ideas of vengeance and forgiveness. We find her most explicit examination of these notions in *The Human Condition*, where she positions vengeance in opposition to forgiveness. As Arendt writes:

> [F]orgiveness is the exact opposite of vengeance, which acts in the form of re-acting against an original trespassing, whereby far from putting an end to the consequences of the first misdeed, everybody remains bound to the process, permitting the chain reaction contained in every action to take its unhindered course. In contrast to revenge, which is the natural, automatic reaction to transgression and which because of the irreversibility of the action process can be expected and even calculated, the act of forgiving can never be predicted; it is the only reaction that acts in an unexpected way and thus retains, though being a reaction, something of the original character of action. Forgiving, in other words, is the only reaction which does not merely re-act but acts anew and unexpectedly, unconditioned by the act which provoked it and therefore freeing from its consequences both the one who forgives and the one who is forgiven. The freedom contained in Jesus's teachings of forgiveness is the freedom from vengeance, which encloses both doer and sufferer in the relentless automatism of the action process, which by itself need never come to an end.[22]

Here, Arendt explicitly contrasts the notion of vengeance with the idea of forgiveness, suggesting that the former is the "exact opposite" of the latter, in the sense that revenge perpetuates an endless cycle of reactionary responses. For her, the logic of vengeance is therefore predictable, since acts of revenge exhibit a cyclicality, whereby every reaction remains tethered to the "original trespassing." According to the vicious character of this "chain" of reactions, there is no newness, no novelty of action, or no freedom. Rather, acts of vengeance merely serve to spin the wheel of violence and counterviolence, which will revolve so long as this economy of retribution is maintained and/ or a new course of action does not break this cycle of revenge. Inserting both an end and a new beginning into this circular movement of (counter-) violence, forgiveness is a form of practice that transforms the changeless, cyclical pattern engendered by vengeance, entering into the flow of time a new course of action that is no longer trapped in an endless loop of vengeful "automatism."

Although Arendt references the teachings of Jesus while conceptualizing forgiveness as the act which frees people from the endless cycle of vengeance, she does not theorize a transcendental understanding of this idea, nor does she express a desire for what Derrida—in *Specters of Marx* (1994)—describes as a "messianic" form of "justice that one day, a day belonging no longer to history [. . .] would be removed from the fatality of vengeance."[23] That is, unlike Derrida, whose notion of justice is bound up with his exceedingly radical understanding of responsibility, Arendt conceptualizes forgiveness in relation to a more traditional, "common sense" conception of retributive punishment, limiting her views about this notably Judeo-Christian idea to what is possible in the realm of human affairs. Emphasizing that forgiving and punishing "trespasses" are human practices capable of interrupting vicious cycles of reactionary violence, Arendt states that the "alternative to forgiveness, but by no means its opposite, is punishment [. . .] both have in common that they attempt to put an end to something that without interference could go on endlessly."[24] Forgiveness, for her, is thus not a matter of doing the impossible, in a Derridean sense of experiencing the "madness" of undecidability; rather, it is an act that must be understood as a powerful—though thoroughly human—practice of public, political care, related to but different from punishment, which can also be said to put an end to pernicious cycles of vengeful violence. Here, however, we run up against a significant limitation within an Arendtian theory of human relations: that processes of punishment *and* forgiveness are only capable of dealing with misdeeds and forms of wrongdoing that can be fathomed by people, which is a prerequisite of our ability to respond to them, whether that be in terms of the law and/or in more informal, private manner. This, of course, is not always the case.

As was noted in my discussion of forgiveness and the unforgivable in the previous chapter, human beings can put an end to cycles of (vengeful) violence only so long as the trespasses that need to be redressed or "dismissed"[25]—which is to say punitively rectified or forgiven—can be understood in terms of existing "frameworks" of moral, political, and/or legal knowledge.[26] Arendt recognizes that acts of vengeance, punishment, and forgiveness rely upon humankind's ability to be reconciled to an original trespassing, as well as to the world within which such an act appeared. As a scholar well known for her efforts to confront—on a theoretical level—the unprecedented evil associated with totalitarianism, Arendt was deeply concerned with understanding the crimes committed under totalitarian regimes, which, she contends, "exploded our traditional categories of political thought [. . .] and the standards of our moral judgment."[27] When they first appeared in the realm of human affairs, the acts of evil committed under the Third Reich shattered humankind's capacity to think, understand and, ultimately, to take action in response to these crimes of atrocity. Humanity was left unable to respond proportionality to the crimes of the Nazis, which Jankélévitch describes as "metaphysical crimes" that sought—in an unprecedented way—to eradicate the humanness of being human, that is, to eliminate the "'hominity' of human beings in general."[28] Given their severity, magnitude, and the heinous nature of their intentions, totalitarian crimes and willed acts of evil effectively "dispossess[ed] humankind of all [its] power."[29] This is a point that Arendt illustrates in *The Origins of Totalitarianism*:

> When the impossible was made possible it became the unpunishable, unforgivable absolute evil which could no longer be understood and explained by the evil motives of self-interest, greed, covetousness, resentment, lust for power, and cowardice; and which therefore anger could not revenge, love could not endure, friendship could not forgive. Just as the victims in the death factories or the holes of oblivion are no longer "human" in the eyes of their executioners, so this newest species of criminals is beyond the pale even of solidarity in human sinfulness.[30]

Totalitarian acts of "radical evil" consequently demonstrate that human beings are unable to forgive what they cannot punish, and that they are not able to punish what they cannot fully fathom, understand, or judge. In short, there is a limit to humankind's "power to" act in the world.[31]

Set against the historical and conceptual context of totalitarianism, which underscores humankind's limited abilities to punish/forgive acts of evil, Arendt highlights the need to make a distinction between ordinary transgressions, which she refers to as "trespasses" in terms of the Greek word "*hamartanein*,"[32] and extraordinary "offenses," which she conceptualizes in reference to the Greek word *skandalon* and the Hebrew word *mikhshol* or *zur mikhshol*.[33] In particular, Arendt suggests that *skandalon* refers to a trap laid for one's enemies and is a term that she uses synonymously with the word *mikhshol* or *ẓur mikhshol*, which means "stumbling block." For her, then, such "deadly stumbling blocks [. . .] cannot be removed from our path as can mere transgressions" and are representative of a wrong that exceeds even the "current distinction between venial and mortal sins."[34] Accordingly, totalitarian crimes of "radical evil" were "deadly stumbling blocks" for humanity that could not be overcome—which is to say, punished or forgiven—and are offenses "where all we can say is that 'this should have never happened,'"[35] or "only repeat with Jesus: 'It were better for [an offender] that a millstone were hanged about [their] neck, and [they be] cast into the sea.'"[36] Arendt therefore highlights that doers of radically evil deeds "should never have been born at all,"[37] and that such persons—if and when they have come to exist and committed thought-defying crimes—ought to be expelled entirely from the Earth.

According to Arendt, then, the execution of persons guilty of laying such "traps" and committing "metaphysical crimes" against "human beings in general"—such as, for example, Adolf Eichmann (whose 1961 trial Arendt reported on for *The New Yorker*, as a correspondent)—is merited not because such retaliatory measures are forms of just punishment but rather because, by carrying out policies of "not wanting to share the earth with the Jewish people and the people of a number of other nations [. . .], no member of the human race can be expected to want to share the earth with [him]."[38] In a significant passage from *Eichmann in Jerusalem*, Arendt references Yosal Rogat's work and recognizes that when a "great crime offends nature," the "very Earth cries out for vengeance," as this evil "violates a natural harmony which only retribution can restore."[39] In addition to having several reservations about various aspects of this trial's proceedings, Arendt was skeptical of the more thoroughly vengeful character of Eichmann's sentencing, though—despite her misgivings about what might arguably be considered in Baconian terms, as a "kind of wild justice"[40]—she ultimately accepted the court's verdict. She did so, however, on the grounds that Eichmann's hanging was symbolic of a need to cast this doer of radically evil deeds into the sea with a millstone hung around his neck, leaving him "to be taken care of by God in the Last Judgment." The decision to execute Eichmann should be understood neither as an act of vengeance, nor of just punishment; rather, it she be considered an attempt to remove this criminal completely from the realm of human affairs, which is a testament to the limitations of humankind's ability to act in the world. Where Derrida contends that the possibility of forgiveness becomes possible only at the level of the impossible, then, an Arendtian understanding of this act is conceptualized in terms of what is actionable in the realm of human affairs. In this sense, as Paige Digeser observes in her book, *Political Forgiveness* (2001), "forgiveness may have a place in politics, but it is not one without bounds."[41]

Focusing upon Arendt's understanding of how "radically evil" crimes defy human comprehension, Roger Berkowitz is a scholar who has—in several places[42]—theorized an Arendtian understanding of reconciliation and non-reconciliation in relation to the notion of revenge—an approach that has led him to consider how responding vengefully to acts of "radical evil" can facilitate the (re-)building of worldly, common spaces in the wake of such "willed crime." While he does not use the term "care" explicitly, the implications of his study arguably suggest that it is possible to "care for the world" through practices of revenge; this is a controversial—though thought provoking—point, given how Arendt appears to understand the conceptual relations between vengeance/violence, punishment/forgiveness, and forgiveness/power. Berkowitz suggests that Arendt "finds a return to revenge" at the limits of reconcilability, and he argues that the "enduring political power of revenge to unite a people comes not simply from raw emotions, but also from the aesthetic satisfaction that accompanies a well-wrought act of vengeance."[43] More specifically, he suggests that acts of vengeance—in the very rare circumstances that certain conditions are met—can be said to satisfy the public need for justice, as well as to serve a political purpose as the common focal point around which a shared, political world can be (re-)formed.[44] Stressing the significance of how the "world" is (re)constructed by people during the activity of "work," Berkowitz contends that revenge is politically pertinent insofar as *homo faber* carries out an act of vengeance in order to (re)build the "common home" which was lost when the appearance of radical acts of evil in world caused an abyss to open in human history. Accordingly, he finds there to be a "political power of revenge," with acts of vengeance giving rise to new worlds, within which once alienated persons and peoples can reconcile themselves to vengeful deeds.

While such an interpretation of Arendt's body of thought provides an intriguing means of considering revenge and (non-)reconciliation (as it is interesting to think about how "vengeful non-reconciliation" can form the foundation upon which a new common sense and a shared world can be cultivated in the wake of extreme evil),[45] Berkowitz conflates several important aspects of Arendt's nuanced understandings of reconciliation, vengeance, punishment, and forgiveness. In particular, I take issue with his suggestion that vengeance is a powerful from of work, as such a configuration of ideas confuses violence with power. Although Berkowitz is correct to suggest that vengeance is associated with the work of *homo faber*, we cannot rightly overlook the ways in which revenge operates according to a violent, instrumental logic incommensurable with the nonviolent, free character of political action: an activity that occurs in public when a plurality of distinct but equal people speak and act together. Although the products produced by *homo faber* are artifacts that can give rise to and stabilize worldly spaces within which human affairs can take place, it is my contention that vengeance is *not* a powerful response to violence but, rather, it is a mere form of counterviolence put to use according to a logic of utility. Such a means-ends mentality exhibits a certain viciousness or a cyclicality that effectively perpetuates the pernicious cycle of revenge. Taking issue with Berkowitz's understanding that acts of vengeance can be understood as powerful actions capable of caring for worldly public spaces, a conceptualization that frames revenge as a type of redemptive act of an "enduring political power," I argue that vengeance is a violent practice: a powerless form of human activity that leaves the "sword of Damocles" suspended "over every generation." Developing this point, the subsequent section examines revenge in terms of Arendt's understandings of "labor" and "work," before investigating how the act of forgiving is associated with "action." This is a discussion of how the act of forgiving—unlike violent practices of revenge—can be said to care for the intangible, worldly "web of human relationships" that comprise political spaces of freedom and power, allowing us to "care for the world."

2. VENGEANCE, FORGIVENESS, AND THE *VITA ACTIVA*

Conceptualizing the powerlessness of vengeance and the power of forgiveness in terms of Arendt's trichotomous conceptualization of the *vita activa* requires recognition of the important spatial distinction that she makes between the private and public realms: a demarcation that undergirds the entirety of her conceptualization of the human condition. Affirming the importance of the ancient distinction "between a private and public sphere of life," which corresponds, respectively, to "the household and the political realms,"[46] Arendt highlights how these two separate, but indissociable, realms are each dedicated to the various activities that comprise the human condition. The private realm is a space that is characterized by the singularity of an isolated individual's activities, while the public realm is conditioned by the presence of plural persons. For Arendt, each of the three activities that comprise the human condition—"labor," "work," and "action"—can be understood in terms of the private/public spatial distinction. "Labor," being an entirely private activity, does not require the presence of any other people. The process of "work" is completed in the private realm, but leads to the production of a thing capable of being shared between a plurality of people in worldly public spaces. "Action," being a thoroughly public activity, always transpires in the presence of others who appear to speak and act together in the world.

According to Arendt, the activities of "labor" and "work" go on in private, during moments when a person is secluded from other people and the affairs of the world. Privacy "lies in the absence of others" and, as far as we are concerned, "private man does not appear [before others]."[47] By contrast, the public realm is the non-private space of worldly affairs, as it is the sphere of existence where people and things can be said to make their appearance before a plurality of other people, such as—for example—when they choose to speak and act in the world during the doing of "action." The public realm is where plurality and appearance correlate to her notion of worldliness. I introduced Arendt's notion of "world" in the introduction to this book, but it is necessary to re-state the following about her understanding of the relationship between "public" and "private":

> The term "public" signifies two closely interrelated but not altogether identical phenomena: It means, first, that everything that appears in public can be seen and heard by everybody and has the widest possible publicity. For us, appearance—something that is being seen and heard by others as well as by ourselves—constitutes reality [. . .] Second, the term "public" signifies the world itself, in so far as it is common to all of us and distinguished from our privately owned place in it. [. . .][The world] is related [. . .] to the human artifact, the fabrication of human hands, as well as to affairs which go on among those who inhabit the man-made world together. To live together in the world means essentially that a world of things is between those who have it in common [. . .] the world, like every in-between, relates and separates men at the same time.[48]

Unlike the private realm, where people do not make an appearance, the publicness of the public realm corresponds to that which can be experienced by a plurality of people in the "world." For Arendt, the world is a "common home," a shared place of dwelling where a collection of people can be said to exist in relation to the tangible and intangible "artifacts" that have been produced during both the activities of work and action. Though a state of "worldliness" forms as a result of doing each of these two activities, the products of *homo faber* tend to appear in the world as tangible "things," while action—which corresponds to the affairs of *zoon politikon* (people as a "political animal")—generates a much more intangible, but not any less "real," "in-between" when a plurality of people appear to speak and act publicly together in the commonly shared "home" of the "world." Action, therefore, gives rise to what Arendt calls a "web of human relationships," which comes to exist "wherever men live together."[49] The intangible "web of human relations" possesses the same worldly quality as a physical, fabricated good (Arendt—as one might recall—refers to the example of a "table"). However, unlike tangible things, which—as a result of their materiality—can remain in the world and endure the test of time, the "web of human relations" is not lasting since acts of speech (*lexis*) are impermanent, performative forms of communication. For me, vengeance is but a violent form of work, while forgiveness is a type of action capable of caring for "web of human relationships," or for maintaining, preserving, and (re)developing that which makes political action possible at all.

A. Labor: The Private Activity of "Producing" Life

As the foundation of Arendt's understanding of the *vita activa*, labor is the existential basis of human life, corresponding to the "biological process of the human body."[50] This activity is associated with the fulfillment of a person's most basic biological needs, or the necessities of being adequately fed and hydrated, preserving one's health, reproduction, etc. Laboring is about caring for the biologic needs of the human body, whose "spontaneous growth, metabolism, and eventual decay are bound to the vital necessities produced and fed into the life process by labor."[51] Labor is therefore what people "share with all other forms of animal life,"[52] and it is an activity which must forever be repeated so long as a human creature is a living, breathing being. Moreover, labor is the most private of human affairs; the doing of this existentially basic activity "does not need the presence of others," as a person "laboring" in "complete solitude" is "not human" but, rather, an "*animal laborans*."[53] When "compared with the reality which comes from being seen and heard" by a plurality of other people in the public realm, the laboring individual leads an outwardly unreal, "uncertain, shadowy kind of existence."[54] Because the private realm is the space of non-appearance, and because this activity "never 'produces' anything but life,"[55] labor is a characteristically worldless mode of existence. In servicing a person's biologic needs, and thereby (re)producing human life in the most fundamental of ways, however, *animal laborans* lays the existential foundation for all human life: the base of existence which must be maintained if people are to do "work" in the mode of *homo faber* (man the maker) or to "act" as *zoon politikon* (political animal).

Because labor is the activity dedicated to the process of overcoming our everyday needs, or of repeatedly and unceasingly servicing the demands of biologic necessity, it could be argued that the logic of the laboring process mirrors that of the logic of vengeance, which is the "natural, automatic reaction to transgression" that "can be expected and even calculated." Like the ever-recurring activity of labor, which adheres to a decidedly economic logic, there is a notably cyclical movement informing vengeance, a predictable response that ensnares people in a vicious loop of unending "automatism." This is a cyclical course of reactionary violence and counterviolence structured by the repetitive dynamic that informs the entire existence of *animal laborans*: a loop characterized by a perpetual return of violence. We might even go so far as to suggest that the closed nature of this circle of (counter-) violence forms a trap not unlike the "*skandalon*" or "*mikhshol*" of which Arendt speaks.

Unlike labor, which only (re)produces more life, vengeance does not share the same aim of *animal laborans*: survival. Rather, to seek revenge is to pursue a reconfiguration of the power arrangement between persons or people within a sociopolitical system, aiming to "produce" an intangible—though thoroughly "real"—end product: a hierarchy. This is a relation of power that would see an avenging party establish a state of domination over the party that has trespassed against them. In a philosophic debate with Jeffrie Murphy, Jean Hampton illustrates how vengeance—as a form of retaliation—works to create an asymmetrical relation of power through the practice of retributively responding to a perceived injustice:

> Perhaps the retributivist's *lex talionis*, his "eye for an eye, tooth for a tooth" conception of punishment, is just a restatement of vengeance which victims frequently want. The wrongdoer inflicts one pain; the victim (or the society which represents him) reciprocates with a second. Aren't both parties simply engaged in a kind of competitive struggle for standing, in which harm is taken either to effect or to prove a diminishment of the other's position relative to one's own, a diminishment in which one glories?[56]

Questioning the dynamics of power associated with revenge, Hampton draws attention to acts of vengeance as a means to alter the anatomy of power between two parties; she highlights, in particular, how an injured person/ group—by seeking to vindicate themselves through an act of vengeful retaliation—imposes their will upon the wrongdoer, engaging in what can be understood as a "competitive struggle" for a position of power. In this fight for power, and thus, in an effort to assume power over those who have committed an offense, we can understand acts of vengeance as being akin to a type of "symbolic communication," a message that reads: "I am here up high and you are there down below."[57] Understood in this manner, vengeance is a means of crafting a new relationship between parties, or of transforming a victim into a vindicator, effectively empowering—or re-empowering—the victimized party at the expense of the original transgressor. As a means to an end, vengeance is a way for a wronged party to craft a new order, which is to say, people seeking revenge are fabricators who employ this retaliatory measure as if it were a tool to be utilized in the construction of a preconceived product: a new structure of power, one which sees them standing "up high" and their opposition positioned "down below." Unlike the activity of labor, which (re)produces life by caring for a person's private needs of survival, then, the active pursuit of vengeance corresponds to the fabrication of a new dynamic of power within the "web of worldly relationships." This is a conceptualization of vengeance that aligns well with Arendt's understanding of "work" and the utilitarian, violent, and means-end mentality of *homo faber*.

B. Work: The Private Activity of Producing (Public) Things

According to Berkowitz, "There is a beauty to a well-wrought act of revenge—the symmetry of an eye for an eye and a life for a life and the glorious heroism of an avenger who risks himself for the doing of justice."[58] For him, acts of vengeance can be beautiful, in the sense that a well-crafted act of revenge can become a "worldly" "adornment" made by a heroic individual; this is a figure who acts for the sake of the (re)creation of a common world, where "action" can occur and new, meaningful stories can be enacted.[59] He suggests that revenge can produce or re-produce the world in a manner akin to which *homo faber* works to provide human affairs with a beautiful, publicly shared world. In reference to *The Human Condition*, Berkowitz writes:

> [A]cting and speaking men need the help of *homo faber* in his highest capacity [...] because without them the only product of their activity, the story they enact and tell, would not survive at all." What unites work and action in Arendt's exploration of the human condition is that works can only work insofar as they embody the originality and newness, and action can only appear in public when it is adorned by beauty. The enduring political power of revenge to unite a people comes not simply from raw emotions, but also from the aesthetic satisfaction that accompanies a well-wrought act of vengeance.[60]

As previously mentioned, this conceptualization of both vengeance and work contradicts an Arendtian conceptualization of "power," which is—for Arendt—antithetical to the "power over" logic associated with the violent notion of revenge. Though he is right to suggest that vengeance is a form of work, Berkowitz's alignment of revenge with this human activity contradicts how an Arendtian understanding of power is non-hierarchical, nonviolent, and non-instrumental. Moreover, acts of revenge do not put an end to vicious cycles of violence and counterviolence; rather, they ensure that parties to this violent act remain subjected to a re-occurring process that therefore perpetuates, as Arendt observes, "the chain reaction contained in every action to take its unhindered course." Thinking both with and against Berkowitz, I contend that vengeance is a private activity of work completed in isolation; crafted in accordance with a preconceived conceptual model; carried out through violent means; and considered part of a thoroughly instrumental logic.

While acts of revenge carried out by one party against another do not necessarily produce a worldly "thing," the anatomy of power fabricated by an avenging party is an intangible construct "wrought" in private by the work of a single party for a worldly, public purpose. That is, if Jeffrie Murphy is correct to argue that vengeance is a rational pursuit,[61] one which is carried out with intent by a thinking being, then revenge can be considered as a deliberate activity that produces a new sociopolitical hierarchy between parties within the worldly "web of human relationships." This "power over" dynamic is a product of work, and the raw materials which were used to produce such a product are, arguably, the very people targeted for subjectification. This is a most distressing and anti-political idea: people-come-resources to be used in the production of a new worldly "thing." For Arendt, work is completed by an isolated *homo faber*, yet the products of such a private process can appear in the public realm, and therefore be held in common by all who enter this space of appearance. *Homo faber*'s process of "fabrication (*poiēsis*, the making of things)," is always "performed in a certain isolation [. . .], no matter whether the result is a piece of craftsmanship or of art."[62] The product of *homo faber*'s efforts contribute directly to the worldliness of the public realm, providing— through the work of their hands—an "'artificial' world of things, distinctly different from all natural surroundings."[63] As a coercive activity that culminates in a state of domination, whereby one party has "power over" another, vengeance is a form of "work" because an avenger is a *homo faber* who willfully fabricates their hierarchical position over others. This established dynamic can become a sociopolitical framework that undergirds and informs interactions that occur in the "world." It is through acts of revenge, then, that an avenging party reifies a hierarchy and (re-)produces a state of inequality. Such hierarchical constructs are not associated with the public realm of the political, which is—for Arendt—a space of equality and distinction. Rather, acts of vengeance correspond to the activities that occur in the private realm: the space characterized by "the strictest inequality."[64]

In addition to the private nature of the fabrication process, Arendt contends that the process of work is carried out in accordance with a preconceived conceptual model.[65] *Homo faber* makes something in concordance with a predetermined template and for a predestined purpose, destroying and manipulating some material resource(s)—such as wood, metal, dirt, and so on—in order to fabricate something else. In making something, such as—in the case of vengeance—a new anatomy of power, *homo faber* privately produces an end product in accordance with an understanding, idea, or desire that precedes the actual process of work. According to Arendt, the actual work of fabrication is performed under the guidance of a mental model which is an "image beheld by the eye of the mind or a blueprint in which the image has already found a tentative materialization through work."[66] Work is ordered and completed in accordance with a preconceived conception; this model is not an image conjured from the dark abysses of the utterly unknown but, rather, one which is formed in relation to something or some idea that has previously existed in the world.[67] While *homo faber* may create a new "thing" that has never been fabricated before, the ideas, components, and very language that inform processes of production precede the doing of this individual's work of fabrication. Vengeance adheres to the same conceptual logic, since the hierarchical state of domination inherent to this notion is based upon an age-old understanding of violent retaliation—a model thoroughly engrained in the human realm. The "blueprint" for revenge is so familiar, in fact, that vengeance is often considered to be "humankind's natural sense of retribution."[68] The individual *homo faber* who fabricates a new sociopolitical hierarchy, through the pursuit of vindictive domination, no doubt operates in accordance with this "natural sense" of vengeful retaliation.

In terms of work, a vengeful *homo faber* actualizes their preconceived blueprint for a coercive sociopolitical hierarchy through violence. Work and vengeance are both violent since *homo faber*—the creator of worldly things—is a "destroyer of nature."[69] As Arendt writes:

> Material is already a product of human hands which have removed it from its natural location, either killing a life process [. . .] or interrupting one of nature's slower processes [. . .] *homo faber* conducts himself as lord and master of the whole earth.[70]

As "lord and master," *homo faber* has "power over" that with which they are working, and it is through violent strength that they violate, break, and bend a material in accordance with their will. This display of strength occurs when a single party dominates something or someone in order to make manifest an idea which had only previously been seen in the eye of the mind. The notion and practice of vengeance is therefore violent because an avenging party imposes their will upon a wrongdoer in an act of strength that aims to (re-)produce a state of domination. If Eichmann's trial—for example—is considered in terms of what Arendt describes as the "long-forgotten propositions" of vengeance,[71] then his death sentence was an imposition of the court's vengeful will upon the entirety of this man's being, as the tribunal subjected him to the violent force of the long drop and the tightening noose around his neck. Through coercive forms of violence, that is, people can be said to create—in the mode of *homo faber*—a new hierarchy, which is to say (re-)fabricate a "power over" dynamic, thereby making manifest the understanding that—as Hampton suggests—"I am up here and you there down below."

The violent domination that *homo faber* imposes on a material throughout the work process is justified in utilitarian terms, whereby the violent means used throughout the process of work is validated by the end product produced. "Everything," as Arendt observes, "is judged in terms of suitability and usefulness for the desired end and for nothing else."[72] Revenge is similar in that the means are justified by the end state of domination. This is not to say that vengeance is "legitimate." It is not. Legitimacy, as Arendt maintains, is rooted in action and the base of power formed when a plurality of persons speak and act together. Violent pursuits, such as vengeance, can therefore be justified but never legitimate precisely because they involve the domination of a single party over another party.[73] Vengeance is therefore a type of "work" because the end state of vindication can be seen to justify, without legitimating, the violent process of fabrication. In this way, the means/ends logic that characterizes work is also prevalent in vengeance—the state of domination becomes a fabricated end that justifies the violence done in its name. If Berkowitz's interpretation of Arendt's work is correct, the "aesthetic satisfaction that accompanies a well-wrought act of vengeance"—which he contends has the power to reestablish the "natural order" (Rogat)—is a process of coercive violence whose end state justifies the means by which the "power over" framework was created.

Extending further Arendt's thinking about the instrumentalism inherent to the logic of *homo faber*'s work, Arendt contends that the fabricated good produced during the activity of work is an end product that becomes part of the means to some other end. In other words, a fabricated good is an end, but "the same standards of means and end apply to the product itself [. . .] [it] never becomes, so to speak, an end in itself, at least not as long as it remains an object for use."[74] According to this logic, work is entirely instrumental, and the fabrications of *homo faber* are products that become the means by which to produce something else. As Paul Voice observes, "Work is locked into a never-ending chain of means and ends and it is therefore chained to an instrumental view of life," since, for *homo faber*, "everything is a means and so transcendence here is impossible."[75] The sociopolitical hierarchy that emerges when the work of vengeance is completed is a hierarchical construction, which becomes the framework for further acts of violent coercion. In this sense, the (re)established state of domination engendered through vengeance becomes a springboard for further domination, which ultimately means that a dominator's will can be further demonstrated, increased, and multiplied across time and space. Furthermore, a counterforce is often triggered in response to such a process of (continuous) violence. This cycle of domination, and the never-ending nature of work, undergirds Arendt's understanding of vengeance, which—"far from putting an end to the consequences of the first misdeed"—keeps "everybody [. . .] bound to the process [of revenge]."[76] Acts of revenge circulate violence, with each reaction becoming yet another retaliatory response in an unending process.

While Berkowitz suggests that acts of revenge—as a type of product wrought by a vengeful *homo faber*—may be capable of "adorning" the public realm of human affairs and ultimately "inaugurating a new legal consciousness founded upon a new common world,"[77] it is my belief that such violent practices ultimately impede the doing of politics. As a violent notion that operates in accordance with a means-ends and unfree logic, revenge is a powerless practice of work which inhibits the experience of power and freedom engendered when a plurality of people appear to speak and act freely together in the public realm. Because political action should be—as I subsequently discuss—a nonviolent public affair, aligned with the "power to" conceptualization of power and the experience of freedom, the instrumental logic that characterizes the work of *homo faber*, who—as "lord and master of the whole earth"—breaks and bends the world according to their singular vision, hinders rather than helps people to overcome states of alienation and to do (once again) politics with one another. In short, revenge is not a practice of caring for the world but, rather, a violent form of work that engenders a pernicious, cyclical dynamic that directly inhibits the doing of politics.

C. Action: The Public Realm, Plurality, and the Power of Forgiveness

Turning now to "action," the third and highest level of Arendt's tripartite conceptualization of the *vita activa*, I investigate how—as an act which cares for the relationships that bind together "the political"—forgiveness, unlike vengeance, is a powerful form of public practice. Forgiveness does not reproduce an economy of violence or pursue any predetermined aims; rather, it cares for the experience of freedom, which corresponds to the cultivation of power in the "world." In an effort to theorize more fully the power of forgiveness as a form of action, then, this section emphasizes how Arendt's understanding of action differs from work: the private, violent activity which is completed in accordance with a preconceived model, and in terms of a utilitarian, means-ends logic. While I consider the narrativity and temporality of action in the subsequent chapters, I theorize this activity here as the powerful, worldly activity of plurality, which is conceptually informed by the ideas of civic equality and distinction. It is in these terms that forgiveness can be understood as an act of public, political care.

While "labor" is the private activity that *animal laborans* undertakes in order to overcome biologic necessity, and "work" is the private process of producing public "things" in humankind's capacity as a *homo faber*, "action" is a thoroughly public form of speaking and acting among, and with, a collection of people in spaces of appearance. For Arendt, action is always public—as it is the "only activity that goes on directly between men"[78]—and is a mode of human existence that takes place entirely in spaces of appearance, where everything or everyone empirically present in the "world" can be observed by all who move and act in this realm. This activity, one might say, is the antithesis of the "self-reflective" mode of being theorized by Heidegger, who suggests that *Dasein* can be revealed only in isolation from—or freedom from—the public affairs of the world. As an activity performed through speech (*lexis*) and/or deeds that are disclosed through acts of speech,[79] action is consequently an *inter*active experience that occurs between people, giving rise to a nonhierarchical conception of power: the "power to" act freely with a plurality of other people in the public realm.

Spaces of appearance are only political realms of public action if and when the condition of human plurality is met. Human plurality, for Arendt, is "specifically *the* condition—not only the *conditio sine qua non*, but the *conditio per quam*—of all political life."[80] Plurality corresponds to the fact that plural persons—rather than a singular person—live on Earth and inhabit the world.[81] This is an understanding of humankind she develops in contradistinction from Heidegger's phenomenology and in relation to an Augustinian conceptualization of the biblical story of Genesis (particularly the passage from Genesis 1:27), where it is written that "God created man in his own image, in the image of God he created him; male and female he created *them*."[82] Embracing the understanding that the Genesis story is predominately about the creation of a "them" on Earth, Arendt highlights that this biblical narrative "offers a welcome opportunity to stress the species character of animal life, as distinguished from the singularity of human existence."[83] Accordingly, human life is life lived in relation to other people, since God created a "them" to share the Garden of Eden. Additionally, and in terms of the human "them" on Earth, Arendt suggests that to be a human being is to be a unique person within a worldwide community of other beings, who are equally unique in their humanness. In other words, human plurality is a "paradoxical plurality of unique beings,"[84] for, in the broadest of terms, the human community of all humankind, is comprised of a plurality of distinct equals. A seemingly contradictory conceptualization of humankind's plural existence on Earth, it is nevertheless the equality and distinction of "them" that Arendt bases her understanding of human plurality upon: the "*conditio per quam* of all political life." Consequently, it is necessary to explore the interrelated notions of equality and distinction, as these two ideas are the key to accessing an Arendtian understanding of power.

C.1. Equality and Freedom

Although contemporary conceptions of equality invoke the idea that all people are equal in the eyes of God, and/or are born equal—an Arendtian conceptualization of equality corresponds to the ancient Greek notion of civic equality, or *isonomy*. According to Arendt, who credits Herodotus (c.

484—425 BC) with first introducing this notion,[85] *isonomy* corresponds to a state of "no-rule," whereby there is no "division between rulers and ruled."[86] Such a state of non-rule is not an essentially provided, natural state of equality inherent to humankind. Rather, it is a construct established by human beings within human communities, such as—for example—the ancient Greek *polis*. Arendt writes the following about civic equality in the *polis*:

> Isonomy guaranteed ἰσότης, equality, but not because all men were born or created equal, but, on the contrary, because men were by nature (φύσει) not equal, and needed an artificial institution, the *polis*, which by virtue of its νόμος [laws] would make them equal.[87]

As an attribute of life in the ancient Greek *polis*, the equality guaranteed by *isonomy* was a product of law, and it was a status provided by virtue of a person's citizenship and not merely their birth in the community.[88] This law, however, "does not mean that all men are equal before the law, or that the law is the same for all, but merely that all have the same claim to political activity," namely of "speaking with [one's fellow citizens]."[89] Civic equality, then, is a status endowed by the community, and it is that which corresponds to an individual's equal right to speak in the world. It is useful here to call to mind Norman Rockwell's 1943 painting, *Freedom of Speech*, which depicts a man standing—poised and just about to speak—among a plurality of his fellow citizens during a town hall meeting. In contrast to the finely dressed and well-groomed men and women who sit around him, this man's plaid, blue-collared shirt, well-worn, and seemingly stained leather jacket, as well as his noticeably dirty, calloused hands, are indicative of his humble origins and working-class background. Within this public space (which appears to be a schoolroom), however, he speaks as an equal among all those who appear with him, though they appear to be of a higher social standing within this community.

This painting depicts the form of civic equality engendered by the notion of *isonomy*, which does not imply that people are all naturally equal but, rather, that all people have an equal right to speak and participate in the doing of politics with their fellow citizens. Such a form of equality can be an institutionalized aspect of a community's laws, as was the case in the Greek *polis*, and the American town portrayed in Rockwell's painting. This being said, the equal right to speak need not be limited to any particular institutional spaces of political action. Civic equality can be found within informal political contexts where actors—out of a sense of *amor mundi*—have spontaneously created new public realms and have chosen to uphold the principle of *isonomy* without any formal, legal implements to ensure its application in the world. The examples Arendt presents of such instances are the Revolutionary moment in American history, as well as the February Revolution of 1917 in Russia, and the Hungarian Revolution of 1956, all of which demonstrate how civic equality can be an informally established understanding, since—in each of these instances—the "spirit of revolution" and the "elementary conditions of action itself" (equality, freedom, power, etc.) gave rise to the "federal principle, the principle of league and alliance among separate units."[90] Civic equality, an "elementary condition of action itself," is the conceptual crux of theorizing how the act of forgiving can be understood in non-hierarchical terms, which—as one will recall—is one of the issues Derrida uncovers at the heart of the faculty of forgiving, since a "forgiveness worthy of its name, would be a forgiveness without power: *unconditional but without sovereignty.*"[91] While this aspect of an Arendtian conceptualization of forgiveness is explored more fully in the coming pages, my point here is that such a sense of civic equality is a human construct directly associated with action and the doing of politics in worldly spaces of appearance, where freedom—the *raison d'être* of politics—can be experienced.[92]

From an Arendtian perspective, the notion of freedom is considered in dual terms: first, it is a freedom from rule, which corresponds directly to Arendt's understanding of *isonomy*, and, second, it is a freedom to act politically in the world. In other words, freedom has both a negative and positive form, which is an understanding she acknowledges when she writes about the ancient Greek understanding of politics:

> "Politics," in the Greek sense of the word, is [. . .] centered around freedom, whereby freedom is understood negatively as not being ruled or ruling, and positively as a space which can be created only by men and in which each man moves among his peers.[93]

From this perspective, to be free is not, as Jonathan Schell observes, "merely to be unobstructed" but, rather, "it is to take positive action with others."[94] Although Arendt is well known for her prioritization of "positive freedom," which is an aspect of her body of thought that sits in opposition to—for example—the work of scholars such as Isaiah Berlin,[95] she nevertheless recognizes the significance of "negative freedom" as the conceptual and existential foundation upon which all positive action rests. Synonymous with the notion of "no-rule" (*isonomy*), negative freedom implies that "to be free mean[s] both not to be subject to the necessity of life or to the command of another *and* not to be in command oneself."[96] Corresponding to the state of being both liberated[97] from necessity, and the coerciveness of the "power over" framework, each of which impede the experience of acting in the world, negative freedom is a preliminary form of liberation needed to begin positively acting with a plurality of other people, who—from an Arendtian perspective—can be understood as civic friends.

Without pursuing a tangential discussion of political friendship, which is an aspect of political theory that demands far more attention than I can give within the scope of this book, it is important to note that an Arendtian conceptualization of the political is informed by Aristotle's understanding of *philia politikē*.[98] Arendt's conceptualization of equality and negative freedom is directly related to her understanding of civic friendship, which is—as she writes—a "kind of 'friendship' without intimacy and without closeness, it is a [respect for others] from the distance which the space of the world puts between [parties]."[99] The equality inherent to the notion of negative freedom, which informs Arendt's understanding of human plurality, corresponds to her belief that the political community of civically equal persons, which is engendered when people appear to speak and act together in the world, is one constituted by friends. As she writes:

> The equalization in friendship does not of course mean that the friends become the same or equal to each other, but rather that they become equal partners in a common world—that they together constitute a community. Community is what friendship achieves.[100]

Unlike the notion that a "friend is another self,"[101] the form of friendship theorized by Arendt is conceptualized in terms of civically equal persons who share the worldly space of the political realm. Hers is an understanding of friendship that "is not intimately personal," but one which "makes political demands and preserves reference to the world."[102] Graham Smith, in his book, *Friendship and The Political: Kierkegaard, Nietzsche, Schmitt*, similarly, maintains that the doing of politics is a non-hierarchical activity, one which goes on between "friends" in relation to a world shared among a plurality of people:

> Friendship [. . .] point[s] to the horizontal, the shared and the open. [. . .][It is] indispensable to the political because just as friendship is understood to denote the bonds between person and person, the political is understood to denote a concern with the *shared* world of order and value. This shared world rests upon and is shaped by the bonds of friendship.[103]

Rooted in the "world" shared between people, politics is a mode of human interaction that is shaped by the ways in which friends speak and act upon a plane of commonality, one which supports "horizontal" rather than vertical relationships within a sociopolitical community. From an Arendtian perspective, such "bonds" are supported by civic equality and can be understood as the fabric of the "web of human relationships" that forms betwixt all those who speak and act within the realm of human affairs: civic friends who appear to act freely together in the world, doing so for the purpose of preserving or caring for the world they share in common. Accordingly, Arendt's understanding of civic friendship corresponds directly to her understanding of negative freedom, which in turn informs her understanding of positive freedom.

In the positive sense, freedom is about acting politically in the world with a collective of civically equal "friends." Moreover, it corresponds to the instigation of new courses of political action within the public spaces of appearance shared by these distinct, equal persons. Experienced among a plurality of "civic friends," then, Arendt's understanding of positive freedom is synonymous with the activity of action precisely because, as she indicates, "to act, in its most general sense, means to take an initiative, to begin (as the Greek word *archein*, "to begin," "to lead," and eventually to "to rule," indicates), to set something into motion (which is the original meaning of the Latin *agere*)."[104] Free from the rule of necessity and the hierarchical trappings of sovereignty, being free to act is thus a matter of being able "to begin" and to initiate a new course of action within the realm of the political with one's civic friends. Because Arendt's conceptualization of action is theorized in terms of beginnings, it is clear that freedom and the doing of politics relates to her notion "natality": the Augustinian-inspired term she uses to describe "the fact that we have entered the world through birth."[105] Arendt suggests that all human life, and thus the entirety of her tripartite conceptualization of the *vita activa*, is "ontologically rooted" in natality.[106] It is the activity of "action," however, that "has the closest connection with the human condition of natality," since "the new beginning inherent in birth can make itself felt in the world only because the newcomer possesses the capacity of beginning something anew, that is, of acting."[107] Theorizing action in the very terms with which she conceptualizes human life, Arendt highlights how it is in birth that human beings originally come to be on Earth: each new child can be understood as a new beginning "thrown"—to borrow Heidegger's term for human facticity—into the phenomenological realm. And yet, it is in acting politically that people experience a "second birth,"[108] entering into the "world" as if being reborn as a member of the *polis*, where words spoken and deeds shared, insert new beginnings into the historical, meta-narrative of human history.

Unlike the "death-driven phenomenology" theorized by Heidegger, who—in *Being and Time*—elaborates upon his distinctive understanding of "being-toward-death," Arendt focuses upon new beginnings and argues that the capacity to begin anew is the promise contained in every human being *and* the activity of acting with other people in the public realm of the political. Echoing the work of Saint Augustine (AD 354—430), Arendt maintains that "beginning, before it becomes a historical event, is the supreme capacity of man [. . .] *Initium ut esset homo creatus est*—'that a beginning be made man was created.'"[109] Considered in terms of the language and logic of humankind's most fundamental moment of being in the world, that of becoming a being by *being* born, she contends that both the "beginning [that] is guaranteed by each new birth," as well as the "second birth" experienced in political action, is "identical with man's freedom."[110] "Because he *is* a beginning," Arendt writes, "man can begin, to be human and to be free are one and the same; God created man in order to introduce into the world the faculty of beginning: freedom."[111] In sum, all people are equally new beginnings, and it is in the public realm that the beginning inherent to all of humankind can, under certain conditions, be made manifest in the world during the experiential activity of freedom: action. The new beginning made manifest in acting freely with a plurality of others is precisely that which forgiveness preserves, as it is a practice that frees people from the cyclicality inherent to cycles of revenge: the act of forgiving liberates people from the rule of revenge.

C.2. Acting Distinctively

Insofar as it pertains to political life, plurality requires equality—which Arendt disassociates from contemporary conceptions of justice[112]—since the public realm is a space comprised of unequal people, "who stand in need of being 'equalized in certain respects and [for] specific purposes."[113] Additionally, plurality is informed by the notion of distinction: the fact that individual persons are different from any people who currently exist, have existed, and will ever exist in the world. Maintaining the conceptual difference between the notions of "distinction" and "otherness," the latter of which is "found only in the sheer multiplication of inorganic objects," Arendt suggests that distinction corresponds to the uniqueness of individual human beings: to be a distinct human being is to be a unique being within the human community.[114] The distinctiveness of which Arendt speaks is bound up with the unique perspective people each have of the world and the understandings they have formed from their individual experiences in life. In reference to the Heideggerian recognition that *"Dasein is its disclosedness,"*[115] Arendt avers that an individual's distinct perspective—which corresponds directly to the understandings they have developed in relation to their position in the "world"—is precisely that which is disclosed when one speaks publicly in the world before a plurality of other people.[116] Foreshadowing the subsequent chapter's discussion, the publicly disclosed understanding shared through acts of speech is that of their distinct, unique story. In response to Heidegger's notion of *Dasein*, or "human existence," Arendt suggests that people "distinguish themselves," as distinct human beings through speech, and appear to others not as "physical objects," but *"qua* men." That is, people disclose their unique account of their phenomenological experience—what might be understood as their "story"—by speaking and acting in the world, which effectively reveals "who" they are as a distinctive person.[117]

People distinguish themselves most fully during the activity of political action, as this phenomenological endeavor occurs entirely between people in the public realm of the political, which effectively reveals the "who-ness" of each actor as a human being. In this sense, there is a centrally significant conceptual association inherent to Arendt's theory of action: that acts of speech simultaneously insert a person into the public realm, as if they were born again in the world, and disclose their "who-ness" as a human being. Arendt writes:

> If action as beginning corresponds to the fact of birth, if it is the actualization of the human condition of natality, then speech corresponds to the fact of distinctiveness and is the actualization of the human condition of plurality, that is, of living as a distinct and unique being among equals.[118]

Action is an interactive experience that reveals to the world a person's beingness as a being who can act and begin anew throughout the course of their life. Action is a phenomenological activity of disclosing one's uniqueness *and* of reaffirming that which is guaranteed by each new human birth: a new beginning, which is, indeed, in every human being.[119]

Conceptualized in this manner, action is the public, political activity of disclosure that reveals and renews the "supreme capacity of man,"[120] which is the freedom to act in the world with a plurality of civically equal and distinct people. This "capacity" to act with other people (understood as a person's civic friends) is the conceptual core of her understanding of action, the most *human* of human activities. For her, action is the highest, most human activity within her tripartite conceptualization of the *vita activa* because acting and speaking in the public realm of appearance discloses a person's humanness as a human being to all those people who have appeared in the world: action publicly reveals one's unique perspective (or narrated understanding), which corresponds to one's distinctive ability to begin. While all people are beings capable of beginning anew, as all people are human beginnings that have entered the world through birth, each person has a distinctive capacity to begin which is unique to them and that is revealed when they make their appearance in the public realm of the political. From an Arendtian perspective, then, acting and speaking in the world embodies the unique beginning inherent to human beings, which is the capacity to act—or initiate—new courses of action with other people, who are similarly unique and free to reveal their own distinctiveness in public spaces of appearance. It is this capacity to act that corresponds to an individual's understanding of "power," which refers—as she writes in *On Violence* (1969)—to "the human ability not just to act but to act in concert."[121] Power is not a hierarchical, coercive concept but, rather, a potentiality: the "power to" act and thus to begin new courses of action with our civic friends. This power, and the web of civic friendship which accompanies it, is what a caring forgiveness seeks to preserve.

C.3. The "Power to" Act

Arendt's conceptualization of "power" challenges the "power over" understanding of power that is inherent to, for example, the logic of vengeance and traditional conceptualizations of sovereignty, which see one party establish—through a violent process of work—a state of domination over another. From an Arendtian perspective, such notions cannot be understood in terms of "power," since they are manifestations of violence and/or strength, which—as Arendt writes—"designate something in the singular,"[122] and are thus not dependent upon "numbers or opinions but on implements—and the implements of violence [. . .] like all other tools—increase and multiply human strength."[123] Arguing that power is associated with the presence of human plurality, which is a matter of a "they" or "we" on Earth, Arendt writes about the relationship between violence, power and, ultimately, freedom:

> This We arises wherever men live together [. . .] it can be constituted in many different ways, all of which rest ultimately on some form of consent [. . .] Consent entails the recognition that no man can act alone, that men—if they wish to achieve something in the world—must act in concert, which would be a platitude if there were not always some members of the community determined to disregard it and who in arrogance or in despair try to act alone. These are tyrants or criminals, depending on the final goal they aim at; what they have in common is that they put their trust in the use of the instruments of violence as a substitute for power. [. . .] [P]olitical power, even if the tyrant's supporters consent to terror—that is, the use of violence—is always a limited power, and since power and freedom in the sphere of human plurality are in fact synonyms, this means that political freedom is always a limited freedom.[124]

Here, Arendt demonstrates how power stems from "consent," which is precisely what is lacking when tyrants and criminals strike out on their own in order to act alone—as consent requires the presence and support of a plurality of people. Arendt does not write of a consent formed through domination, since her notion of civic equality ensures that consent corresponds to a form of legitimacy derived "from the initial getting together," or of a plurality of people appearing in the "world," where "they" can speak and act in concert.[125] This initial getting together of people in the public realm is that which engenders power and, as has been emphasized throughout this discussion, which corresponds to freedom. Arendt suggests that "power and freedom in the sphere of human plurality are in fact synonyms," though—by contrast—as she writes elsewhere, "power and violence are opposites."[126] Power is therefore formed in human togetherness when a collective of people—as civically equal yet distinct friends—appear with one another to experience freedom during the activity of political action. Violence, however, is an illegitimate exertion of a singular actor's strength.

In Arendtian terms, power is a potentiality inherent to plurality; as a capacity for action, it is present solely in instances when, and where, people appear to speak and act freely together in the world. At its most fundamental level, power is a dispositional concept, which is an understanding encapsulated in the word "power" itself—"like its Greek equivalent '*dynamis*,' like the Latin '*potentia*' with its various modern derivatives or the German '*Macht*,' indicates its 'potential' character."[127] Considered as a "potential," an Arendtian understanding of power aligns with what is often referred to as the "power to" conceptualization of power, which—as Pamela Pansardi observes—"refers to the ability to cause certain outcomes or states of affairs [and] is a dispositional concept [that] refers to the capacity actors possess to bring about specific outcomes, not to their action of producing those results."[128] Affirming this definition, Peter Morriss contends that "power" is foremost a dispositional concept, for power "is neither a *thing* (a resource or vehicle) nor an *event* (an exercise of power): it is a *capacity*."[129] He highlights that typical conceptions of "power" fall prey to the "exercise fallacy," whereby the "'power to' do something is nothing more than the doing of it [and] that [to] talk of [. . .] *having* power is simply a metaphysically illegitimate way of saying that you are *exercising* that power."[130] Similarly, Arendt maintains that power does not reside in expressions of power, whether such expressions be a verbal recognition of one's abilities and/or the phenomenological act of taking action. Rather, power corresponds to the very capacity to act. From this perspective, the outcomes produced when people take action are merely manifestations of an already present "power to" act, which is the fundamental capacity engendered when a plurality of people appear to speak and act together in the world. For Arendt, whose understanding of political action is "ontologically rooted" in natality, this "power to" act refers explicitly to the human capacity to begin new courses of action in the world. Power is an ability to begin that exists insofar as a collection of civically equal and distinct people remain and act together in the "world": the "space for politics" where freedom can be experienced and new courses of action can be originated.

C.4. The "Power" of a Caring Forgiveness

As an impermanent potentiality present only so long as people are actively enacting their freedom in the world during the activity of action, power is a capacity ever in need of being renewed, which is why political institutions—as "manifestations and materializations of power—petrify and decay as soon as the living power of the people ceases to uphold them."[131] This is the fundamental reason why we need to "care for the world": there is a ceaseless need to preserve "power" and its accompanying experience of freedom. Bringing together the various strands of this chapter's discussion of Arendt's theory of the political, this section highlights how power must be cared for and, subsequently, that forgiveness can be understood as a centrally significant practice of "caring for the world." It is a public practice capable of caring for the potentiality contained within the "world": the ability to act freely and to begin new courses of "action" with a plurality of other people. A "caring forgiveness," cares for the capacity to begin new courses of action in the public realm: the "common home" shared with a plurality of people.

Arendt suggests that forgiveness is an act that can interrupt vicious cycles of vengeance by actively overcoming worldless states of alienation, which prevent people from experiencing freedom during action. Forgiveness is thus a safeguard for the activity of action, or a form of insurance against the unpredictability and irreversibility that characterizes the experience of freedom. Because contigency is the "price" people must pay for freedom, or the "gift" of being able to spontaneously begin new courses of action in the "world,"[132] there is a supreme need to be able to forgive—which is to say, "dismiss"[133]—wrongs that have been done, so that the "power to" act can be (re-)engendered in the world during the activity of action. The miraculous, redemptive power of forgiveness is apparent: the "power to" act that characterizes the phenomenological experience of freedom is the capacity that similarly informs the faculty of forgiveness. This promise of a new beginning is the very reason the act of forgiving can protect and preserve the power inherent to action. It is, arguably, for this reason that Phelps-Roper suggests that—despite her offensive, alienating, and hateful actions against the people of the world and the "world" itself—"forgiveness," and "the benefit of the doubt," is still wonderous: "it still amazes [her]." That her "friends" on Twitter could call forth the power to "undo the deeds of the past," and thus access the promise of the new beginning contained within them (as human beings who are themselves a new beginning), is a testament to humankind's power to perform miracles: to forgive is to perform a miracle.

Rather than establishing a new hierarchy within the world, effectively fabricating the subject-sovereign dynamic inherent to the "power over" logic (which Derrida is concerened with in his conceptualization of forgiveness), Arendt suggests that the act of forgiving cares for the powerful experience of freedom because it is a form of action that is, itself, a capacity enacted *between* civic friends. Forgiveness, in other words, "does not arise out of another and possibly higher faculty," which is to say, that it is *not*—as Derrida might describe it—messianic; rather, the faculty of forgiving is, according to Arendt, "one of the potentialities of action itself." As a thoroughly worldly potentiality, or a practice which contains its own type of power, forgiveness is a form of *praxis* that cares for the "world": the "space for politics," where power is generated in the mode of human togetherness, between civically equal persons who have appeared to speak and act publicly together.

Similar to power, forgiveness is a capacity that "can never be fully actualized."[134] Unlike the "work" of both vengeance and retribution, power and forgiveness do not adhere to the means/ends logic, in that there is no final, fabricated product that political action aspires to achieve. Instead, the doing of action, which enacts power, can only be said to cultivate more power as a plurality of people embody freedom. This is an experience that is—in theory—free from the trappings of sovereignty, utilitarian logics, and preestablished end goals. While "violence is instrumental by nature," and always stands in need of guidance and justification through the end it pursues," power is, "as they say, 'an end in itself.'"[135] Forgiveness, as a "potentiality," consequently contributes to the same process that results in further action and whose end is "power." As Arendt writes, "forgiving is an action that guarantees the *continuity of the capacity for action*, for beginning anew" which is "in every single human being."[136] For her, then, forgiveness and action are both capacities capable of (re)generating "power," or of engendering more power, which is cultivated in the public realm of the political *with* a plurality of distinct but equal people. In the "world," which is a space of *equal* relations, then, both action and the faculty of forgiveness beget power. Recalling Derrida's observation that forgiveness—if it is to be understood as forgiveness at all—cannot serve any reconciliatory purpose and/or be used in the process of producing some end state, it is important to note that an Arendtian conceptualization of forgiving is undergirded by the notion that the "end" result of this action is a renewed state of power, which is synonymous with the experience of freedom. Forgiveness protects the power of freedom: the capacity *to begin* spontaneously new courses of unconstrained action with a plurality of other people. In this sense, the end of "power" is further action, the unpredictable and irreversible activity that occurs between civic friends in the public realm of the political. This means that the "end" produced by forgiveness is not really an "end" at all: it is a new beginning to a course of action whose "end" cannot be known in advance.

The difference between the potentiality of action and the faculty of forgiving is, however, that the latter is an act that cares for the doing of the former. Forgiveness effectively cares for the world, since it maintains, preserves, and enhances the public realm—and therefore "power"—when relationships between people have become broken and/or vengeance has created a vicious cycle of work (which are instances when violent acts of domination have established a hierarchy within a given sociopolitical community). Because "what first undermines and then kills political communities is the loss of power,"[137] forgiveness is a centrally significant public form of practice, as it has the potential to re-invigorate the public realm by renewing the capacity for new action. Forgiving (re-)imbues the "power to" act into the public realm by undoing what had previously been done to impede the doing of politics. Forgiveness overcomes past deeds that have put an end to action so that fractured relationships, and thus the public realm, can be tended to and power can be preserved. In arguing that "power" is only actualized when a plurality of people communicate together to "disclose realities [. . .] [and] to establish relations and create new realities,"[138] it becomes clear that action and forgiveness are closely linked, since this faculty can renew "power" by caring for the "power to" begin anew when action has been impeded by a state of worldless alienation. Forgiveness is consequently the corrective, "conservative" faculty for action, as it cares for the world by "undoing the deeds" of the past and dismissing the trespasses that have put an end to or inhibited the (re)development of power.

Forgiveness is a powerful practice of care. An Arendtian form of "care" is antithetical to the self-centric idea theorized by Heidegger and free from the conceptual pitfalls of the "power over" dynamic identified by a Derridean deconstruction of the notion of forgiving. In Arendtian terms, a "caring forgiveness" is a world-centric understanding that allows people to overcome transgressions and to begin, or resume, the activity of speaking and acting with other distinct but equal people in the mode of human togetherness, that is, of experiencing freedom with one's civic friends. Forgiveness is a powerful act precisely because it cares for the worldly "web of human relationships" that comprise the "world," the political space of freedom. It is thus a "caring forgiveness" that preserves and (re-)enhances our world, and it is the act of forgiving which ensures that the powerful experience of being able to begin new courses of action with one's civic friends is preserved. In sum, forgiveness is a powerful act of tending to and preserving humankind's "common home," and thus, by forgiving, we "care for the world." We perform miracles, which—if I might borrow Phelps-Ropers line—truly "amazes me."

NOTES

1. Phelps-Roper, *Unfollow*, 256.
2. Ibid., 254.
3. Ibid.
4. Ibid., 260.
5. The public apology Phelps-Roper refers to when she discusses her disassociation from the WBC is that of the one she made via her 2013 post on Medium,

where she writes: "[My sister Grace and I] know that we've done and said things that hurt people. Inflicting pain on others wasn't the goal, but it was one of the outcomes. We wish it weren't so, and regret that hurt." [Megan Phelps-Roper, "Head Full of Doubt/Road Full of Promise," Medium, 2013, https://medium.com/@meganphelps/head-full-of-doubt-road-full-of-promise-83d2ef8ba4f5.] It is interesting to note here that this expression of regret lacks a certain particularity, leading me to question this declaration of remorse. I question not the sincerity of her and her sister's apologetic intentions but, rather, wonder if such an "apology" holds much meaning at all, since she problematically equalizes and lumps together all of her prior actions into one all-encompassing, vague expression of "regret."

    6. Phelps-Roper, "I Grew up in the Westboro Baptist Church. Here's Why I Left."

    7. Phelps-Roper, *Unfollow*, 260.

    8. Phelps-Roper, "I Grew up in the Westboro Baptist Church. Here's Why I Left."

    9. Arendt, *The Human Condition*, 183.

    10. Nicolas de Warren, "For the Love of the World: Redemption and Forgiveness in Arendt," in *Phenomenology and Forgiveness*, ed. Marguerite La Caze (London: Rowman & Littlefield International, 2018), 26.

    11. Arendt, *The Human Condition*, 236–37.

    12. Ibid., 237.

    13. Ibid.

    14. Derrida, *On Cosmopolitanism and Forgiveness*, 59. Original emphasis.

    15. Arendt, *The Human Condition*, 240–41.

    16. Ibid., 239–40. As it is written in Matthew 16:27—"For the Son of Man is going to come in his Father's glory with his angels, and then he will reward each person according to what he has done."

    17. Ibid., 240–41. Arendt was concerned with the question of "evil" throughout the course of her life, as her thought developed and as she came to terms with the evils of Nazism and Stalinism. Accordingly, scholars now speak in terms of her "early" and "late" work on evil, the latter of which is arguably more well known, corresponding to her writings about Adolf Eichmann and what she describes as the "fearsome, word-and-though-defying *banality of evil*." [Hannah Arendt, *Eichmann in Jerusalem: A Report on the Banality of Evil* (London: Penguin Books, 2006), 252. Original emphasis.] In this book, my focus revolves most fully around her earlier conceptualization of willed evil; these are crimes that she explores in reference to Kant's notion of "radical evil."

    18. Arendt, *The Human Condition*, 236–37.

    19. Ibid.

    20. Ibid., 236.

    21. Hannah Arendt, "What Is Freedom?" in *Between Past and Future: Eight Exercises in Political Thought* (London: Penguin Books, 2006), 145; Arendt, *The Human Condition*, 204; Hannah Arendt, *On Violence* (New York: Harcourt Publishing Company, 1969), 81–82.

    22. Arendt, *The Human Condition*, 240–41.

23. Derrida, *Specters of Marx*, 25.
24. Arendt, *The Human Condition*, 241.
25. Ibid., 240.
26. Hannah Arendt, "Social Science Techniques and the Study of Concentration Camps," in *Essays in Understanding, 1930–1954: Formation, Exile, and Totalitarianism*, ed. Jerome Kohn (New York: Schocken Books, 1994), 234.
27. Arendt, "A Reply to Eric Voegelin," 405.
28. Jankélévitch, "Should We Pardon Them?," 555.
29. Arendt, *The Human Condition*, 240–41. It should be noted that "good" is used here in reference to a specific conceptualization of "goodness" that Arendt identifies in the New Testament, when—as she writes—"Good works, because they must be forgotten instantly, can never become part of the world; they come and go, leaving no trace. They are truly not of the world." [Arendt, 76. Cf. Matthew 6:1-4.] For Derrida, forgiveness would be an example of a "good" deed, as it must be given unconditionally and in a manner that such a gift is given without instigating any reciprocal action.
30. Arendt, *The Origins of Totalitarianism*, 459.
31. Arendt, *The Human Condition*, 240–41; Arendt, *The Origins of Totalitarianism*, 458–59.
32. Arendt, *The Human Condition*, 240, n. 80.
33. Hannah Arendt, *Responsibility and Judgment*, ed. Jerome Kohn (New York: Schocken Books, 2003), 109; Arendt, *The Human Condition*, 240, n. 80.
34. Arendt, *Responsibility and Judgment*, 109.
35. Ibid.
36. Arendt, *The Human Condition*, 240–41.
37. Arendt, *Responsibility and Judgment*, 74 and 109.
38. Arendt, *Eichmann in Jerusalem*, 279.
39. Cf. Yosal Rogat, *The Eichmann Trial and the Rule of Law* (Santa Barbara, CA: Center for the Study of Democratic Institutions, 1961), 22.
40. Francis Bacon, *The Essays of Francis Bacon*, ed. Mary Augusta Scott (New York: Charles Scribner's Sons, 1908), 19.
41. P.E. Digeser, *Political Forgiveness* (Ithaca: Cornell University Press, 2001), 206.
42. See Roger Berkowitz, "Bearing Logs On Our Shoulders: Reconciliation, Non-Reconciliation, and the Building of a Common World," *Theory & Event* 14, no. 1 (2011); Roger Berkowitz, "'The Angry Jew Has Gotten His Revenge': Hannah Arendt on Revenge and Reconciliation," *Philosophical Topics* 39, no. 2 (2011): 1–20; Roger Berkowitz, "Reconciling Oneself to the Impossibility of Reconciliation: Judgment and Worldliness in Hannah Arendt's Politics," in *Artifacts of Thinking: Reading Hannah Arendt's Denktagebuch*, eds. Roger Berkowitz and Ian Storey (New York: Fordham University Press, 2017), 9–36.
43. Berkowitz, "'The Angry Jew Has Gotten His Revenge,'" 17.
44. For Berkowitz, two conditions determine when Arendt might be said to embrace revenge as means of enacting justice in the world, and of cultivating a new "common home": first, the crime calling forth vengeance must be extraordinary and

therefore burst the bounds of traditional legality; and second, the avenger must give himself up for judgment to a public judge/jury to determine if his act was just despite its illegality. [Ibid., 5.]

45. Ibid.
46. Arendt, *The Human Condition*, 28.
47. Ibid., 58.
48. Ibid., 50–52.
49. Ibid., 183–84.
50. Ibid., 7.
51. Ibid.
52. Ibid., 84.
53. Ibid., 22.
54. Ibid., 50.
55. Ibid., 88.
56. Jeffrie G. Murphy and Jean Hampton, *Forgiveness and Mercy* (Cambridge: Cambridge University Press, 1988), 119.
57. Ibid., 25.
58. Berkowitz, "'The Angry Jew Has Gotten His Revenge,'" 17.
59. Ibid.
60. Ibid. Here, Berkowitz refers to: Arendt, *The Human Condition*, 173.
61. For Murphy, resentment and vengeance are morally legitimate and rational. [Jeffrie G. Murphy, *Getting Even: Forgiveness and Its Limits* (Oxford: Oxford University Press, 2003), 17.] This conception is rooted in a cognitivist theory of emotion, whereby emotions "involve certain distinctive evaluative beliefs and desires which accompany any feelings or psychological changes in the person who experience them." [Murphy and Hampton, *Forgiveness and Mercy*, 54, nt. 14.] See also Robert C. Roberts's work, as he similarly contends that emotions ought to be understood in rational terms and as moral assessments within specific contexts. [Roberts C. Roberts, *Emotions: An Essay in Aid of Moral Psychology* (Cambridge: Cambridge University Press, 2003).]
62. Arendt, *The Origins of Totalitarianism*, 475.
63. Arendt, *The Human Condition*, 7.
64. Ibid., 32.
65. Ibid., 140–41.
66. Ibid., 140.
67. Theorizing the *vita contemplativa*, Arendt underscores how all "thinking always implies remembrance [since] every thought is strictly speaking an afterthought." [Hannah Arendt, *The Life of Mind* (London: Harvest Book, 1978), pt. I, pg. 78.] I return to this idea in chapter 4.
68. Robert C. Solomon, "Justice and the Passion for Vengeance," in *What Is Justice?: Classic and Contemporary Readings*, eds. Robert C. Solomon and Mark C. Murphy (Oxford: Oxford University Press, 1990), 297.
69. Arendt, *The Human Condition*, 139.
70. Ibid.
71. Arendt, *Eichmann in Jerusalem*, 277.

72. Ibid., 153.
73. Arendt, *On Violence*, 52.
74. Arendt, *The Human Condition*, 153.
75. Paul Voice, "Labour, Work and Action," in *Hannah Arendt: Key Concepts*, ed. Patrick Hayden (Durham, UK: Acumen Publishing, 2014), 43.
76. Arendt, *The Human Condition*, 240.
77. Berkowitz, "'The Angry Jew Has Gotten His Revenge,'" 17.
78. Arendt, *The Human Condition*, 7.
79. Arendt does not equate action with speech, or words with deeds. Rather, she underscores that "speechless action would no longer be action," as acting, for her, "becomes relevant only through the spoken word in which [an actor] identifies himself as the actor, announcing what he does, has done, and intends to do." That is, action "requires speech." [Ibid., 178–79.]
80. Ibid., 7. Original emphasis.
81. Ibid.
82. Emphasis added. In terms of Arendt's discussion of this passage, see both: Arendt, *The Promise of Politics*, 61; Arendt, *The Human Condition*, 7–8.
83. Arendt, *The Human Condition*, 8, n. 1. Arendt finds biblical support for her argument in that the creation story acknowledges human plurality in the New Testament, where—in Matthew 19:4—Jesus states the following to a group of Pharisees in a discussion about relations between husband and wife: "Haven't you read [. . .] that at the beginning the Creator 'made *them* male and female.'" [Arendt, 8, n. 1. Emphasis added.]
84. Ibid., 176.
85. See *Herodotus* (Book III, 83), where Otanes—the defender of *isonomy*—states, "I desire neither to rule nor to be ruled." [Arendt, 32, n. 22; Herodotus, *Herodotus*, trans. A.D. Godley, vol. II (London: William Heinemann, 1928), 111.]
86. Hannah Arendt, *On Revolution* (London: Penguin Books, 2006), 20. On this topic, also see: Hannah Arendt, "The Great Tradition: II. Ruling and Being Ruled," *Social Research* 74, no. 4 (2007): 941–54.
87. Arendt, *On Revolution*, 21.
88. Ibid.
89. Arendt, *The Promise of Politics*, 118.
90. Arendt, *On Revolution*, 258–59.
91. Derrida, *On Cosmopolitanism and Forgiveness*, 59. Original emphasis.
92. Arendt, "What Is Freedom?" 145.
93. Arendt, *The Promise of Politics*, 117.
94. Jonathan Schell, "Introduction," in *On Revolution* (London: Penguin Books, 2006), xv.
95. Berlin prioritizes negative freedom, whereby "being free [. . .] [is] not being interfered with by others—the wider the area of non-interference the wider my freedom." [Isaiah Berlin, "Two Concepts of Liberty," in *Liberty*, ed. Henry Hardy (Oxford: Oxford University Press, 2002), 170.]
96. Arendt, *The Human Condition*, 32. Original emphasis.
97. For Arendt, the notion of "liberation" should not be conflated with "freedom," since "liberation may be the condition of freedom but by no means leads

automatically to it [. . .] the notion of liberty implied in liberation can only be negative." If revolutions and rebellions are to be more than a futile attempt to liberate a people from being ruled by another party, they must be followed by the constitution of the newly won freedom, as it is necessary to secure and stabilize the newly formed body politic. [Arendt, *On Revolution*, 19–20.]

98. Arendt, *The Human Condition*, 243.
99. Ibid.
100. Arendt, *The Promise of Politics*, 17.
101. Aristotle, *The Complete Works of Aristotle: Volume II*, ed. Jonathan Barnes (Princeton: Princeton University Press, 1984), 142.
102. Arendt, *Men in Dark Times*, 25.
103. Graham M. Smith, *Friendship and the Political: Kierkegaard, Nietzsche, Schmitt* (Exeter, UK: Imprint Academic, 2011), vii. Original emphasis.
104. Arendt, *The Promise of Politics*, 114; Arendt, *The Human Condition*, 177.
105. Arendt, *Love and Saint Augustine*, 51.
106. Arendt, *The Human Condition*, 247.
107. Ibid., 9.
108. Ibid., 176.
109. Arendt, *The Origins of Totalitarianism*, 479; Arendt, "What Is Freedom?" 165–66; Arendt, *The Human Condition*, 177.
110. Arendt, *The Origins of Totalitarianism*, 479; Arendt, "What Is Freedom?" 166.
111. Arendt, "What Is Freedom?" 166. Original emphasis.
112. Arendt, *The Promise of Politics*, 118.
113. Arendt, *The Human Condition*, 215.
114. Ibid., 176.
115. Heidegger, *Being and Time*, 171. Original emphasis.
116. Dana Villa examines well the influence of Heidegger's body of thought on Arendt's work. See: Villa, *Arendt and Heidegger*; Dana R. Villa, "Arendt, Heidegger, and the Tradition," *Social Research* 74, no. 4 (2007): 983–1002. See also: Lewis P. Hinchman and Sandra K. Hinchman, "In Heidegger's Shadow: Hannah Arendt's Phenomenological Humanism," *The Review of Politics* 46, no. 2 (1984): 183–211; Jacques Taminiaux, *The Thracian Maid and the Professional Thinker: Arendt and Heidegger*, trans. Michael Gendre (Albany, NY: State University of New York Press, 1992).
117. Arendt, *The Human Condition*, 176. Original emphasis.
118. Ibid., 178.
119. Arendt, *The Origins of Totalitarianism*, 479.
120. Ibid.
121. Arendt, *On Violence*, 44.
122. Ibid., 46.
123. Ibid., 53.
124. Arendt, *The Life of Mind*, pt. II, pgs. 200–1.
125. Arendt, *On Violence*, 52.
126. Ibid., 56.

127. Arendt, *The Human Condition*, 200.
128. Pamela Pansardi, "Power to and Power Over," in *Encyclopedia of Power*, ed. Keith Dowding (Thousand Oaks, CA: Sage Publications, 2011), 522.
129. Peter Morriss, *Power: A Philosophical Analysis* (Manchester: Manchester University Press, 1987), 19. Original emphasis.
130. Ibid., 15.
131. Arendt, *On Violence*, 41.
132. Arendt, *The Life of Mind*, pt. II, pg. 198.
133. Arendt, *The Human Condition*, 240.
134. Ibid., 200.
135. Arendt, *On Violence*, 51.
136. Arendt, *The Promise of Politics*, 59. Emphasis added.
137. Arendt, *The Human Condition*, 200.
138. Ibid.

Chapter 3

Caring Cosmopolitanism
Worldly Stories and Narrative Voices

We understand the world through the stories we tell. Megan Phelps-Roper tells her story in her book, *Unfollow: A Journey from Hatred to Hope, Leaving the Westboro Baptist Church* (2019). It is a story of an "Us" and "Them," a narrative of a people—the WBC—so thoroughly blinded by their ideology and their skewed worldviews that they have been, arguably, alienated from global civil society. Though it is true that everyone's view of the world is biased and subjective to some extent, the WBC's "vilification of compromise," and "knee-jerk expulsion of insiders who violate group orthodoxy," as well as their "demonization of outsiders and the inability to substantively engage with their ideas," happens because they "cannot step outside" of their own ways and perspectives.[1] And yet, through her interactions on social media, Phelps-Roper discovers that "open discourse and dialectic is the most effective enabler of the evolution of individuals and societies."[2] Her entire life, she had been told one story, one which she—for many years—also recounted to herself, to those around her, and to the people of the world at large. As she writes:

> We had been claiming to *love thy neighbor* all my life. We claimed we were the *only* ones who *truly* cared about anyone else. [. . .] And at the same time, we had been wholly dedicated to antagonizing the world. We mocked and delighted in their suffering. We demanded they repent, and then asked God to preserve them in their sin. We prayed for Him to destroy them.[3]

This is, of course, an entirely paradoxical narrative, pulling in two different directions, which shaped the course of her life: love and hatred. As she further elaborates: "Two diametrically opposed positions, held strongly and sincerely by the same mind at the same time—just never in the same moment."[4] Never admitting, even to herself, that her beliefs could be wrong, she adhered, instead, to her grandfather's oft-repeated adage that "there's something wonderfully liberating in the notion that you're one hundred percent right."[5] There was no room for any other story. That you can keep more than one story in your mind—be it a coherent narrative or otherwise—is not in question here but, rather, in what ways we can "open" further our "discourse," or expand the public spaces for discussion and dialectical argumentation, in such a manner that we welcome the (unknown) Other as a co-narrator in the "world." Phelps-Roper's position was "inherently arrogant and full of hubris," though she notes that she "felt humble."[6] In spite of her hateful actions and perceived disdain for the world, and her belief that she "would not find the world a hospitable place,"[7] her narrative voice was welcomed. She was subsequently liberated from the cycle of eternal enmity for the people and affairs of the world. She was released from a circular logic of hatred, which—by reducing the "nuance, complexity, and humanity" of other people's existence—maintains an inescapably Schmittian narrative: an "us" versus "them," or "friend" versus "enemy" paradigm.

"Before Twitter," Phelps-Roper writes, "friendship with outsiders had always been easy to avoid."[8] She could keep outsiders at "arm's length," interacting with classmates at school, but eschewing "interaction outside of that."[9] Further, the WBC's self-identification with Jacob, "chosen by God for love, mercy, honor, glory," put them at odds with the figure of Esau, symbolic of the "reprobate"—here representing the people of the world, who are marked by "hatred, cruelty, wrath, destruction."[10] This self-conceptualization is antithetical to an Arendtian conceptualization of the "world," political action, and Arendt's related views about civic friendship, or the Aristotelian *philia politikē*: a kind of friendship mediated by "the distance of the space of the world puts between [people]."[11] From this perspective, the WBC's worldview consequently opposes an Arendtian world-centric conception of politics and prohibits "friendship with the world." This ultimately inhibits Arendtian forms of friendship that are theorized by scholars such as Patrick Hayden, for example, who argues that there is a "need to make political friendship more 'worldly' by fostering triadic interconnections between, self, world, and other [. . .] [a] befriending of the world."[12] Rather than "befriend the world" or recognize that, as Graham Smith does, "all forms of politics are dependent on the bonds between person and person and their shared world of order and value,"[13] the WBC vehemently embraces the understanding that "friendship with the world is enmity with God." The world—and the friendships between the people who share this space—is opposed by the WBC's position. As is evinced by their unique "picketing ministry,"[14] the WBC has paradoxically managed to politicize their thoroughly anti-political message (in an Arendtian sense of "the political"): "God Hates the World."

This chapter re-examines cosmopolitanism in terms similar to the conceptualization of forgiveness in chapter two. The act of forgiving is understood as a distinctly political practice of caring for the "world." Here, however, the notion of "care for the world" is examined in greater detail in order to theorize what I have described as a *caring cosmopolitanism*: an ethico-political form of cosmopolitan theory characterized by the desire to care for the worldly space of action that emerges when plural persons speak and act together in the public realm. More specifically, my Arendtian-inspired conception of cosmopolitanism is concerned with the narrative nature of this political interaction, in that cosmopolitan care can be understood as a means of taking care of the storied realm of public, political action.

The first section of this chapter departs from the argument put forth by Ella Myers in her book *Worldly Ethics: Democratic Politics and Care for the World* (2013), a text that makes a case for a care-based, democratic ethos fashioned from the idea of "caring for the world" rather than caring for the self or for the Other. Unlike Derrida's distinctly Levinasian conception of hospitality, which is thoroughly Other-centric, a caring cosmopolitanism is a world-centric, ethico-political theory concerned with the worldly "thingness"[15] of stories and the active welcoming of the Other's narrative voice. Bringing together several different lines of thought, specifically Myers's critique of Other-centric ethics and Arendt's narrative-driven conception of action, as well as her understanding of political theorizing as a type of narration, this chapter lays the conceptual foundations for a theory of cosmopolitanism devoted to storytelling, understood here as an intersubjective interaction between plural persons who speak and act together in the public space of appearance. This chapter consequently highlights the cosmopolitan potential of public storytelling. Moreover, it demonstrates how the welcoming of the Other's narrative voice allows us to move beyond the paradoxes uncovered by Derrida's deconstruction of cosmopolitan hospitality, namely, the inescapable conditionality of an unconditional welcoming of the face of the Other, and the dynamic of "power over" associated with giving an Other a place in one's home. A caring cosmopolitanism necessitates a care for the story enacted with (global) others as a means of beginning to preserve, maintain, and enhance the world in which a plurality of narrative voices "produce" a worldly, narrated "thing" capable of fostering political action and, ultimately, becoming a lasting part of human history, that is, in Arendt's words, "the storybook of mankind."[16] Emphasizing the "thing-character" of the world, then, I illustrate how public storytelling fosters worldliness when narratives are enacted between people in the public, political sphere.

Storytelling is by no means alien to Arendt's thinking, as she understands action—the third and highest activity within her tripartite conception of the *vita activa*—in narrative terms, leading Allen Speight to describe her as a "narrative theorist of action."[17] Arendt developed what Seyla Benhabib suggests is a "conception of political theory as 'storytelling.'"[18] And indeed, Arendt referred to her way of doing political theory as "my old-fashion story-telling."[19] Despite the fact that she wrote very little about her method of doing political theory, however, mentioning her conception of theorizing as a form storytelling in only a few scattered remarks, she clarifies, at least to some small degree, her approach in a letter to Karl Jaspers, her doctoral supervisor and long-time friend: "I've become a kind of freelance writer, something between a historian and a political journalist."[20] Even though this self-identification fails to capture fully the nuanced nature of her writings,[21] this self-labeling is significant because it demonstrates how she understands herself to be a type of storyteller concerned with specific, worldly historical and political phenomena.[22] Remarkably, this self-classification positions her outside the disciplinary boundaries of both the social sciences and political philosophy—the two academic disciplines most typically associated with the study of politics. Arendt identifies with this type of storytelling because she believes that social scientists and philosophers fail to understand human affairs and the particularity of worldly occurrences. By distilling the kaleidoscopic character of human life into simplistic abstractions, political scientists, in Arendt's view, problematically reduce the complexities of sociopolitical, economic, and cultural affairs. Philosophers, meanwhile, prioritize the life of the mind, forsaking the common world shared between people. For Arendt, social scientific modes of inquiry tend to negate the inescapable effects of natality on human life, while the philosophic tradition wrongly privileges the *vita contemplativa* over the *vita activa*.

While this chapter ultimately focuses on Arendt's narrative conception of action, I introduce briefly her approach to political theory here since her method of storytelling supplements her body of thought, and informs my theory of a caring cosmopolitanism. In particular, Arendt's narrative method of doing theory reflects what Maša Mrovlje describes as her "phenomenological-existentialist sensibility"[23]: storytelling is a means of coming to terms with one's ineluctable thrownness in the world. In light of this, we might wonder how Arendt's narrative approach—her form of "old-fashion storytelling"—developed throughout the course her life, and how she interwove this narrative mode of thought into her scholarly work. We might reflect upon, for instance, how storytelling allowed her to narratively come to terms with the turmoil that surrounded her as a German Jewish woman living in Berlin when Hitler came to power (1933) and, subsequently, as an *émigré* compelled to flee Europe in 1941. In an effort to understand her experience of totalitarian domination—and the accompanying terror, war, and statelessness—Arendt told "stories," developing a narrative approach to political theory that offers an epistemological alternative to abstract, preconceived, and prefabricated forms of social scientific inquiry. For her, such forms of inquiry were "exposed and exploded" by the "altogether unexpected phenomena" of totalitarianism, which could not be "understood within the framework" offered by their "categories."[24] Arendt's efforts to confront totalitarianism in all its novelty, and to tell the story of this never-before experienced phenomena, is evidenced by the significance she attributes to understanding historical events in terms of their unique appearance in the world. It is this attentiveness to newness—associated with natality and human unpredictability—that makes her storytelling relevant to this book: a caring cosmopolitanism is concerned with worldly relationships and the particularity of individual stories. Although a caring cosmopolitanism is bound up with Arendt's narrative conception of action, her understanding of political theory as a form of storytelling suggests that, if the narrative voices of the Other are to be welcomed, it is necessary to consider the Other's story in terms of its particularity and unique emergence in the world.

The strangers with whom Phelps-Roper interacted on Twitter were largely anonymous, hidden behind a digital wall of sorts: they were faceless. She had succeeded in keeping the world at arm's length. But when we speak of facelessness in these terms, of welcoming the unknown Other—paradoxically, a faceless being whose face represents all of humanity—and regard a stranger in this way, do we disregard this person's voice? This is not so much, just yet, a question of empowering the Other to speak, but rather—in the first instance—a question of giving place to their voice, and ultimately, of a willingness to listen. Are we prepared to welcome the voice of, or give place to, the voice of the faceless stranger? In law, we speak of a "hearing" and, in this sense, one's voice is defined as a "right to be heard."[25] In terms "the political," such a "right to be heard" corresponds to the act of giving place to the voice of an individual, or a group, in a public space. This is where the "common voice" of democracy emerges, typically being understood in narrative terms and thus as a story *in medias res*. These stories are, of course, significant to particular groups, as political narratives form the histories of communities. But yet, they are also so much more, existing and informing people's lives in a much more all-encompassing manner. To call upon the work of Roland Barthes, narrative is "international, transhistorical, transcultural: it is simply there, like life itself."[26] As part of the "text," about which Derrida so famously writes, narrative does not belong to a particular culture or language; it is universal in scope. What gives it *character*, then, so to speak—at least in this paradigm—is perhaps our ability to "hear" the distinct voices—both single and plural—which speak it into existence. To care for the narrative voices of strangers, then, is to engender worldly spaces for political discussion and action; it is to act in an inherently cosmopolitan manner because we are radically welcoming the (unknown) Other *by* giving place to their voice.

1. CARE FOR THE SELF, OTHER, OR THE WORLD?

When thinking about what it means to care for the "world" shared with a plurality of people, Myers's work offers a sturdy foundation upon which to build a caring cosmopolitanism: my theory for how we might more fully and radically "dilate" (Hugo) the political realm, allowing for the "face" of humanity to make its appearance in the "world." In her book, *Worldly Ethics*, Myers theorizes a world-centric ethos of democracy, one which aligns political action with "care for the world." Focusing on what she describes as the "turn to ethics" in the field of political theory, Myers contends that attempts to establish a flourishing democracy from models of care that either focus on the self, as Michel Foucault suggests (in his theory of "the care of the self"),[27] or the Other, as Levinas advocates, are depoliticizing and ultimately insufficient. In pursuit of a "worldly ethics," Myers argues that both self-centric and Other-oriented ethical approaches disproportionately privilege their respective foci of care, to the detriment of the "world" (understood in Arendtian terms). Myers draws heavily on the work of Arendt in order to demonstrate how a democratic ethos might better operate in a world where worldly "things" are shared between one's self and others. As Myers writes:

> Foucauldian and Levinasian approaches, each focused on a different dyadic of care, are inclined to enervate rather than enrich associative action by democratic citizens. [. . .] I conceptualize and defend an alternative ethical orientation, one focused on inciting citizens' collective care for worldly things. And I argue that worldly ethics, implicit in certain collective citizen efforts, is a promising resource for democratic action today.[28]

Democratic action is not, for Myers, fostered as a result of extensively caring for one's self, nor is it in devoting one's self to the task of caring for the needs of others. Myers problematizes Foucault's argument that caring for one's self "renders one competent to occupy a place in the city,"[29] and she challenges Other-centric models of care, such as Levinas's ethics of responsibility to the face of the Other, whereby "the Other who dominates me in his transcendence is the stranger, the widow, and the orphan, to whom I am obligated."[30] For Myers, it is the act of caring for the world and worldly things, as the focal point of political acting and speaking, which best conditions democratic action. Her work is an umbrella under which my own theory of a caring cosmopolitanism is sheltered.

Myers asks us to consider what motivates democratic political action, and to consider the ways in which people can care for the world and worldly "things"; I propose a caring approach that emphasizes the welcoming of the (unknown) Other and, specifically, their narrative voice. Walking with Myers, under the cover provided by her Arendtian-inspired, world-centric theory of care, my aim is to investigate how we might go about creating an even more radically inclusive public realm: this is a space where the "stranger," "widow," and "orphan" are equally welcome to become co-storytellers in our ever-unfolding narrative. These are figures who have traditionally had limited power to speak and act politically; and indeed, with his own choice to use both the words "widow" and "orphan," Levinas implies a certain element of passivity. We speak of *being* widow-*ed* and of *being* orphan-*ed*. The widow and the orphan are two vulnerable figures who, having experienced a rupture of relationships (loss of a husband and parents, respectively), frequently find themselves on the fringe of society. But who is caring for their respective voices, and do their stories form part of our "world"? In Isaiah 1:16-18, God's command to the people is to "take your evil deeds out of my sight; stop doing wrong. Learn to do right; seek justice. Defend the oppressed. *Take up the cause of the fatherless; plead the case of the widow.*" But is this enough? Perhaps it is time to go beyond simply taking up the cause of the orphan and pleading the case of the widow. Instead, we need to find ways to give place to their voices, and to "hear" them as equal speakers in the public realm of "the political."

A. Moving Past Derrida's Other-Centric Ethic of Hospitality

Like Levinas, Derrida presents an Other-centric conception of hospitality: this is an unconditional responsibility to the (unknown) Other engendered when someone is "taken hostage" in "face-to-face" interactions. Like Myers, I take issue with both Levinas and Derrida's similarly aligned belief in the obligation owed to the face of the Other, as such a debt and hyperbolic sense of responsibility does not allow for a world to develop in-between political parties. For Myers, the Levinasian/Derridean conception of responsibility to care for the Other is deficient since acts of welcoming the face of the Other "focus on a 'transcendental horizon' that substitutes an ethical understanding of otherness for a political one."[31] Accordingly, as previously discussed, the arrival of the Other is, in terms of the Levinasian/Derridean account, a matter of transcendence in which one welcomes infinitude: "the messianic, or messianicity without messianism."[32] This conception of transcendence and the welcoming of the infinite is problematic for Myers because she contends that this unconditional responsibility to the face of the Other permits no space for the emergence of political action. She argues that Levinasian/Derridean acts of care for the Other are depoliticizing for the reason that they do not care for any worldly "thing" in particular. That is, Other-centric acts of hospitality care for the infinite since, as Levinas remarks, "the epiphany of the face qua face opens humanity."[33]

From Myers's perspective, Other-centric acts, such as welcoming the Other into one's home or city, are consequently depoliticizing because their focus on the Other impedes the development of a worldly and political "in-between,"[34] a "thingly" entity capable of fostering democratic deliberation, contestation, and/or joint action. From Myers's Arendtian-inspired perspective, neither a democratic ethos nor a cosmopolitics can be fashioned from an Other-centric conception of care, precisely because acts that seek to care solely for the Other do not constitute any "in-between." Here, the significance of the "in-between" cannot be overstated, for, as Arendt observes, "action and speech go on between men."[35] The Other-centric models of care hinder the emergence of a common world by being unconcerned with the common interest of political actors. "Interests," as Arendt writes, "constitute, in the word's most literal sense, something which *inter-est*, which lies between people and therefore can relate and bind them together."[36] Caring for the Other bypasses an intermediating in-between "thing," in favor of an idealized, unmediated, and direct form of face-to-face contact. Because Other-centric acts of care generate no in-between—as they are completed solely for the Other's benefit—they do not allow for the development of a worldly, political space that might have otherwise been cultivated if these caring actions had been carried out for the sake of the world and the "thing-ness" of this public space.

Arendt's understanding of "love" highlights the apolitical character of Other-centric ethico-political understandings, such as Derrida's and Levinas's respective conceptions of hospitality. Cosmopolitan hospitality is not presented in this book as a type of love, though it is nevertheless possible to recognize the similarly apolitical character of these two conceptions: both are Other-centric in the sense that they do not take into account the worldly space of the political, nor of any worldly "things," in their respective processes of care.[37] Arendt's views on the worldless character of love are explained succinctly in a 1964 television interview with Günter Gaus, during which she states:

> The directly personal relationship, where one can speak of love, exists of course foremost in real love. [. . .] There a person is addressed directly, independent of his relation to the world [. . .] if you bring love to the negotiating table, to put it bluntly, I find that fatal. [. . .] I find it apolitical. I find it worldless. And I really find it to be a great disaster.[38]

Arendt's understanding of love, which is both private and personal,[39] illuminates how Other-centric sentiments are "apolitical" because they are aimed specifically at the Other in a way that circumvents the worldly intermediary. In a loving relationship, there is a direct, worldless, and emotional connection between two people—the self and the Other. Moreover, love need not be expressed through acts of speech (*lexis*) and can be experienced in silence.⁴⁰ Like love, then, acts of hospitality, from the Levinasian/Derridean point of view, establish a dyadic interaction, without referring to any worldly "thing," or interest, that sits in-between the self and the Other. Rather, there is simply the face of the Other and the *ipseity* of the self, mutually holding each other hostage in a (silent) worldless, depoliticizing situation.

Without engaging directly with an Arendtian conception of interpersonal love, Myers's position against a Levinasian model of caring for the Other stems from her belief that democracies ought to cultivate ethico-political frameworks that take the world as their locus of care. According to Myers's critique of Other-centric ethics, Derrida's vision for a "new charter of hospitality," a new "cosmopolitics" of the "democracy to come," would seem undesirable for liberal, democratic societies, as this model of hospitality is rooted too fully in Levinas's work: his notion of radical responsibility to the "face" the Other. From Myers's perspective, then, Derrida's body of thought, like that of Levinas's, would effectively destroy the "in-between" that characterizes democratic politics, because the unconditional welcoming of the Other that characterizes a Derridean cosmopolitanism is ultimately a worldless welcoming. While I would agree with Myers that political action must consider and, ultimately, take care of the world—rather than simply one's self or the Other—her criticism of Levinas, while salient, cannot be applied unproblematically to Derrida's work; to do so is effectively to deny the conception of politics with which Derrida identifies when he suggests that "ethics is hospitality."⁴¹

As discussed in chapter 1, a Derridean account of ethics is inherently a matter of hospitality, yet ethics cannot be disassociated from politics because hospitable acts of welcome are a matter of giving the Other a place in one's home, city, and/or nation-state; this act of giving space to the Other consequently relates ethics to the political issues of belonging and sovereignty. Consequently, for Derrida, ethics and politics are inextricably linked through the idea of hospitality, or the giving of place to the Other. With this in mind, Derrida's Other-centric model of hospitality, despite its similarities to Levinas's work, is depoliticizing only if we consider politics in terms of an Arendtian conception of the political. While this conceptual difference may, arguably, indicate the theoretical incommensurability of Derrida's understanding of the political and Arendt's conception of politics, I suggest that it is, in fact, *precisely* this conceptual differentiation that allows a pairing of a Derridean conception of hospitality with an Arendtian conception of "world."

More than simply welcoming the "face" of the Other, it is imperative to welcome the Other's narrative voice as a means of caring for the worldly story produced in the doing of politics with a plurality of others in the public realm. Accordingly, the world, as an "in-between," ought to be considered in terms of its "thing-ness," as a story produced during the course of political action. Furthermore, the Other should be welcomed as a co-narrator, responsible for the narrative production of this worldly "thing." This chapter consequently re-orients Derrida's work on hospitality and develops from it a conception of cosmopolitan care, the central premise of which is the caring about worldly stories and caring for the narrative voice of the (unknown) Other. The subsequent sections of this chapter examine more closely Arendt's conception of "world," the narrative character of her understanding of action, and why stories are worldly political "things" in need of care. Because Arendt's narrative conception of action is directly related to her beliefs about the inextricability of the *vita activa* and the *vita contemplativa*, it is also important to explore briefly the themes of understanding and *logos* ("coherent speech"): the two human faculties through which thinking is, as Steve Buckler suggests, "implicated in the fate of the world."[42]

B. (Re)considering the "World" in Narrative Terms

Whereas Derrida presents the notion of "*monde*" in terms of the Apostle Paul's Judeo-Christian conception of human brotherhood, Arendt's conception of "world," although strongly influenced by Heidegger's work (most especially *Being and Time*), draws heavily upon the ideas of the ancient Greeks in order to theorize this notion in relation to the three primary activities that comprise the *vita activa*—"labor," "work," and "action." While both Derrida and Arendt understand the term "world" (or *monde*) in human terms, the latter contends that the world is produced from human practice; the former, however, suggests that the notion of *monde* refers to a human brotherhood, whose members are called "*citizens of the world*," or "brothers, fellow men, neighbors, insofar as they are creatures and sons of God."[43] Though such a conceptualization of world citizenship is expansive and, perhaps, helpful in understanding the more distinctly Levinasian aspects of Derrida's thought, it is Arendt's focus on the "things" made by people—both tangible and intangible—that is of particular relevance here, in seeking to understand how stories are "thingly" entities that bind together the "web of human relationships." Arendt's notion of world is not rooted in Judeo-Christian theology, nor is it "identical with the earth or with nature."[44] It relates, instead, to her interpretation of the ancient Greek distinction between the activities that occur in the private realm and those that take place in the public space of appearance. Moreover, Arendt illustrates how the world consists of "things" produced in these two spaces and how "the objectivity of the world–its object- or thing-character–and the human condition supplement each other."[45] In this sense, to examine the Arendtian notion of world is to consider worldly "things" and their significance for human life.

For Arendt, labor occurs in the private realm and is an activity devoted to the perpetuation of one's life cycle—that is, the satisfaction of one's basic, biological needs. Labor, as Arendt writes, "never 'produces' anything but life";[46] therefore, it is the only thoroughly worldless activity within her tripartite conception of the *vita activa*. That is, labor produces no worldly things that can sit in-between people in the public space of appearance, which is a realm of human activity characterized by publicity—the ability by which something/someone can be seen and heard by a plurality of people. In terms of Arendt's understanding of the *vita activa*, worldliness is consequently associated with the activities of work and action, for the world is, as she writes, "related to human artefact, the fabrication of human hands, as well as to affairs which go on among those who inhabit the man-made world together."[47] Worldliness refers to those things that are produced in the process of work as well as in acting and speaking (action).

While products of work (such as paintings, sculptures, buildings, etc.) are tangible things, action does not leave behind any physical end products. Despite the intangibility of products generated through action, however, the in-between produced by acting and speaking is "no less real": this reality being termed "the 'web' of human relationships."[48] Highlighting the distinction between tangible, objective and intangible, subjective in-betweens, Arendt writes:

> Distinguished from [. . .] consumer goods and use objects, there are [. . .] the "products" of action and speech, which together constitute the fabric of human relationships and affairs [. . .] Their reality depends entirely upon human plurality, upon the constant presence of others who can see and hear and therefore testify to their existence.[49]

Here, there are clear links between the end results of work and action, while acting and speaking leave no permanent trace, for the world exists only so long as people continue the doing of politics together in the public realm. In this sense, the human artifacts produced through work are different from those generated in action, but the doing of these two activities brings into existence some-*thing* that can simultaneously link and separate people in the public space of appearance. Accordingly, the end results of work and action are both worldly because the products of *homo faber*, (wo)man as the maker of things, and a plurality of *zōon politikon*, (wo)men as a political animals, are characterized by their "thing-ness": their capacity to sit in-between people in the public realm. In particular, political action, which occurs between people in the public realm, is an activity that results in a "*story* with enough coherence to be told."[50] Action, as Arendt further writes, "'produces' stories," just "as naturally as fabrication produces tangible things."[51] Stories are therefore

B.1. Action, Stories, and the World

This subsection examines more closely Arendt's conception of action, exploring the narrative nature of this public activity. Because a caring cosmopolitan is premised upon the idea of caring about, as well as caring for, the worldly stories "produced" through and/or in response to action, it is important to look in greater depth at the notion of narrative Arendt employs within her understanding of the political. I therefore highlight how stories are worldly reifications of action that can form a lasting part of human history, contributing to the narrative that is in Barthes's words "international, transhistorical, transcultural," or "simply there, like life itself." Although not all stories become a part of history, I nevertheless use the phrase "historical stories/narratives" as a means of drawing a distinction between reified stories and "enacted stories." In terms of Arendt's narrative understanding of action, there is an inextricable (but not dialectical) link between enacted stories and historical narratives. For her, historical narratives refer to the stories that have already occurred, while enacted stories correspond to the stories currently unfolding in the world; enacted stories can one day be represented in a complete, coherent historical narrative by a storyteller. A story-oriented ethics ought therefore to be the conceptual starting point for beginning to care for the world because it is by caring about the story "produced" with the Other that we begin to think and act in a cosmopolitan manner.

As an end product, a story is worldly in terms of its "thing-ness," and the ways in which it is "produced" by a storyteller in the process of re-presenting action as a definable and delimited thing: an emplotted story.[52] While discussing the reification of acting and speaking in her chapter on "Action," in *The Human Condition*, Arendt suggests that the "living flux of acting and speaking" can be "represented and 'reified' only through a kind of repetition [. . .] imitation or *mimēsis*."[53] The words and deeds that are shared between people during action become a worldly "thing" through the mimetic process of narration, which transforms impermanent happenings into a reified representation of that which has occurred. Thus, when Arendt suggests that action "produces" stories just as naturally as work fabricates things, she effectively means that public acting and speaking can be *transformed*, so to speak, into a "thing" by a storyteller. This is an "historian" of sorts, whose position in space and time provides them with the perspectival distance to account for and re-*present* the words and deeds that transpired between people. This process of reification is significant within Arendt's body of thought, especially with regards to her understanding of history, as she avers that "what goes on between mortals directly, the spoken word and all the actions and deeds which the Greeks called πράξεις and πράγματα" can "never outlast the moment of their realization."⁵⁴ Action, if it is to be made a part of human history (the "storybook of mankind"), requires reification for things to be remembered; Arendt consequently argues that it is the task of the poet and/or historiographer, as storytellers, "to make *something* lasting out of remembrance," which they do by "translating πρᾶξις and λέξις, action and speech, into that kind of ποίησις or fabrication, which eventually becomes the written word."⁵⁵ Action can therefore be said to assume a sort of durability through its "thing-ness" as a story. Moreover, history, as the all-encompassing metastory of humanity, is comprised of these narrated things, these historical narratives which are the mimetic representations of completed courses of action. As a narrated "thing," a story therefore allows the words and deeds shared in the public realm to be remembered, (re)told, and to (re)appear in the world, as a part of the world itself and/or as a narrated object around which further political deliberation, contestation, or joint action may take place.

Inextricably linked to this aspect of Arendt's storied conception of action is her notion of "enacted stories."⁵⁶ While the word "enact" can be defined in a number of different ways, Arendt uses this term in the sense of a theatrical performance, according to which a character is impersonated or personified dramatically on, or as if on, the stage. Different from a reified story, which is most often recorded (historically, in writing, but more recently in a wide variety of digital mediums), an enacted narrative is a story that is acted out in person, and in real-time. Enacted stories differ from those reified by a single storyteller because they have no author and are a coproduction in which a plurality of actors effectively serve as co-storytellers in a currently developing narrative. This is not to say that the actors involved in this production are moving and acting in accordance with some already known plan but, rather, that this group of people are acting in such a way that they are effectively co-producing a story that has not been, and cannot yet be, told as a story. Each person is a co-narrator, whose individual narrative voice contributes to the developing story by advancing political action toward some end (one that is unknown and unforeseeable).⁵⁷ In this sense, enacted stories refer to the *praxis* of action itself, while historical narratives recount events, words, and/or deeds that have already taken place in the public realm. Historical narratives are reified accounts of the story that has already been enacted. Because enacted stories can only become "things" in hindsight, the form of worldliness that action engenders is of an entirely alternative sort. Unlike historical narratives, which require a single storyteller to transform a course of action into a "thing" of remembrance, enacted stories correspond to the intangible state of worldliness characteristic of the "web of human relationships," which is—as Arendt writes—"an altogether different in-between [as it] consists of deeds and words and owes its origins exclusively to men's acting and speaking *to* one another."[58] Although action generates worldly "things," in the sense that acting can be reified by a storyteller, acting and speaking in public also engender the world as it occurs. The worldliness of action corresponds, for Arendt, to the most human form of "in-betweens," because the world engendered through the enactment of stories emerges entirely through the sharing of words and deeds between people. It is in the mode of human togetherness that enacted stories generate the "world." To care about stories enacted with the Other is to care about the world shared with them.

To emphasize how stories are enacted through acts of speech is to underscore Arendt's belief that a "life without speech and action [. . .] is literally dead to the world, it has ceased to be a human life because it is no longer lived among men."[59] In caring for the narrative voices of the Other, we care about the most human aspect of their beingness as a human being. This point is related to Arendt's Heideggerian-inspired understanding of disclosure. As Heidegger writes, *"Dasein is its disclosedness."*[60] According to Arendt, then, action and the enactment of stories revolves around people speaking together in the public realm and, as she maintains, "to be political, to live in a *polis*," means that "everything" is "decided through words and persuasion and not through force and violence."[61] The worldliness of the *polis* is established as a result of words shared between people: Aristotle's *zōon politikon* "can only be fully understood," if we take into account his "second famous definition of man as *zōon logon ekhon* ('a living being capable of speech')."[62] We might be tempted to assume that people are political beings simply because they possess the ability to communicate with one another; however, such an understanding is flawed because the ability to communicate is not synonymous with Arendt's distinctly Aristotelian conception of speech as *logos*, that is, coherent speech. In *The Life of the Mind*, Arendt illustrates how *logos* is more than a mere form of communication, which other mammals—through sounds, signs, gestures—are also capable of making. *Logos* is reasoned speech, which emerges in the process of assembling one's words into coherent sentences and, ultimately, into stories.[63] A word is the commonly accepted label for a specific worldly referent, but the meaningfulness expressed through *logos* is derived from the process of synthesizing certain combinations of words. It is in this way that *logos* reveals meaning, disclosing how the world appears to an individual "in the mode of it-seems-to-me."[64] The distinctly human character of *logos* stems from the disclosure of an individual, subjective account of the world, as speech conveys understanding: "the specifically human way of being alive."[65]

Arendt's conception of "understanding," which is an idea that I consider in the preceding chapter's reflections on "radically evil" crimes, helps us bridge the gap between her thoughts about the *vita activa* and the *vita contemplativa*:

the "active life" and the "contemplative life" (or the life of the mind). Understanding is an "unending activity" by which we "come to terms with and reconcile ourselves to reality, that is, try to be at home in the world."[66] It is not a simply a process of rationalization or logical pursuit of knowledge, although such cognitive processes are inextricably connected to understanding. Rather, understanding is an activity by which people attempt to come to grips with their "thrownness" in the world. Such thinking is critical; it is both reflective and reflexive. It is an attempt to make sense of the phenomena that appear in the world, in order to come to terms with our own existence and, ultimately, to reconcile ourselves to the ever-changing realities that constrain and condition our lives. Understanding, then, is foremost a matter of self-understanding, or of reconciling ourselves to the never-static phenomenological world into which we are born and to which we will forever remain a stranger.

For an outlander in a state of perpetual foreignness to the world, understanding is a necessarily ceaseless pursuit, one that can never produce a single, definitive account of human affairs. Instead, it results in the uncovering of "meaning," which people "originate in the very process of living" insofar as the "try to reconcile" themselves "to what [they] do and what [they] suffer."[67] Meaning is therefore thoroughly subjective, since it refers to an individual sense of being at home in the world, which Arendt equates with "the familiarity of daily life."[68] When someone speaks in the political realm, as a co-narrator in a developing story, they are effectively revealing and making public a part of their individual, private world. If a mind can be understood in spatial terms, to speak publicly is to cast open the doors and windows of a person's mental abode—allowing a public body of people to peer into a space which is typically shielded from prying eyes. Through speech, once hidden thoughts and understandings become the political content from which the doing of politics can occur, culminating in a story to be told. In revealing one's self to the world through a coherent act of public speech, a person communicates—at least to some degree—part of their story, while contributing to a political narrative which is unfolding with all those who have appeared publicly together in the world. Conceptualized in this way, it is through the act of appearing to others, through words and deeds, that the voice of each individual—who is both an actor and a co-narrator in an enacted story—facilitates the emergence of the world by speaking and acting with other actors/narrators.

The world that is formed through the enactment of stories is therefore one comprised of a complex web of human relationships and publicly expressed meanings, which, upon being shared, are woven into the preexisting and continuously evolving meta-story of human history: "the storybook of mankind." While Arendt's two differing conceptions of stories are linked, since historical narratives are comprised of enacted stories, it is the public act of co-storytelling that is of primary concern here; it is the joint character of co-producing a story that is the key to overcoming the aporia of power inherent to Derrida's understanding of cosmopolitan hospitality. Considering the worldly story generated through the process of co-storytelling and the worldly web comprised of vocalized meanings, it is possible to act hospitably to the Other without being trapped by the paradox of power that characterizes Derrida's conception of cosmopolitanism: the self being held hostage by the face of the Other and the Other being held hostage by the self. It is through caring about stories and caring for the narrative voice of the Other that it becomes possible to act in a cosmopolitan manner that does not lead to a pernicious depoliticization of interactions with the Other and/or the development of any hierarchical anatomies of power between people. An Arendtian understanding of stories, as both worldly things and dramatic enactments, reveals the ways in which narratives can be said to accomplish two important tasks for the doing of politics: they first reveal some-*thing* around which political deliberation can occur, and, second, they disclose "who" the storyteller is in a non-coercive manner. The two subsequent subsections examine these two aspects of storytelling in order to illustrate how the welcoming of stories is crucial to theorizing a "worldly ethics."

C. Arendtian Storytelling and Derridean Cosmopolitanism

In terms of Derrida's understanding of cosmopolitan hospitality, it is necessary to shift the focus from the "face" of the Other to the world, if a "democracy to come" is to be realized more fully. Arendt's conception of enacted stories allows for hospitable action to occur without depoliticizing the act of welcoming the Other. Moreover, a narrative conception of the political highlights how the welcoming of the Other's story overcomes the dynamic of power that Derrida suggests is characteristic of the "face-to-face." Although this renewed focus on stories does not eliminate the issue of space, in the sense that hospitality requires the giving of a place in our home to the Other, it does, however, change the coercive relationship of power formed by the face-to-face interaction into a non-coercive and non-hierarchical relationship of plural persons, who—as civically equal friends—can act together in the world. In other words, a "thing"-oriented politics of public storytelling dissolves the Derridean framework of responsibility for the Other, which forms in face-to-face interactions: the insertion of a worldly "in-between" serving to bind people together in a non-hierarchical relationship, with a "worldly" space opening between those who appear to speak and act with one another. Through the enactment of a story and the co-narration of a currently unfolding narrative, a vertical power structure is transformed into a horizontal one. Recalling the Arendtian conception of power (as presented in chapter 2), storytelling transforms an asymmetrical relationship—whereby one party dominates or has "power over" another—into a non-dominative dynamic. As a result, people have the capacity to act together, that is, the "power to" do the work of politics with one another, on equal footing, as civic friends.

Emphasizing that storytelling is a non-hierarchical, noncoercive means of doing politics, Shari Stone-Mediatore suggests that "when we share stories, we speak not from "above" but from within a community of storytellers [and] we address our audience as fellow storytellers, people who have perspectives of their own to contribute to an ongoing narrative."[69] Although we cannot overlook the fact that a society's code of law and legal institutions are largely responsible for (not) bringing citizens to the bar of equality within delimited sociopolitical communities, action and co-storytelling—by reorienting the doing of politics around acts of speech—equalize the voice of political actors, making them both co-narrators and fellow members of an audience to an ongoing story. Furthermore, the non-hierarchical dynamic of power established by a worldly politics of storytelling is premised upon the notion that no single party possesses the sole claim to truth, since the truth of a worldly story is inherently contestable. In other words, the nature of co-storytelling with others creates a political dynamic in which stories make a claim about the world without putting an end to action. "When one tells a story *as a story*," as Stone-Mediatore observes, "that is, as a historically located person's attempt to render intelligible distant phenomena," we do not "replace" a single "explanation of the world with another."[70] While some might posit that storytelling is therefore mere subjectivism, Arendt's narrative account of the political generates a form of objectivity, whereby we assume a form of "situated impartiality"[71] in relation to worldly stories. Because stories are only a single account of something, a narrative politics recognizes that impartiality is generated not by some objective position removed from the world but, rather, by an object-oriented focus, and a storyteller's account is appraised from the positions of all those who are gathered together as co-narrators.[72]

Reconsidered in terms of worldly stories, cosmopolitan hospitality calls for a form of care aimed at worldly "things" shared between plural persons, which ultimately amounts to a welcoming of the Other's narrative voice and their individual understandings. This process of welcoming (re)establishes the web of human relationships by connecting people through the enactment of a story, thereby cultivating further political action and generating a horizontal anatomy of power ("power to") in a relationship formerly mired by issues associated with the "power over" dynamic. By focusing our attention on the worldly story held common between people, we begin to care for specific issues shared by individual narratives, as acts of speech make public that which is most familiar and unique to specific speakers. Here, caring for the worldly narratives "produced" in the doing of politics, with a plurality of people, is a means of caring for the Other through that which they themselves care about. This is the basic premise of a caring cosmopolitanism, a cosmopolitan theory dedicated to caring for the (unknown) Other through the welcoming of their narrative voice, which leads to the cultivation of a more nuanced, democratic world.

D. Revealing Who Someone Is through Storytelling

A caring cosmopolitanism is world-centric. By welcoming the narrative voice of the Other, we care for both the worldly story "produced," and for the worldly state engendered during the enactment of this yet to be completed narrative. While worldly stories are commonly held manifestations of a once private thought, feeling, concern, and so forth, narratives are ultimately about some-"thing" that the storyteller consequently wishes to discuss, debate, or change. Therefore, to welcome the Other's story is to acknowledge publicly and to begin caring for the very thing that the Other (does not) need, (does not) want, or (does not) believe in. Storytelling consequently discloses the concerns of the Other and cultivates political action around these "things"; additionally, it is a process that reveals "who" a storyteller is. By telling a story in public, we not only introduce an issue for debate or discussion, but also disclose who we are. A caring cosmopolitanism, by focusing on worldly stories and public action, welcomes the Other in a manner that allows them to reveal who they are without being coerced or even asked to do so.

As Derrida's deconstruction of cosmopolitan hospitality indicates, acts of welcoming the Other are reliant upon the process of taking from someone, even if only on a nominal level in order to ask what someone's name is. As he writes:

> You begin by asking [the foreigner his] name; you enjoin him to state and to guarantee his identity, as you would a witness before a court. This is someone to whom you put a question and address a demand, the first demand, the minimal demand being: "What is your name?"[73]

Though a seemingly harmless request, the act of asking someone's name can, under certain circumstances, establish a hierarchical relationship since such a demand has the potential to (re)affirm the "power over" dynamic. Derrida, I believe, has in mind situations where an empowered party acts upon another party, such as—for example—when a border agent asks an individual's name as a condition of their entrance into a given sociopolitical community. In such circumstances, welcoming the Other is rooted in an imbalance of power, which has been manifested when a powerful agent has taken something—if only a name—from a powerless party. To reconsider this Derridean notion in a different light, a caring cosmopolitanism allows people to reveal themselves on their own terms, free to tell their story as they wish since they are equal co-narrators within a space of distinct but equal people. In other words, as a result of the notion of civic equality theorized by Arendt, storytelling welcomes the Other on equal terms and in such a way that no person or institution assumes "power over" them in demanding to know who someone is, where they are from, what they do for a living, and so on—all of which being questions that can effectively further condition hospitable acts, as well as further subject the Other to the whims of a figure of authority. A caring cosmopolitanism, then, in allowing the Other to reveal themselves on their own terms, is a (re)humanizing form of caring for the Other and, more broadly, humanity itself.

Just as in the work of Derrida, the question of *who* someone is sits at the heart of Arendt's thinking about the political. The specifically human activity of speaking and acting in public with others revolves around the revelation of "who" someone is as a distinct (but equal) person. In *The Human Condition*, Arendt writes:

> Action and speech are so closely related because the primordial and specifically human act must at the same time contain the answer to the question asked of every newcomer: "Who are you?" This disclosure of who somebody is, is *implicit* in both his words and his deeds.[74]

There are clear similarities between Arendt and Derrida's body of thought, almost certainly an indication of Heidegger's strong influence on these two scholars, and yet, an Arendtian conception of action draws attention to its implicit revelatory character. Unlike Derrida, however, both the question "who are you?" and its answer are implied in action itself: a speaker reveals themselves through the very doing of acting and speaking. Examining Arendt's narrative theory of the political, in *Hannah Arendt: Life is a Narrative*, Julia Kristeva observes: "The art of narrative resides in the ability to condense action into an exemplary moment, to extract from the flow of time, and reveal a *who*."[75] For Arendt, it is in action that people "show who they are, reveal actively their unique personal identities and thus make their appearance in the human world."[76] Drawing once again upon the Greek tradition, Arendt contends that speaking/acting publicly is to reveal a person's personality, which, as she writes in *Men in Dark Times*, "most closely resembles the Greek *daimōn*," or "this personal element in man" which "can only appear where a public space exists."[77] By conceptualizing human personality in terms of this Greek "guardian spirit,"[78] Arendt illustrates that "who" we are can never be fully known to us. This is a point which throws Arendt's thought into sharp relief against a Heideggerian conceptualization of Being: whereby *Dasein* is revealed in the self-reflective mode of a person's "beingness-towards-death," when they can "run ahead" toward that which is distinctly their own: death. For Arendt, "who" a person is only becomes apparent to others when this individual acts/speaks before other people in the public, political realm, where the "identity of a person, though disclosing itself intangibly in act and speech," becomes "tangible only in the story of the actor's and speaker's life."[79] While writing about Arendt, Suzanne Jacobitti observes that the "actor loses control of the meaning and consequences of the action the instant the action occurs" and that a "story is the only way to tell who someone was [. . .] such a story is not written by actors but by others."[80] The "who-ness" of someone, their *daimōn*, is therefore, as Allen Speight suggests, "*something essential about an agent that may not be personally accessible to that agent but that is accessible to others*."[81] For Arendt, then, who someone is, like their *daimōn*, only appears in the presence of others through the act of public storytelling.[82]

A cornerstone for a caring cosmopolitanism and the welcoming of stories is the disclosure of the Other's "who-ness,"[83] which is revealed in the doing of public action by those who appear throughout the political process of conarration. According to Arendt, "This revelatory quality of speech and action comes to the fore where people are *with* others and neither for nor against them—that is, in sheer human togetherness."[84] A person's "who-ness" is disclosed in the context of the world, where no single, powerful party coerces us or an Other to reveal themselves in the process of storytelling. Rather, this form of political *praxis* is characterized by freedom, with political agents disclosing themselves freely to a collection of civically equal friends while sharing their own unique story. For Arendt, the moment that "human togetherness is lost, that is, when people are only for or against other people, as for instance in modern warfare," action devolves into a mere form of work, and a person's activity is "indeed no less a means to an end than making is a means to produce an object."[85] From this perspective, "sheer human togetherness" generates and maintains a "power to" act, while dominative dynamics of "power over" effectively depoliticize public interactions in a manner not unlike the self- and Other-centric forms of caring that Myers criticizes. It is, therefore, necessary to welcome and care for stories because public storytelling engenders worldly states of political togetherness, which ultimately allow people to disclose "who" they are. A thing-oriented politics that cares about—and cares for—the process of storytelling can consequently be understood as empowering, in the sense of maintaining the capacity for a collection of people to act and speak together, and humanizing or rehumanizing.

A caring cosmopolitanism, then, is an ethico-political theory premised upon the understanding that welcoming the Other's story encourages human togetherness by (re)engendering worldly relationships through narratives, "things" which are "produced" freely and which are shared between a plurality of persons on equal terms. Accordingly, this strand of cosmopolitanism is crafted from Derrida's conception of cosmopolitan hospitality, but its theoretical core is Arendtian, as Arendt's narrative approach to political theory and her notion of "care for the world" inform directly what it means to care about the Other via their actions. Returning, once again, to Phelps-Roper's narrative, the final section of this chapter considers how her experience of being welcomed by her friends on Twitter offers an example of a caring cosmopolitanism at work in the world.

2. MEGAN PHELPS-ROPER AND A CARING COSMOPOLITANISM

From 2009 onward, Phelps-Roper began using Twitter and became an active user of this online platform, which is often referred to in colloquial terms as the "Twitterverse," "Twitosphere," or "Twittersphere." This foray into a digital "worldly" space can be understood as an act that instigated her transition from a Schmittian "us" versus "them" worldview, to a more Arendtian understanding of the political. It was this perspectival transformation that was a catalyst for her disassociation from the WBC. In the following excerpt from her 2017 TED Talk, Phelps-Roper elaborates upon the ideological shift that occurred as a result of her decision to insert herself into the Twitterverse, which represents what Arendt might describe as a "second birth" into the public world beyond the private confines of her church/family and where she experienced a worldly form of "friendship" for the first time:

> In 2009, [my zeal for the WBC's agenda] brought me to Twitter. Initially, the people I encountered on the platform were just as hostile as I expected. They were the digital version of the screaming hordes I'd been seeing at protests since I was a kid. But in the midst of that digital brawl a strange pattern developed. Someone would arrive at my profile with the usual rage and scorn, I would respond with a custom mix of Bible verses, pop culture references, and smiley faces. They would be understandably confused and caught off guard, but then a conversation would ensue. [. . .] There was no confusion about our positions, but the line between friend and foe was becoming blurred. We'd started to see each other as human beings, and it changed the way we spoke to one another.[86]

Here, Phelps-Roper indicates how her "worldly" interactions on Twitter eroded the Schmittian mindset "drummed" into her by the WBC because the exchanges that occurred there evolved from mere forms of verbal antagonism—whereby users only appeared to "lob rhetorical grenades at the other camp"—to a "worldly" dialogue that she describes in positive terms as a confabulation between herself and her "friends on Twitter."[87] This evolution caused a blurring of the "line between friend and foe" that corresponds to the Arendtian conception of humanization associated with speaking in the public realm of appearance, where differing parties at the worldly "table" (to borrow Arendt's metaphor for the "world") each fully assume their status as *human* beings through acts of speech (*lexis*) shared publicly before a plurality of other people. In other words, speaking and acting in public, which Arendt suggests is the most human of human activities, fundamentally altered the nature of this virtual space, as this online realm became—as Phelps-Roper states—"civil" and "full of genuine curiosity," where apparent "enemies [. . .] became my beloved friends."[88] The Twittersphere became, for Phelps-Roper, the public space of civic friendship where she could enter into the world as a human being capable of experiencing the "joy of inhabiting [a world] together with others."[89] For Phelps-Roper, the seemingly banal, or ordinary, act of using Twitter not only helped her to see "the bigger picture, that we're all just human beings," but it also allowed her to experience the pleasure as well as "the power of engaging with the other."[90]

While it could be argued that this worldly engagement with the Other is predominately a matter of mutual recognition between various interlocutors on Twitter, with the reciprocally recognized humanness of each party providing—as Smith suggests—"the political with a starting point which represents a kind of foundation,"[91] I would like to highlight here how the dynamic of which Phelps-Roper speaks also further exemplifies my cosmopolitan theory of hospitality: the welcoming of the narrative voice of the (unknown) Other into a worldly space where a plurality of co-narrators create a meaningful story together. Though Twitter is an internet-based, social media phenomenon that challenges traditional conceptions of public, political action, this technology allowed Phelps-Roper to recognize her shared humanity with her Twitter acquaintances, illustrating—for theorists of "the political"—how her worldly interactions can be interpreted as hospitable acts of welcoming the narrative voice of the (unknown) Other. Describing her interlocutions on Twitter, she gestures toward how a caring cosmopolitanism is arguably at play in her interactions online, when, in her TED Talk, she presents the "four things" her Twitter friends did to make "real conversation possible."[92] Although I am most interested here in her first and second points, Phelps-Roper explains that "real conversation" was fostered by her friends" dedication to (1) not assuming that a speaker has bad intentions, (2) asking questions, (3) staying calm, and (4) making arguments.[93] The first two steps are significant since they correspond to a sovereign-less form of power as theorized by Arendt, the "power to" conceptualization of power and the giving of space in the world to the (unknown) Other so that their argument/story can be heard.

Her initial points about "assum[ing] good or neutral intent" and "asking questions" correspond to a caring cosmopolitanism because they are part of the process of creating a "framework for dialogue"[94] in which the distinctive story of the Other is welcomed on equal terms: an important part of facilitating the emergence of power within this virtual space. Her first point about assuming good/neutral intent corresponds specifically to the notion of equality, ensuring that the worldly space of the public realm—where people speak and act together—is nonhierarchical and free from the coerciveness of the "power over" logic. Accordingly, and recalling an Arendtian understanding of political action, equality is considered to be the counterpart to her conception of distinction; when considered together, equality and distinction are the two defining characteristics of human plurality: the *conditio per quam* of all political life.[95] Assuming good/neutral intent refers to treating each distinct speaker and their argument/story from a common conceptual foundation, upon which no party is given a privileged position. Rather, Phelps-Roper acknowledges that all people ought to be given an equal platform from which to distinguish themselves through acts of speech. In other words, her simple point underscores the importance of fostering a foundation of equality within the world of Twitter, which is an invaluable aspect of acting hospitably to the distinctive narrative voice of the Other, and sharing in the co-narrative activity of public action that can occur in public spaces of appearance.

Relatedly, Phelps-Roper's second point about asking questions also alters fundamentally the worldly "dynamic of [her] conversations" since her friends' proactive asking of "questions gave [her] room to speak," which in turn also "gave" her "permission to ask them questions and truly hear their responses."[96] Another pivotal aspect of welcoming the narrative voice of the (unknown) Other, asking questions is a matter of giving space in the world to the narrative contributions of a plurality of diverse perspectives, which further engenders a horizontal form of power during the discursive practice of public speaking and acting among a collection of distinct but equal *human* beings. In conjunction with the conceptualization of equality cultivated when political actors assume good/neutral intentions, then, asking questions helps foster a hospitable "framework" within worldly spaces, whether they be online or in person. This seemingly banal practice creates dialogue between people in a non-dominative manner, transforming the space into one of civic friendship and human action. Such a dynamic is central to the practice of public co-storytelling theorized in this chapter. Asking questions and assuming good/neutral intent allowed Phelps-Roper's "friends on Twitter" to "approach her as a human being"[97] during the public activity of speaking and acting in the world, which—from an Arendtian perspective—is understood as the most human of human activities. Phelps-Roper's civic friends' approach allowed her narrative voice to be welcomed on equal terms and in such a manner that she was capable of becoming a co-narrator in a broader public story. They put into practice a caring cosmopolitanism, and Phelps-Roper was welcomed into a public world beyond the private confines of the WBC.

Though my focus throughout this chapter has been on my more thoroughly discursive form of hospitality, it is interesting to note that it was Phelps-Roper's "beloved" Twitter friends who ultimately cared for her and her sister's private needs when they first left their church and family in Topeka. To think more broadly about the topic of (cosmopolitan) hospitality, it is particularly remarkable to note that Phelps-Roper and her sister were welcomed into communities that the WBC had previously picketed. Speaking of her experience of being welcomed by those whom she had once vitriolically rebuked, Phelps-Roper explains, "My friend from Twitter invited us to spend time among a Jewish community in Los Angeles," where "we slept on the couches in the home of a Hasidic rabbi [. . .] the same rabbi that I'd protested three years earlier with a sign that said, 'Your Rabbi is a Whore.'"[98] This friend from Twitter was David Abitbol (Twitter handle: @Jewlicious), who once "joked" with Phelps-Roper about this "dramatic role reversal": "Your Rabbi is a Whore? Your rabbi is a *host*."[99] Once again, the lines between different forms of hospitality blur, with a more discursive form of hospitable action and forgiveness giving rise to a type of welcome that saw Phelps-Roper and her sister become guests in the home of a family they had once antagonized.

While Phelps-Roper and her sister were not "orphans" per se, they were—when excommunicated from their former church—shunned by their family, which is to say, excluded from the home in which they had lived the entirety of their lives. A rupture not only in familial relations, this act of exclusion also marked what is arguably the culminating point in her story of transitioning away from the WBC. This is the point in time when her very sense of self was fully called into question. Having given up her place in the WBC, she could no longer identify herself as a "Jacob," and she ceased being one of the "good guys" fighting "against the bad" in the "quarrel of the covenant."[100] Having relinquished her status as a "cherished daughter" who had built her "life and identity around the church," and who was "well-beloved,"[101] Phelps-Roper became an "Esau," or an outsider, left wondering:

> Who was I on the outside? I was the perpetrator of untold amounts of harm in the world. I was a lover of tragedy, cruelly attacking the grieving at their most vulnerable. [. . .] What reason did anyone have to give me a second chance?[102]

Though suggestive of how Phelps-Roper was beginning to think and act from a position of "doubt" and "epistemological humility,"[103] these questions cannot—in the first instance—be answered, least of all by Phelps-Roper herself. Because, as Arendt suggests, the "who-ness" of a person—or "who" this individual is as a distinctive human being—is knowable only to those with whom someone shares the "world," such questions of identity, or of changing someone's perceived identity in the eyes of the world, demands a renewal of this individual's place in the storied realm of "the political." Renewing a person's relationship with the "world" is where we can see a caring cosmopolitanism at play: the narrative voice of the (unknown) Other being welcomed into the "world," (re)connecting this person to the "web of human relationships" in such a way that a new "worldly" thing can be created with them. In the case of Phelps-Roper, it was because her narrative voice was welcomed into the public realm that she had a "second chance" to disclose her identity to the "world," which is to say, she was able to show herself to be more than a "lover of tragedy"—an individual who "cruelly" attacked "the grieving at their most vulnerable"—as a consequence of a discursive act of hospitality opening a "worldly" space for her story to be (re)told and her "who-ness" to be revealed.

Though it may perhaps be too soon to discern "who" Phelps-Roper is, her very presence in the "world"—and how she came to find refuge in this "common home"—is a testament to those who acted hospitably toward her: the people who welcomed her as a co-storyteller in the public realm of "political" and, in some instances, who offered her a space in their private places of residence. In particular, the cosmopolitan care shown to Phelps-Roper—the acts of hospitality that gave place to her narrative voice—disclose the character and "who-ness" of those persons who welcomed her (such as the rabbi she called a "whore" and her friend @Jewlicious). In spite of the fact that these people will very likely remain faceless (to us), they showed—through their actions—an important aspect of "who" they are: individuals capable of acting in the mode of civic friendship, and of fostering "worldly" relationships between people who hold the most divergent of views. This is a caring cosmopolitanism in action: an act of discursive "dilatation," of opening more fully the public realm of the political, so that the "world" can become, remain, and/or be refurbished as a "home" common to all of humanity.

"Among many others, *it* happened," Phelps-Roper writes, "with a friendly college student in Canada, a sassy start-up employee in Chicago, a hilarious Australian guy who tweeted political jokes, even an American soldier to whom I had sent a care package in Afghanistan."[104] The manifestation of cosmopolitan hospitality, this "it" is the creation of a "world" shared between people; this is an "in-between" created within the digital *milieu* of Twitter, a social media platform which has—for better and for worse—created new ways for people to connect with one another, to speak to each other, and to act politically together. With access to the internet, people are no longer able to speak and act only with those they encounter physically in their local public realms, but also with persons from around the globe. Conceptualized in terms of Arendt's notion of "world," which refers to the "web of human relationships," the internet is by definition a *world*wide web of human relations, through which people from all over the planet can interact publicly with others to speak and act together. While the strength/weakness of the relational connections made between people who connect in this virtual space is contestable,[105] it is undeniable that the worldwide web links people in a manner hitherto unknown in history, since this global network provides humanity with an unprecedented ability to speak and act with (infinite) others from across the world in real-time. If Arendt is correct to suggest that "the *polis*, properly speaking, is not the city-state in its physical location [but rather] the organization of the people as it arises out of acting and speaking together,"[106] then the internet, it may be argued, has made possible the development of global public realms where action can occur unencumbered by the conditions imposed upon humanity by time and space. Twitter exists within this unbounded virtual space; moreover, it is a microcosm of this public realm, since it allows people from around the globe to speak and act together within a quasi-universal space of appearance.

Within such digital spaces, there is a need for certain types of rules and regulations, just like those which govern life in cities. This is indisputable, most especially given the ways in which Twitter, and other social media platforms have been leveraged in recent times for good and evil. But, as Trevor Smith maintains, "the Internet is no longer new or strange, but is now simply a normal part of our lives."[107] With this in mind, though it is not within our scope here to address wider questions of internet governance, security, and digital ethics, I acknowledge instead that online space is "malleable" and that politics can be reinvigorated within the digital realm because the internet "can provide possibilities for beginning something new."[108] Further, and perhaps most importantly, it can help to "facilitate various aspects of politics in a way that is simply not possible offline."[109] This is evident in Phelps-Roper's case. But beyond the ways in which the internet offers new possibilities, and new sites for potential political action, we must not be so caught up in the novelty of our evolving technologies so as to forget to consider the implications of more basic practices and forms of human interaction, especially when they are transposed to the digital realm. Where Michael Ignatieff writes about the need to think and act in terms of "ordinary virtues,"[110] I believe we should reconsider the seemingly basic, or "ordinary," forms of public, political care that allow us to maintain and enhance the web of relations that connect us, whether this "fabric," or worldly "thing," is created in the phenomenological realm, online, or both. It is in terms of these more fundamental practices of care, such as the act of giving place to the narrative voices of the (unknown) Other, that we "care for the world." Such acts give rise to a "world" that is more democratic, hospitable, and capable of holding a true plurality of storytellers; a place where the "stranger," "widow," "orphan," rabbi, and former member of the WBC can act freely with one another, as co-narrators of the "storybook of mankind," thereby contributing to a narrative—that is, to borrow the words of Barthes, "international, transhistorical, transcultural: it is simply there, like life itself."

NOTES

1. Phelps-Roper, *Unfollow*, 276.
2. Ibid., 277.
3. Ibid., 162. Original emphasis.
4. Ibid.
5. Ibid., 145.
6. Ibid., 146.
7. Ibid., 167.
8. Ibid., 115.
9. Ibid.
10. Ibid., 19.
11. Arendt, *The Human Condition*, 243.
12. Patrick Hayden, "From Political Friendship to Befriending the World," *The European Legacy* 20, no. 7 (2015): 745.
13. Smith, *Friendship and the Political*, 226.
14. Phelps-Roper, *Unfollow*, 31.
15. Although the notion of a "thing" invokes the rich philosophic debate surrounding the concepts of both "thing" and "object," I understand the former term in terms of the latter, whereby an object is that which can be placed before or presented to the eyes and/or other senses. That is, a thing is an object, and an object is understood in relation to its etymological root, *obiectum* (Latin): something presented to the senses. Refraining from a foray into "Thing Theory," I present here an Arendtian-inspired interpretation of an object-oriented theory of political action.
16. Arendt, *The Human Condition*, 184.
17. Allen Speight, "Arendt on Narrative Theory and Practice," *College Literature* 38, no. 1 (2011): 116.
18. Seyla Benhabib, "Hannah Arendt and the Redemptive Power of Narrative," *Social Research* 57, no. 1 (1990): 170.
19. Hannah Arendt, "Action and the 'Pursuit of Happiness': A Lecture," in *Annual Meeting of the American Political Science Association* (New York, 1960), 11.
20. Hannah Arendt and Karl Jaspers, *Hannah Arendt Karl Jaspers Correspondence: 1926-1969*, ed. Lotte Kohler and Hans Saner, trans. Robert and Rita Kimber (London: Harvest Book, 1985), 23.
21. While Arendt described herself to Jaspers in terms of these two professions, Benhabib asserts that her work is "too systematically ambitious and over-interpreted to be strictly a historical account [. . .] and although it has the vivacity and the stylistic flair of a work of political journalism, it is too philosophical to be accessible to a broad public." [Benhabib, "Hannah Arendt and the Redemptive Power of Narrative,"

173.] Highlighting further the difficulty of classifying Arendt's work, Peter Baehr goes so far as to suggest that Arendt was not an academic in the traditional sense but, rather, a "political writer [. . .] for whom the university was a secondary and erratic site of convenience." [Peter Baehr, *Hannah Arendt, Totalitarianism, and the Social Sciences* (Stanford: Stanford University Press, 2010), 36.] In short, Arendt's approach, style, and focus defy scholastic categorization, so much so that some commentators have placed her work outside the academy entirely.

22. Arendt warns against scholarship that deals solely in the abstract. To deal solely in the abstract is akin to "not thinking through experience," and doing so in manner that "we lose the ground of experience. [Hannah Arendt, "On Hannah Arendt," in *Hannah Arendt: The Recovery of the Public World*, ed. Melvyn Hill (New York: St. Martin's Press, 1979), 308.]

23. Maša Mrovlje, "Narrating and Understanding," in *Hannah Arendt: Key Concepts*, ed. Patrick Hayden (Durham, UK: Acumen Publishing, 2014), 67. Benhabib has a similar term for Arendt's existential tendencies: Arendt's "phenomenological essentialism." [Seyla Benhabib, *The Reluctant Modernism of Hannah Arendt* (London: Sage Publications, 1996), 123.]

24. Arendt, "Social Science Techniques and the Study of Concentration Camps," 232; Hannah Arendt, "Mankind and Terror," in *Essays in Understanding, 1930-1954: Formation, Exile, and Totalitarianism*, ed. Jerome Kohn (New York: Schocken Books, 1994), 302.

25. *Oxford English Dictionary*, s.v. "voice."

26. Roland Barthes, *Image-Music-Text*, trans. Stephen Heath (New York: Fontana Press, 1977), 79.

27. Michel Foucault, *The Care of the Self* (New York: Pantheon Books, 1986).

28. Myers, *Worldly Ethics*, 11.

29. Foucault, *The Care of the Self*, 118.

30. Levinas, *Totality and Infinity*, 215.

31. Myers, *Worldly Ethics*, 70. Myers argues this point with the help of Jacques Rancière, who writes: "Derrida places liberal democracy as a form of government, on one side, and the infinite openness to the newcomer and wait for the event that evades all expectation, on the other. In my view something gets lost in this opposition between an *institution* and a *transcendental horizon*. What disappears is democracy as a practice." [Jacques Rancière, *Dissensus: On Politics and Aesthetics*, trans. Steven Cocroran (London: Continuum, 2010), 59. Original emphasis.]

32. Derrida, *Acts of Religion*, 56.

33. Ibid., 213.

34. Arendt, *The Human Condition*, 182.

35. Ibid.

36. Ibid.

37. Derrida gestures toward the link between love and hospitality when he writes: "Does [hospitality] begin with the question addressed to the newcomer (which seems very human and sometimes loving, assuming that hospitality should be linked to love—an enigma that we will leave in reserve for the moment): what is your name?" [Derrida, *Of Hospitality*, 27.]

38. Arendt, "'What Remains? The Language Remains,'" 17.

39. For Arendt, "private" is a distinct spatial category, while "personal" refers to relationships between specific persons. One can have personal relationships in both the public realm of politics and the private realm of the household.

40. Here, it is useful to recall the poet Rūmī's words: "Reason says, 'I will beguile [one] with the tongue'; Love says, 'Be silent. I will beguile [one] with the soul.'" [Jalāl ad-Dīn Muhammad Rūmī, *Mystical Poems of Rūmī: Second Selection, Poems 201-400*, trans. A.J. Arberry (London: The University of Chicago Press, 1979), 2.]

41. Derrida, *On Cosmopolitanism and Forgiveness*, 16–17.

42. Steve Buckler, *Hannah Arendt and Political Theory: Challenging the Tradition* (Edinburgh: Edinburgh University Press, 2011), 162.

43. Derrida, *Negotiations*, 375.

44. Arendt, *The Human Condition*, 52.

45. Ibid., 9. Original punctuation.

46. Ibid., 88.

47. Ibid., 52.

48. Ibid., 183.

49. Ibid., 94–95.

50. Ibid., 97. Emphasis added.

51. Ibid., 184.

52. Aristotle's work strongly influences Arendt here, as his conception of tragedy directly informs her understanding of narrative, and her belief that action—like human life (*bíoς*)—can be narrated. For Arendt, a truly human life is a life capable of being narrated.

53. Ibid., 187.

54. Arendt, *Between Past and Future*, 44.

55. Ibid., 44. Emphasis added to the word "something."

56. Arendt, *The Human Condition*, 181–88.

57. It is worth noting how action, unlike work, proceeds to an "end" and not a "goal." Whereas work is teleological, action is nonviolent, non-teleological, and nonutilitarian.

58. Ibid., 183. Original emphasis.

59. Ibid., 176.

60. Heidegger, *Being and Time*, 171. Original emphasis.

61. Arendt, *The Human Condition*, 26.

62. Ibid., 27. See also Hannah Arendt, "Concern with Politics in Recent European Philosophical Thought," in *Essays in Understanding, 1930-1954: Formation, Exile, and Totalitarianism*, ed. Jerome Kohn (New York: Schocken Books, 1994), 442–43.

63. As Arendt writes: "*Logos* is speech in which words are put together to form a sentence that is totally meaningful by virtue of synthesis (*synthēkē*)." [Hannah Arendt, *The Life of Mind* (London: Harvest Book, 1978), pt. I, pgs. 98–99.]

64. Ibid., 49.

65. Hannah Arendt, "Understanding and Politics," in *Essays in Understanding, 1930-1954: Formation, Exile, and Totalitarianism*, ed. Jerome Kohn (New York: Schocken Books, 1994), 308.

66. Ibid.

67. Ibid., 309.

68. Hannah Arendt, *The Jewish Writings*, ed. Jerome Kohn and Ron H. Feldman (New York: Schocken Books, 2007), 264.

69. Shari Stone-Mediatore, *Reading Across Borders: Storytelling and Knowledges of Resistance* (New York: Palgrave Macmillan, 2003), 64.

70. Ibid., 62.

71. Lisa J. Disch, "More Truth Than Fact: Storytelling as Critical Understanding in the Writings of Hannah Arendt," *Political Theory* 21, no. 4 (1993): 665–94.

72. While this chapter has refrained from a discussion of Arendt's conception of judgment, she emphasizes the role of judging in her considerations of the both thinking and action. Her understanding of this cognitive activity, one tied closely to understanding, reinvigorates a form of impartiality from an ancient conception of objectivity, whereby one critically considers an idea or phenomena from a plurality of perspectives while remaining securely situated in one's own position in the world. That is, judgment, for Arendt, is a cognitive activity during which one thinks "with an enlarged mentality" and uses "one's imagination to go visiting"; in this way, one enlarges one's thinking and adopts the impartial, disinterested "position of Kant's world citizen." [Hannah Arendt, *Lectures on Kant's Political Philosophy*, ed. Ronald Beiner (Chicago: University of Chicago Press, 1992), 42–43.]

73. Derrida, *Of Hospitality*, 27.

74. Arendt, *The Human Condition*, 178. Emphasis added.

75. Julia Kristeva, *Hannah Arendt: Life Is a Narrative* (London: University of Toronto Press, 2001), 17.

76. Arendt, *The Human Condition*, 179.

77. Arendt, *Men in Dark Times*, 73.

78. Ibid., 73.

79. Arendt, *The Human Condition*, 192–93.

80. Suzanne D. Jacobitti, "Thinking about the Self," in *Hannah Arendt: Twenty Years Later*, ed. Larry May and Jerome Kohn (Cambridge, MA: The MIT Press, 1997), 213–14.

81. Speight, "Arendt on Narrative Theory and Practice," 123–24. Original emphasis.

82. Though the purpose of this chapter is not to theorize an Arendtian conceptualization of the "self," it is worth noting that an Arendtian conceptualization of the self is a nuanced one. According to Jacobitti, an Arendtian understanding of the self cannot be understood in simple, clear-cut terms, such as—for example—within the conceptual frame formed by either/or dichotomies that imply the self is *either* a fragmented being *or* a unitary, changeless entity that persists through time and space. An Arendtian notion of the self implies that an individual's unique identity corresponds, at once, to their unique experience of the dark, labyrinth-like space of the *vita contemplativa*, within which people think, feel, and navigate the vast maze of the mind in the singular mode of "I," and the varied non-private spaces of human existence where people are capable of appearing and acting publicly with other human beings.

83. Anna Yeatman, "Individuality and Politics: Thinking with and beyond Hannah Arendt," in *Action and Appearance: Ethics and the Politics of Writing in Hannah Arendt*, ed. Anna Yeatman et al. (London: Continuum, 2011), 69–86.
84. Arendt, *The Human Condition*, 180.
85. Ibid.
86. Phelps-Roper, "I Grew up in the Westboro Baptist Church. Here's Why I Left."
87. Ibid.
88. Ibid.
89. Arendt, *The Human Condition*, 244.
90. Phelps-Roper, "I Grew up in the Westboro Baptist Church. Here's Why I Left."
91. Smith, *Friendship and the Political*, 227.
92. Sam Harris, *Leaving the Church: A Conversation with Megan Phelps-Roper*.
93. Ibid.
94. Phelps-Roper, "I Grew up in the Westboro Baptist Church. Here's Why I Left."
95. Arendt, *The Human Condition*, 7.
96. Phelps-Roper, "I Grew up in the Westboro Baptist Church. Here's Why I Left."
97. Ibid.
98. Adrian Chen, "Unfollow: How a Prized Daughter of the Westboro Baptist Church Came to Question Its Beliefs," *The New Yorker*, November 16, 2015, https://www.newyorker.com/magazine/2015/11/23/conversion-via-twitter-westboro-baptist-church-megan-phelps-roper.
99. Ibid. Original emphasis.
100. Phelps-Roper, *Unfollow*, 8.
101. Ibid., 166.
102. Ibid.
103. Ibid., 273–77.
104. Ibid., 102. Emphasis added.
105. Sociologist Mark Granovetter is well known for his 1973 discussion of the "strength of weak ties" in social networks. If one were to employ Granovetter's understanding here, relationships and networks founded on the internet are very likely to be described as "weak," as his framework suggests that "the strength of a tie is a [. . .] combination of the amount of time, the emotional intensity, the intimacy (mutual confiding), and the reciprocal services which characterize the tie." [Mark S. Granovetter, "The Strength of Weak Ties," *American Journal of Sociology* 78, no. 6 (1973): 1361.] Because such factors are difficult to cultivate online with people who are not physically present, internet-based connections are unlikely to be as "strong" as others forms of in-person networking.
106. Arendt, *The Human Condition*, 198.
107. Trevor G. Smith, *Politicizing Digital Space: Theory, the Internet and Renewing Democracy* (London: University of Westminster Press, 2017), 3.
108. Ibid.
109. Ibid.
110. Michael Ignatieff, *The Ordinary Virtues: Moral Order in a Divided World* (Cambridge, MA: Harvard University Press, 2017).

Chapter 4

Caring in Time

Negotiating the Gap "between Past and Future"

Theorizing a type of Janus-faced form of being in time, negotiating within the moment of "now" requires political actors to a maintain a forward-looking, backward-focused gaze, that is, to think imaginatively beyond the limits of their place in both time and space. By examining the temporal character of Arendt's understanding of the "gap" between past and future, doing so in conjunction with Derrida's insights into (non-)presence, it is my hope to show more fully how a caring forgiveness and caring cosmopolitanism can be said to care for the worldly experience of freedom. But what pitfalls are there along the way? What traps must we avoid? What aspects, in particular, of the human experience of being in time might inhibit freedom and the formation of power associated with acting politically in the "world"?

Every fox must pay his skin to the furrier, goes the Italian proverb.[1] In other words, the crafty—or the cunning—eventually get their comeuppance, falling victim to their own wiliness. In Arendt's view, Martin Heidegger was a "fox," one who "not only kept getting caught in traps but [who] couldn't even tell the difference between a trap and a non-trap."[2] This description is to be found in a July 1953 entry to her *Denktagebuch*, or "thought journal," where she uses a short allegory to draw attention to the political follies and moral failings of her former mentor, whose affiliations with National Socialism permanently sullied his reputation.[3]

"Why," asks Derrida, "in the great corpus of animal figures that people the fable of the political, do we find this or that animal and not others?"[4] According to Derrida, the fox is often of particular interest "precisely because he knows how to be cunning [. . .], because he has the sense and culture of the snare, the fox is closer to the truth of man and man's fidelity, which he understands and knows how to invert."[5] Although Derrida is not referring to Heidegger in this instance, these words have resonance when read alongside

Arendt's "true story" of "Heidegger the Fox,"[6] a figure who, in her view, believed that all the philosophers who came before him—"foxes" from Plato onward—had, in fact, overlooked one of the most fundamental metaphysical questions: What is the meaning of Being as such? Insofar as his philosophy offers a response to this query, by providing a definitive and fundamental ontology of human existence, it is possible to say that Heidegger had, in Derrida's words, "the sense and culture of the snare" and that he was "closer to the truth of man." However, as portrayed in Arendt's account of our "fox," Heidegger became trapped by the very the understanding of authentic temporality and historicity that had come to characterize his philosophy.

A "fox trap" is the metaphor Arendt uses to conceptualize the history of ontology and to critique Heidegger's decision to build a "trap as his burrow," which was an "idea completely new and unheard of among foxes."[7] Unable— as Leland de la Durantaye writes—"to discern logical inconsistencies and metaphysical mystifications,"[8] Heidegger was trapped in what Arendt describes as the most unlikely of "fox traps," one which he had not-so-cunningly built for himself as his place of dwelling. Because the features of Heidegger's "burrow"—his ideas about the conditions of being and time that comprise his philosophy—were "cut, literally, to his own measurements," Arendt claims that he could not step out of the trap that he himself had built: his ontology conditioning his understanding of what it means to be in the world.[9] Rooted in the notion that the meaning of Being is determined temporally, specifically through the self-reflective practice of projecting one's self toward death (which consequently allows one to view one's life as a totality), Heidegger's philosophy was a "burrow" that came to constrain entirely his life as a "fox" and to limit his ability to evade the traps set by people, notably—for him—the trap contained within the totalitarian ideology of Nazism. Politically incapacitated by his refusal to think in terms of, and for the sake of, the "world," and lured by Nazism's fatalistic account of history and its vision of the German people's spiritual destiny, Heidegger became caught in one of humanity's worst traps. His strength—his cunningness—in being able to elude philosophic traps ultimately costing him his philosophic skin, his work being incessantly and justifiably flayed: his payment to the furrier. I have turned to Arendt's "fox" precisely because this allegory offers a means to "people the fable of the political," that is, to anthropomorphize a notoriously cunning creature as a means of beginning to think about the political and what it means to maintain, repair, and preserve the web of relationships that constitute the "world."

Derrida, in his own way, can also be said to have recognized Heidegger to be "trapped" by the conceptual constraints imposed by his philosophy. Where Arendt is largely concerned with the anti-political character of Heidegger's notion of "being-towards-death," which forms a central part of his distinctive attempts to access the true meaning of Being, Derrida effectively maintains that our "fox"—despite his extensive efforts to develop a supraordinate account of Being in terms of a "fundamental" temporality—does not go far enough in his efforts to decenter the present as the locus of human existence. Our "fox," that is, was trapped within the very tradition of metaphysical thought that he wished to destroy, in the sense that his project of *Destruktion* sought to deconstruct ontological concepts as a means of "shaking off the ontological tradition [. . .] [and] staking out the positive possibilities of that tradition."[10] Derrida calls into question Heidegger's project. Finding in it the sign of its "belonging to metaphysics, or what he calls onto-theology,"[11] Derrida works to go beyond the philosophy of our "fox," specifically Heidegger's criticism of Aristotle's "vulgar" conceptualization of temporality: as "counted time," or time as that which can be clocked as the moment of the "now" moves from earlier to later.[12] In Derrida's particular "ruthless criticism of everything existing," whereby this "everything existing" is understood in terms of the "text" and the (n)ever-present play of *différance* that shapes our world's textuality, Derrida critiques the metaphysics of presence without being caught within the metaphysical *clôture* that ensnared Heidegger.[13] Derrida sought to deconstruct the "text" without attempting to locate the ontological grounds of a truly fundamental ontology, and without seeking a "position of fundamentality or primordiality."[14] This effectively means that Derrida destabilizes the present as the ontological moment of presence but "replaces the 'vulgar concept' of time with nothing."[15] Because—for him—*différance* refers to the confluent movements of "traces" upon a "bottomless chessboard where being is set in play,"[16] time can be said to move "only as a play of *différance*"[17] and the "closure of presence [. . .] is effected in the functioning of traces."[18] Derrida does not understand the "now" as a moment of pure presence or in terms of a measurable sequence of contiguous, clock-able points in time, which is the series of successive "is" moments that Heidegger suggests corresponds with the traditional metaphysical temporalization of time.[19] Instead, for Derrida, the "now" is contaminated by the presence of that which is not currently present: the trace of what has been inherited from the past *and* what has yet to come.

Derrida's notion of time is one that cannot be measured or deconstructed into any undergirding binary logics, such as the "is" and "is not" which structures Aristotle's aporetic understanding of time. In this sense, as Richard Beardsworth writes with regards to the temporality of Derrida's "text," "time is absolutely irreducible [. . .] both 'undeconstructable' and the source of all deconstructions."[20] Constituting a temporality shaped by a movement of "traces," according to which being present is to be presently subjected to the "play" of non-present forces that flow into and through the "now," *différance* is Derrida's means of understanding the all-encompassing temporal conditions of humankind's existence. This is an existence that takes place upon a foundationless plane that lacks a singular, shared gridwork capable of bringing order to each and every chess player's movements. Thus, for him, to think about being is to reconsider what it means to be, move, and act within time, as well as to acknowledge the inability for people to root their decisions, judgments, and/or actions in some singular, universally shared, and truly fundamental understanding of the world, language, and/or system of ideas.

Given the ways in which Arendt's body of thought—like that of Derrida—emerges from the phenomenological tradition of Continental philosophy that flows directly through the work of Heidegger the "fox," to think about his philosophy as a "trap" is to introduce questions about being and time that need be addressed when attempting to understand the power of a caring cosmopolitanism and caring forgiveness. In particular, having theorized "care" in reference to Arendt's tripartite conception of the *vita activa*, we might wonder how to go about understanding the temporalities that structure the affairs of the private and public realms. Does time move similarly in both spaces? In theorizing forgiveness and cosmopolitanism as forms of public care, how should people go about acting politically from within their place in the (n)ever-present moment of the "now," forgiving and welcoming the narrative voice of the (unknown) Other from within this ever-fleeting moment of (non-)presence? A study of political time and the temporality of "caring for the world," then, this chapter explores the "now" of politics, doing so in order to develop more fully my theory of what it means to act caringly for the sake of freedom, power, and the web of human relationships that bind the public realm together. Because cosmopolitanism and forgiveness are forms of public care that instigate new courses of political action from within the non-present, present moment of the "now," it is important to reconsider the experience of being in time and thinking anew about how people negotiate the tensions beset by their factical, temporally-paradoxical existence in the "text."

In the first section of this chapter, I explore, from an Arendtian perspective, how the idea of care relates to time by focusing upon the temporality of caring as both a private and public act.[21] That is, I consider Arendt's thinking about time via her distinction between the spatiality of the public and private realms, returning to her understanding of the private-public divide, precisely because her dichotomous conceptualization of space complements her understanding of time as a cyclical and a rectilinear construct. Though—for Derrida—time moves neither in a strictly cyclical manner nor in a linear manner, as is indicated by his notion of *différance*, I have chosen to bring together Arendt and Derrida's respective approaches to the study of human temporality because the former establishes the "now" as the temporal location of political freedom, while the latter highlights the complexities of negotiating the "play" of non-present forces that permeate this moment of presence.

While Derrida might take issue with an approach that arguably re-establishes the Aristotelian metaphysics of presence,[22] when thinking about the political in Arendtian terms, there is a need to understand the "now" as the ever-fleeting "gap" in time where people exist as temporally-conditioned beings: to consider temporality rectilinearly and as an ever-flowing narrative, the "storybook of mankind." Because this is a story *in medias res*, one which is currently being enacted in the (n)ever fully present moment of the "now," as political actors make their way across a "bottomless chessboard where being is set in play," I contend that it is in terms of both Arendt's and Derrida's works that we can productively reconsider the complexities of negotiating the paradoxes of forgiving and acting hospitably to the (unknown) Other.

Focusing on the temporality of the public realm of the political, the second section of this chapter explores Arendt's action-oriented politics of freedom, an experience conditioned by the temporal limitations of being in the "standing now." This is the moment in time where political action occurs and thus the temporal point of (non-)presence that people must cultivate and carefully negotiate if power is to be (re-)engendered. It is through an examination of political time that one can understand more fully how practices of public care—such as forgiveness and the welcoming of the narrative voice of the (unknown) Other—relate to what Arendt describes as the "abyss of freedom"[23] experienced in the (n)ever fully present moment betwixt past and future: the perpetually fleeting non-present, present moment of the *nunc stans*, or "the standing now."[24] Political actors, as though paying heed to the well-known warning issued throughout the London Underground, must "mind the gap" in time, and subsequently transition through the abyssal temporal moment of the "standing now"; they must take care not to allow the forces of past and future to impinge upon political action just as a speeding train might perilously pin a commuter to the edge of the platform. Presupposing a rectilinear temporality, the second part of this chapter investigates more thoroughly the nature of the temporal tenses of past, present, and future; it casts light on the ever-fleeting nexus point of the "standing now" where Arendt contends the already known and forever unknowable converge. This framing of the "now," though distinct from Derrida's notion of the present, is one that I believe connects well with the Derridean notion of "negotiation" since his understanding of this "leisure-less" mental act is precisely that which is needed to think the unthinkable *sans* any fundamental grounds upon which to stand.

Drawing heavily upon Arendt's writings about the *vita contemplativa* (and thus the three mental activities of thinking, willing, and judging), I highlight the significance of such a gap in time and illustrate—through a critical reading of Arendt's interpretation of Kafka's parable entitled "He"—the type of temporal orientation needed to carry out a Derridean negotiation of the ever-transitory, (n)ever-present moment of the "now."[25] This is not only the moment in time when people exist as temporally-conditioned beings, but it is also the moment of (non-)presence when freedom is experienced and power can be realized. Given the paradoxes of being in time, how then to negotiate the "now"? How, in other words, can we "mind the gap" in time?

In keeping with my use of story as a means of thinking about being and acting politically in the world, I turn to yet another narrative in the final section of this chapter, returning—that is—to Megan Phelps-Roper's account of her departure from the WBC. A "she," not unlike Kafka's eponymous "He," Phelps-Roper is someone whose story demonstrates the Arendtian-inspired, Derridean-informed form of temporal movement theorized throughout this chapter; her narrative illustrates the temporal orientation necessary for political actors to negotiate the gap of the "standing now." Phelps-Roper is a "she" who must re-reconcile herself to the meta-narrative within which she was born and that which she distances herself from when she begins anew from the conflictual moment between past and future. Her story, by revolving around her worldly interactions on Twitter, challenges the boundaries of what might be considered a topic of (international) political theory and, arguably, stretches Arendt's theorizing beyond conventional scholarship; however, Phelps-Roper's narrative, and her narrative understanding, captures the essence of the temporal orientation needed to navigate the abyssal space of the *nunc stans*, or the "small non-time space in the very heart of time"[26]: the between moment of the "now" where—in terms of political action—freedom is experienced.

1. PRIVATE, CYCLICAL TIME AND PUBLIC, RECTILINEAR TIME

Investigating the temporal character of caring as both a private and public form of practice, this section explores two distinct, interrelated conceptions of time which are present in Arendt's work: cyclical time and rectilinear time. Here, I highlight how private and public practices of care are inextricably linked through an examination of the temporal logics that inform Arendt's tripartite conception of the *vita activa*. It is, however, in terms of rectilinear time—which corresponds to both human life, as well as political action—that freedom and the significance of public practices of caring for the world can be understood. The aim of this inquiry into Arendtian temporality is to theorize the conceptual foundation for this chapter's second section, in which I consider the conflictual character of the ever-fleeting present moment of the *nunc stans*—the "small non-time space in the very heart of time"—where one must take care to negotiate the forces of both past and future that antagonize "he" who dwells there and further enacts the (infinitely long) rectilinear story of human history.

For Arendt, the distinction between the private realm of the household (*oikos*) and the public space for gathering (*agora*) is centrally significant to her understanding of the three fundamental activities that comprise the *vita activa*. Arendt orders the activities of labor, work, and action hierarchically, in such a way that they might be described as a three-tiered pyramid, whereby "labor"—the most private, biologically basic activity—serves as the foundation of this tripartite structure; the second level: work; and finally action: its highest, most distinctly human echelon. While the top of this pyramid is reserved for the most thoroughly public activity and the lowest level the most private, this hierarchical ranking is not determined solely in reference to spatiality, or where they take place. Rather, this pyramidal classification is reliant on her understanding of the temporalities that characterize the activities of labor, work, and action. Arendt's hierarchical understanding of these three activities is based upon the temporal cyclicality and/or linearity which structures and therefore informs the phenomenological doing of labor, work, and action. Arendt accords rectilinear time a higher status than that of cyclical time since the former is associated with the narrative nature of human life (*bíoç*), while the latter corresponds with non-human life (*zōē*) incapable of being recounted as a story. Considered in conjunction with her tripartite conception of human activities, then, labor is the most basic activity within the *vita activa* because it operates according to the repetitive rhythm of a cyclical temporality. Work is next in the hierarchy since it is an activity related to both circular and rectilinear time. And action is the highest, as it is informed by a linear temporal logic like that of a narratable, human life. The level of action is supported by the two subordinate levels of work and labor. Accordingly, the distinctly human activity of action follows a rectilinear course only so long as labor reproduces biologic life and work maintains the worldly spaces within which people live, move, and act.

For Arendt, the temporality of laboring in private is understood in terms of biological necessity and the continuous (re)production of life. By contending that labor never "produces" anything but life, Arendt underscores that this activity is one that conforms to a cyclical temporality shaped by the ways in which all (non)human beings are "enslaved by necessity."[27] According to Arendt, as she writes in a section of *The Human Condition* entitled "Labor and Life," "cyclical" is the "movement of the living organism, the human *body* not excluded, as long as it can withstand the process that permeates its being and makes it alive."[28] Here, Arendt's use of the word "body" is significant because labor—as the lowest activity within her pyramidal conceptualization of the *vita activa*—does not refer to the humanness of being human but to the physical beingness of a living creature, like any other, with a body ever in need of care. To take care of one's self in this regard is effectively to care for one's personal needs as an organic being. Because every living creature must—on a daily basis—overcome a need to eat, drink, be sheltered, etc., labor is necessarily repetitious; in other words, this activity—"caught in the cyclical movement of the body's life process—has neither a beginning nor an end."[29] It is an activity whose "particular time is trapped within the *eternal return* of nature, of life in the biological sense of the word."[30] Corresponding with the biological basis of all life, labor can therefore be said to exhibit a temporal circularity that conditions the existentiality of all other private and public activities, as all those people who do work and/or act politically possess bodies that will decay and die without adequate care.

Unlike the thoroughly cyclical temporality of labor, the activity of work operates according to a linear temporal rhythm. This being said, the products of work correspond to a circular flow of time, as things that are produced from nature will—if not properly cared for—return to the natural, cyclical flow of time. In terms of the temporality associated with the production process of fabrication, the temporal character of doing work is that of a certain linearity since working has a "definite beginning and a definite, predictable end."[31] Whereas labor is a never-ending activity and "action" has a beginning but no predictable end, work is an activity in which *homo faber* proceeds according to a preconceived plan/blueprint and from a definable starting point. *Homo faber* works from a known starting point to a predictable end in order to produce a thing capable of existing in the world for an extended period of time. Working is therefore a rectilinear process of producing a product that can appear in the world, and potentially exist well into the future. Without adequate care, however, such objects will not last precisely because the life process that conditions all of humankind will also ultimately affect all human artifacts. If people do not use the things they have produced or if they use them without attending to them properly, they will eventually decay and return into the overall natural process from which they were drawn and against which they were erected.[32] Products of work, such as art, buildings, travel infrastructures, and even sociopolitical institutions are therefore "things" that possess the ability to stand the test of time but which will decay if they are not properly maintained and preserved. If there is indeed a desire to sustain the worldly character of human existence, there is consequently a need to care for the fabricated things that comprise and/or structure both the private and public realms. It is thus necessary to recognize that care plays an important role in caring for the worldly spaces of the political realm, as well as for the worldly web of human relationships, which forms when a plurality of people publicly speak and act together. Without such care, the spaces within which people live, move, and act are unstable and inadequate as homes for either one's private affairs and/or those common to all persons and peoples.

Although the worldly durability of *homo faber*'s products stabilize the human condition by effectively allowing humankind to remove itself from nature's cyclical temporal movement, action is the activity that Arendt considers to be the highest and only truly "human" endeavor. It is also the only activity within her pyramidal conceptualization of the *vita activa* that is entirely structured by a linear temporal logic. In the previous chapter, I illustrated that the humanness of action corresponds with the fact that it is only human beings—in contrast to all other earthly creatures—who are capable of speech (*logos*): the communicative means through which humankind can be said to narrate their existence in a coherent, meaningful manner. In returning to this point, I wish to highlight the rectilinear conception of time found within this understanding of *logos*, as it is a linear temporality which informs her conceptualization of human life and the most human of human activities: action. From Arendt's Aristotelian conception of life, then, human life (*βίος*) is a life which can be narrated and told as an emplotted story that moves linearly from beginning to end. As Arendt writes:

> The word "life" [. . .] has an altogether different meaning if it is related to the world and meant to designate the time interval between birth and death. Limited by a beginning and an end, that is, by the two supreme events of appearance and disappearance within the world, it follows a strictly linear movement whose very motion nevertheless is driven by the motor of biological life which man shares with other living things and which forever retains the cyclical movement of nature. The chief characteristic of this specifically human life, whose appearance and disappearance constitute worldly events, is that it is itself always full of events which ultimately can be told as a story, establish a biography; it is of this life, *bios* as distinguished from mere *zōē*, that Aristotle said that it "somehow is a kind of *praxis*."[33]

While Arendt also mentions the circular temporality of labor within this excerpt, her primary assertion is that "life" is human if it can be mimetically re-*presented* in a narrative form. In other words, a life becomes more than a "mere *zōē*" because it "can be told," which is to say, coherently communicated through acts of speech and—most importantly for this discussion—because it follows a linear trajectory across a line between two terminal, bounding points.[34] Threaded through an individual life from the moment of one's birth to the time of one's death, this line—although only perceivable in its entirety through the eye of the historian (or biographer)—is the plot that comprises the unique, human story of their worldly existence. On this matter, Kristeva is right to suggest that the "possibility of representing birth and death, to conceive of them in time and to explain them to others—that is, *the possibility of narrating*—grounds human life in what is specific to it, in what is non-animal about it, non-physiological."[35] While the "possibility of narrating" a human life also presupposes the ability to remember the details of one's existence and to "relate back to [one's] own origin,"[36] a presupposition that effectively establishes memory as "time's eternal anchor"[37] and *memoria* as the means through which one secures their "ontological bearings,"[38] human life can therefore be said to move in a characteristically linear progression from birth to death, mirroring the plot of a story unfolding from beginning to end. From this perspective, the human condition of natality, and the very appearance of a new human being in the world, effectively begins a new narrative, whose plot corresponds directly with a life lived between life and death, an individual's lifetime. As Arendt notes in the above quotation (referencing Aristotle's *Politics* 1254a7), "[βίος] somehow is a kind of *praxis*," which means that being human corresponds with the real-time practice of emplotting one's own story as one proceeds rectilinearly toward death. While we cannot ever know the end of our own tale and, consequently, cannot ever understand the full meaning of our own existence, life is nevertheless an actively progressing story within the meta-narrative of human history.

Because human time conforms to a narratable, rectilinear temporality and because action is a distinctly human activity, Arendt contends that acting in public is also characterized by a temporal linearity capable of being mimetically represented in the form of a story. Additionally, and similarly to the time of human life, the linear temporality of action is resultant of natality, or—as Arendt writes—"the new beginning inherent in birth [which] can only make itself felt in the world because the newcomer possesses the capacity of beginning something anew, that is, of acting."[39] In reappropriating this existential condition of human beginning to the realm of the political, whereby acting and speaking is understood as a kind of public "second birth," Arendt consequently suggests that action is also "somehow a kind of *praxis*" in which a plurality of civic friends are the co-narrators in a story which progresses through time. This distinctly human story is, however, one whose end will never come so long as people emerge from their private homes to speak and act together publicly in the worldly realm of the political. In other words, the narrative life of the public, political realm can potentially continue to exist *ad infinitum* so long as a plurality of people are publicly reborn, and in so far as these people continue to initiate new courses of free action and effectively "confirm and take upon [themselves] the naked fact of [their] original physical appearance [in the human world]."[40] Here, the "naked fact" of which Arendt speaks refers to the condition of being a human being who is free and capable of initiating a new course of action, that is, of setting something new in motion.[41] For Arendt, the "second birth" experienced in action is therefore coeval with the public emergence of freedom:

> Man does not possess freedom so much as he, or better his coming into the world, is equated with the appearance of freedom in the universe; man is free because he is a beginning and was so created after the universe had already come into existence: [*Initium*] *ut esset, creates est homo, ante quem nemo fuit.* In the birth of each man this initial beginning is reaffirmed, because in each instance something new comes into an already existing world which will continue to exist after each individual's death. Because he *is* a beginning, man can begin; to be human and to be free are one and the same. God created man in order to introduce into the world the faculty of beginning: freedom.[42]

This birth of freedom, which Arendt associates with humankind's coming into the world, is narrated in the biblical story of Genesis. Entering the creation story *in medias res*, Adam and Eve's appearance in the world corresponds to the emergence of freedom in the universe precisely because they can speak and act together, which effectively gives "them"—in terms of their plural existence—the "power to" choose their own fate(s) and/or begin new courses of action. Endowed with free will, and the ability to begin their own narrative(s) within the world, their choice to eat the forbidden fruit casts them out of a theoretically timeless paradise; humankind is subsequently forever bound to the temporal and spatial conditions of an earthly existence. When God says, "cursed is the ground because of you; through painful toil you will eat of it all the days of your life," he is condemning them to a cyclical temporality within an overarching human, rectilinear form of beingness in the world, where it is "by the sweat of [their] brow [they] will eat [their] food until [they] return to the ground [. . .] for dust [they] are and to dust [they] will return."[43] Here is an instance where freedom and the "power to" act together is depicted as having long-standing consequences for the "storybook of mankind."

According to an Arendtian conception of action, then, freedom is not unlike power, which is—so long as a collection of people remain together—a distinctly human capacity or potentiality. As with power, the public experience of being free can occur only so long as people, who are beginnings in and of themselves, enter into the world and initiate new action. This is, of course, the very act that gives rise to the power of which Arendt speaks.[44] In other words, the powerful potential of acting politically, and thus of experiencing freedom, is foremost a matter associated with being a human being, which is—according to Arendt—fundamentally about humankind's beingness as a beginning capable of initiating new action within the context of a broader sociopolitical narrative. Theorizing human temporality as linear time, structured by the miracle of natality, which is the beginning inherent to both human life (*bíos*) and action, the "naked fact" of one's birth—as well as one's "second birth" into the public realm of the political (an appearance made through *logos*)—embodies the freedom people experience as beings capable of beginning anew in the world. In this sense, public, political life is temporally structured by "beginnings" and is characterized by a rectilinear movement through time; this is a linear temporal dynamic that corresponds with the unfolding of a narrative that has both an origin and an end. In order to further explore the linearity of human temporality, more specifically the temporal dynamic ever-occurring in the *nunc stans* (which is the "standing now" within which human beings are always presently situated), the subsequent section of this chapter demonstrates how public acts of caring for the world—such as a caring forgiveness and a caring cosmopolitanism—can be said to care for freedom by facilitating new beginnings within the rectilinear flow of time.

2. "MIND[ING] THE GAP" IN TIME

A temporal condition of a human life is that there is an inescapable uncertainty associated with the inability for people to predict fully the outcome of any decisions they may have made or of the actions they might have taken as they have progressed through time. This uncertainty is central to any discussion of humankind's beingness in time since it is this factor of unknowability that accompanies the experience of being forever trapped in the *nunc stans*. As the ever-fleeting moment between past and future, the *nunc stans* is the (n)ever-present moment of the "now" where all people "stand" temporally, which is to say, it is the focal point of human temporality where human beings dwell in time. Given the ways in which I have—throughout this book—theorized cosmopolitanism and forgiveness as forms of public care, or as two political practices capable of (re)cultivating the power of freedom in worldly political spaces, it is my belief that there is a need to reconsider the *nunc stans* as the temporal site of political action. In particular, it is necessary to rethink both what it means to confront the temporal forces that play upon all people as they stand in the moment of the now, and how they can go about "minding" their way through this (n)ever-present gap in time. What, then, does it mean to be *in* time, or to be trapped in the gap between past and future? In what ways can people be said to "negotiate" this characteristically abyssal temporal space, a place in time where freedom and power are engendered only when a plurality of people appear to speak and act together? In being there, in that place, which is not really a "place" at all, what does it mean to "take care" while transitioning between past and future? What faculties of the mind need be activated for people to move freely across the (historical) timeline, as well as to think anew about the ways in which the "now" is a temporally contaminated moment of (non-)presence, spontaneously and powerfully ending and beginning courses of action, without the ability to transcend the existential conditions of humankind's thrownness in time and space? With these questions in mind, I consequently turn to Arendt's reading of Kafka's "He," doing so in order to outline a theory of the temporal "negotiation" needed to undertake the task of caring for the world.

A. "He" and Arendt

Though the topic of temporality is addressed in various places throughout Arendt's corpus, her discussion of time in terms of Kafka's collection of parables entitled "He" occurs twice in her writings. She refers to "He," first, in the preface to *Between Past and Future* (1961) and, second, in part one of *The Life of the Mind* (posthumously published in 1978).[45] In the former publication, Arendt attempts to "indicate metaphorically and tentatively the contemporary conditions of thought."[46] In *The Life of the Mind*, however, she explores Kafka's work with "the hope of finding out where the thinking ego is located in time" and, as a critique of deterministic theories of history, "[of ascertaining] whether its relentless activity can be temporally determined."[47] In spite of the different purposes that each of the aforementioned texts serve, the observations Arendt makes about human temporality are similar in both publications precisely because her observations about time, as Elisabeth Young-Bruehl acknowledges, "did not change over the years."[48] Although I reference both of her theoretical engagements with Kafka's parable, my own purpose is more closely aligned with Arendt's efforts to locate the thinking ego in time, as I am particularly concerned here with the inner experience of how people move through time as beings constrained—but not fully determined—by their place in the (historical) timeline.[49]

Contending that Kafka's simple story "analyzes poetically our 'inner state' in regard to time,"[50] Arendt uses this short allegory in order to investigate the human experience of being in time, which is a state of beingness that occurs—as Derrida suggests—upon a temporal plane without any firm or fixed foundations, with the forces of past and future both contaminating and conditioning the movements taking place on the "bottomless chessboard where being is set in play." Through Kafka's "He," then, Arendt considers human temporality, exploring in abstract terms how the thinking ego—the inner self, or "me" of thought—experiences time. It is only in terms of this "inner time sensation" that Arendt believes "ordinary time"—that is to say, the "vulgar time" associated with the "business of everyday life"—is "broken up into the tenses of past, present, [and] future," because it is only in thought that the past and future are "absent from our senses."[51] Arising not when people are consumed with the worldly happenings/doings of their lives, instead, this inner experience of time takes place when people have withdrawn from the world.[52] It is only in contemplation, absorbed in the mental activity of thinking (in the sense of having an inner dialogue with oneself), that time is experienced as anything more than the "vulgar" progression of the days of the week, weeks of the month, months of the years, and so on. It is only as a result of the perspectival distance created by stopping, and thinking, that it becomes possible to reflect upon time as a continuum moving from past to future, as it is only in terms of the *vita contemplativa* that the past is "transformed" into "something lying *behind* us and the not-yet of the future into something that *approaches* us from ahead."[53] As a poetic representation of time, Kafka's "He" captures this temporal conceptualization, offering—in figurative terms—an account of how time is experienced by people in the mode of thought.

In both *Between Past and Future* and *The Life of the Mind*, Arendt relies upon the following translation of Kafka's text, from the original German:

> He has two antagonists; the first presses him from behind, from his origin. The second blocks the road in front of him. He gives battle to both. Actually, the first supports him in his fight with the second, for he wants to push him forward, and in the same way the second supports him in his fight with the first, since he drives him back. But it is only theoretically so. For it is not only the two antagonists who are there, but he himself as well, and who really knows his intentions? His dream, though, is that some time in an unguarded moment—and this, it must be admitted, would require a night darker than any night has ever been yet—he will jump out of the fighting line and be promoted, on account of his experience in fighting, to the position of umpire over his antagonists in their fight with each other.[54]

Here, Kafka describes a "thought-event"[55] in which two opposing temporal forces collide at the ever-progressing point where a "he" exists during his unidirectional movement through time. A protagonist permanently situated at the nexus of past and future, "he" must do battle against two diametrically opposed temporal "antagonists": the force of the past pressing him forward into the future and the force of the future pushing him backward into the past. Unable to leave the fight and to become a judge capable of presiding over the temporal conflict of which "he" is a part, "he" cannot transcend his situatedness in time, despite any desire that he might possess to free himself and to ascend to a position from which he can observe the "fight" taking place before him. Incapable of stepping out of time in a manner that philosophers have long imagined, with thinkers from Parmenides to Hegel having dreamed about a "timeless region, an eternal presence in complete quiet, lying beyond human clocks and calendars altogether,"[56] Kafka's "he" is forever fated to dwell in the gap between past and future, where he must hold permanently his place on the "fighting line," and do "battle" in a two-sided conflict that can only come to end when he himself perishes.

Because Arendt—as Jacques Taminiaux suggests—"turns the *nunc stans* into the abode of thought,"[57] Kafka's "he" is a figure whose temporal existence is conditioned by his status as a permanent resident of a dwelling place which lacks any firmly established foundation, in the sense that the "now" is neither a fixed position in time nor—as Derrida suggests—a site of pure presence that is ontologically grounded in a fundamental temporality. Ever-fleeting, the "now" is the "most futile and slippery of the tenses [since] when [one] say[s] 'now' and point[s] to it, it is already gone."[58] The very moment when a person reflexively attempts to identify their place in time, they have already come to be in a new temporal location, as they are beings who exist within a "now" that is ever in motion from past to future. "He," in addition to existing in a perpetually fugacious moment, must take a stand in the "now" that is not exactly a "now" at all—his very presence in the world being characterized by its non-presence. If indeed the "now" contains within it the "traces" of both past and future (and I believe it does), the moment in time where "he" stands is not only fleeting but also conditioned by a "play" of forces that are made manifest as "he" navigates his way across the "bottomless chessboard where being is set in play." Trapped between past and future, human beings must ceaselessly endeavor to make a "home" in this "small non-time-space in the very heart of time": the (n)ever-present temporal moment of the *nunc stans* experienced when people stop and think. Given how the "standing now" is neither fully "now" nor a place in time where one can be said to "stand" still, the temporal "abode" within which Arendt suggests "he" resides ought not to be conceptualized statically. Rather, the *nunc stans* is understood dynamically, specifically in terms of a movement which is ceaseless and rectilinear in nature.

Dwelling in an "abode" that is ever in motion, Kafka's "he" is not only a figure destined to reside indefinitely in the *nunc stans*, but is also a being whose very presence in the "now" engenders the temporal conflict wherein "he" is an active combatant. Though one might argue that "he" is not the original instigator of this "fight," as he did not choose to be born and to be thrown into time, his presence within the present moment nevertheless instigates a temporal "battle" that he must wage as he moves from past to future. In other words, the antagonistic "thought-event" that Arendt explores in terms of Kafka's parable takes place precisely because "he" has come to be in time, whereby the "fact that there is a fight at all seems due exclusively to the presence of the man, without whom the forces of past and of the future, one suspects, would have neutralized or destroyed each other long ago."[59] For Arendt, "he" is therefore understood as a being who disturbs the flow of time, his very presence causing the "stream of time to deflect from whatever its original direction or—assuming a cyclical movement—ultimate non-direction may have been."⁶⁰ Just as Adam and Eve's decision to taste the forbidden fruit interrupts their state of eternal changelessness in paradise—their actions transforming their timeless state of existence in the Garden of Eden into a rectilinear form of temporality comprised of past, present, and future—the presence of "he" in the *nunc stans* introduces a new timeline into history. "He," as a figurative representation of the thinking ego, or the inner self who dwells in the ever-fleeting moment of the "standing now," is consequently a being whose emergence in time creates a new (historical) timeline, structuring his experience of time in terms of his rectilinear movement from birth to death, and engendering the "play" of non-present forces that come to a head where "he" presently stands. While the temporal forces of both past and future originate in a time that has either already been or one which is yet to come, the collision of these two tenses at the point where "he" stands generates a line that extends outward into a future which has an unknown number of potential endings, all which are—of course—points of termination that could go on to form the foundations of an infinite array of new courses of (public) action.⁶¹ To use the Augustinian language that Arendt relies upon throughout her corpus, "he" who stands in the "standing now" alters the trajectory of time because he himself is "the beginning of a beginning," and thus, his existence in time instigates a new course of action from within his place in the "small non-time space in the very heart of time."

Capturing the effects of the temporal collision of past and future, Arendt also illustrates the conflicted relationship between two of the mental faculties associated with the *vita contemplativa*: thinking and willing. As Taminiaux suggests, for Arendt, thinking and willing are "in all respects [. . .] at war."⁶² Thinking is dependent on memory, as "every thought is strictly speaking an after-thought,"⁶³ while the "activity of willing is at the very outset focused on the future."⁶⁴ The activities of thinking and willing further complicate the experience of being in time because they are interrelated but incommensurable. Kafka's "he," then, must manage the temporal pressures imposed by his memories, as well as the forces of the future toward which "he" moves, reconciling the backward-facing-ness of thought with the futural need to will his way forward:

> Man lives in this in-between, and what he calls the present is a life-long fight against the dead weight of the past, driving him forward with hope, and the fear of a future (whose only certainty is death), driving him backward toward "the quiet of the past" with nostalgia for and remembrance of the only reality he can be sure of.⁶⁵

Focusing here upon the conflictual dynamic which plays upon "he" in the *nunc stans*, Arendt challenges the idea that it is the future which pulls humankind forward with "hope." Inducing a state of "fear" akin to the form of existential anxiety associated with Heidegger's notion of "being-towards-death," as well as his understanding of *Sorge* (or "care" as a type of anxiety generated by one's concern for what is yet to come), contemplation of the future drives "he" back in time. Consequently, "he" finds solace in a past that he has previously experienced, preferring to fix his gaze there rather than look ahead to an unknown future where the only certainty is death.

Arendt, too, recognizes how the existential "fear" of the future antagonizes "he" by "block[ing] the road in the front him," though she distances herself from Heidegger's position with her distinctive Augustinian-inspired conception of "natality." As Scott and Stark observe, Arendt "abandons Heidegger's death-driven phenomenology with Augustine as her guide."[66] Whereas Heidegger goes so far as to suggest that the ontological status of a human being is that of "Being-toward-the-end," since death "is a way to be, which *Dasein* takes over as soon as it is,"[67] Arendt argues that the "decisive fact determining man as a conscious, remembering being, is birth or 'natality,' that is, the fact we have entered the world through birth."[68] She challenges Heidegger's notion of "being-toward-death" by theorizing what might be considered a philosophic conception of being-toward-birth. According to Patricia Bowen-Moore, "With Hannah Arendt, the notion of natality is elevated as a philosophical thematic alongside its countercurrent experience: the condition of mortality."[69] There is a kind of conceptual balance in Arendt's work; while giving due consideration to death and its significance, she prioritizes the condition of birth for human existence, thought, and action.

But how do we make sense of life and death, of existence and the conditions of our beingness in the world? How do we make meaningful the time lived between birth and death? In simple terms, we remember and narrate the events in our lives. In Arendt's words, "It is memory and not expectation (for instance, the expectation of death as in Heidegger's approach) that gives unity and wholeness to human existence."[70] Suggesting that remembrance is the cognitive ability that permits people to make coherent the seemingly incoherent occurrences that comprise their lives, Arendt describes remembrance as the "most frequent and most basic thinking experience,"[71] privileging memory as the human capacity to recall and represent the past (both to oneself and others in a variety of different mediums). Because meaning is resultant of the narrative process of self-understanding, remembrance is the "basic thinking experience" that allows people to determine the meaning of certain periods of time. "Meaning," in other words, is what Arendt suggests we create "in the very process of living, insofar as we try to reconcile ourselves to what we do and what we suffer."[72] Without philosophically forsaking the force of the future, or discounting the significance of "expectation," Arendt consequently maintains that memory "gives unity and wholeness to human existence," because remembrance is the mental means through which people can come to understand their thrownness in the world. Though "he" must fight "two antagonists" as he moves rectilinearly through time, doing so from within the (n)ever present of the "now" where he stands, he nevertheless has the power to make meaningful his *bíoç* by remembering and narratively representing, or re-*presenting*, his past.

B. An Arendtian Temporal Orientation

Given the need to make meaningful our existence, to tell the story of our lives and to narrate the "storybook of mankind," we may well wonder how to proceed in these circumstances. The paradoxicality of Kafka's protagonist's dilemma is evident. Should "he" maintain entirely the gaze of an historian, focusing on that which has been, or should he risk being caught in our proverbial "fox trap," in a future-oriented state of "being-toward-death"? How, in other words, should we stand in time? Where should we look in "doing battle" with the forces of both past and future? How should we be in time, taking care and "caring for the world" while being trapped in the *nunc stans*? If we are to stand our ground in the "standing now," we must carefully "mind the gap" in time. But how? We need an almost god-like power to face concurrently both past and future: to adopt a dual-facing perspective. For me, this is a forward-looking, backward-focused temporal orientation, one which allows us to transition through the aporias of being in a(n) (n)ever-present moment contaminated by a "play" of (non)discursive forces.

The Roman god Janus springs to mind, whose ability to see, at once, both past and future, gives him an unparalleled cognizance of that which has been and that which has yet to be from within the (n)ever-present moment of the "now." God of transitions, time, and duality, among other things, Janus presides over both birth and death, the beginnings and endings of conflict, and thus war and peace. Who better to turn to than Derrida in order to think about "negotiating" such extremes, such indissociable but thoroughly incommensurable polarities? For Derrida, the practice of "negotiation" is a ceaseless mental activity characterized by "the impossibility of stopping, of settling in a position."[73] To negotiate is to move "to-and-fro between two positions, two places, two choices."[74] Though this mental activity is typically understood in terms of making a decision during moments of "undecidability," it demands a back-and-forth dynamic, resulting from the need to reconcile the irreconcilable, "when there are two incompatible imperatives that appear incompatible but are equally imperative [...] one negotiates by engaging the nonnegotiable in negotiation."[75] This is, as Marko Zlomislic suggests, "the madness of thinking the impossible,"[76] though it is not necessarily incompatible with an Arendtian understanding of the *vita contemplativa*, after all it is Arendt who contends that "the life of the mind" is "sheer activity."[77] Moreover, she adds, that "thinking inevitably has a destructive undermining effect on all established criteria, values, measurements of good and evil," which "we treat in morals and ethics."[78] When considered from an Arendtian perspective, such a "destructive," leisure-less-ness of negotiation would look a lot less like a frenetic "to-and-fro" between two incompatible, indissociable positions and more like a contemplative process of settling into the moment of the "now," as if one were attempting to be more at "home" in the *nunc stans*.

Home is more than a place, or a site in which we live; it also constitutes the dwelling place of our being in time, which we experience not simply as "vulgar," clock-able time but as something imagined. As Alison Blunt and Robyn Dowling explain, home is an "idea" and an "imaginary that is imbued with feelings."[79] Home is thus a "spatial imaginary," or a set of "intersecting and variable ideas and feelings, which are related to context, and which construct places, extend across spaces and scales, and connect places."[80] Home is temporal. The *nunc stans*, the "now" where we dwell in time, is the "abode of thought." In acknowledging this aspect of human temporality, we are confronted by the notion that perhaps—to live, move, and act in this fleeting "space"—a theoretical form of what might be described as "homemaking" is necessary. This means drawing upon humankind's power of imagination, a mental faculty that allows us to transcend our situatedness in both time and space. For us to "mind the gap" in time, we must draw upon our "gift"[81] of imagination. According to Arendt, the imagination is the "only inner compass" we possess, as it is through the "imagination, which actually is understanding," that we can find our "bearings in the world."[82] Understanding is, according to Arendt, the "specifically human way of being alive," and it is the mental means through which "we come to terms with and reconcile ourselves to reality, that is, to try to be at *home* in the world."[83] While scholars have long explored the role that the imagination plays in Arendt's conceptualization of judgment to political action,[84] I apply here an Arendtian conception of this "gift" specifically as a means of reconsidering the "madness" of thinking the (im)possible from within the (n)ever-present moment of the "now."

The imagination allows us to do away with the constraints of time and space. According to Arendt, the imagination does not need to be "led" by the "temporal associations," of connecting the "no longer" and the "not yet," making "present at will whatever it chooses."[85] In this way, the power of imagination enables people, as she writes, "to see things in their proper perspective," and "to bridge abysses of remoteness until we can see and understand everything that is too far away from us as though it were our own affair."[86] In terms of the temporal conflict that we must endure, the imagination facilitates a Derridean negotiation through time, as we confront the aporetic impasses opened by our state of being in the abyssal moment of the "now," or when we come "face-to-face" with the (unknown) Other. It is thus the mental faculty that allows us to "bridge the abyss of remoteness" which exists between people—in the sense that the imaginative powers of human beings makes communication possible—and that informs how we can theoretically "go visiting"[87] the perspectives of other people, allowing us to fathom more fully the "faces" of the infinite with whom we might share the "world."

The imagination allows people to *look* forward toward the future, while permitting them to *focus* on the past. Although we may be able to look back on what happened ten minutes ago and describe, with narrative authority, what took place, when thinking ahead to ten minutes from now, we cannot say with any true certainty what will happen—though we may have an idea of what is to come. Our lack of prophetic ability leaves us with little option but to face what can be understood, in Arendtian terms, as the possibility of "darkness" and of being plunged into "dark times."[88] The "darkness" of this unknown, impending future ahead can only be partially illuminated and "dispelled,"[89] though we can cast light on the phenomena that have already transpired in the world, and can represent these things and events in narrative terms. While the Augustinian undertones of Arendt's conceptualization of "darkness" can be traced back to her doctoral thesis,[90] she refers to this theme throughout her theorization of the human condition as a mean of considering the ultimate unknowability of human nature and the future. For my particular discussion of human temporality, such "darkness" is characteristic of both past and future, yet the darkness of the unknown ahead is of a different "density"[91] than that which has already been.

Because we can focus upon (aspects) of the narrative from which we have emerged, a backward-focused emphasis allows us to consider the *nunc stans* not as a mere means to some end but, rather, as the end to all that which has already come before. Prioritizing the backward glance of the historian effectively curbs the establishment and/or further entrenchment of overly forward-oriented perspectives, such as that of *homo faber*, who always works toward a predetermined end in accordance with an instrumental logic. This is a mentality that justifies a violent means of work in terms of the ends pursued. If the present moment is indeed the effective terminal point to all that has come before, it brings with it the potential for a new beginning. Because the present moment is effectively the endpoint of the ever-unfolding story of humankind, as human history has progressed only so far as the moment of the "now," we stand in the ideal position to begin anew. As Arendt writes in the final lines of *The Origins of Totalitarianism*:

> [E]very end in history necessarily contains a new beginning; this beginning is the promise, the only "message" which the end can ever produce. Beginning,

before it becomes a historical event, is the supreme capacity of man; politically, it is identical with man's freedom.[92]

If the "standing now" is the end of human history as we know it, then, it is also a beginning point for a new course of action to emerge, a new plotline that originates—not unlike the "thought-event" that Arendt describes in *The Life of the Mind*—from the temporal conflict occurring in the *nunc stans*. We must take care to "mind the gap" in time by assuming a forward-looking, backward-focused temporal orientation that allows us to negotiate the tension between the (n)ever-present forces of past and future, as well as to comprehend the "message" concealed by the *nunc stans*: that the "now" is an end that "promises" a new beginning. At this point (in time), I (now) turn to a consideration of how this dual-facing temporal perspective relates to action and public practices of "caring for the world."

C. The *Nunc Stans* and Public Acts of Caring for the World

While the *polis* does not have a single thinking ego, like that of an individual human being, the temporal conflict Kafka's "he" faces is also one which political actors experience while being present in the non-present moment of the *nunc stans*. The political is, of course, a matter of a plural "we" and not a singular "I" or "he," but it is nevertheless possible to transpose Arendt's thinking about Kafka's "he" to the collective plane, specifically to the public realm of the political, where—in liberal democratic communities—a plurality of distinct but equal persons must together negotiate their way through time; this is the "we" formed when a plurality of political actors speak and act together as they move through a historical narrative *in medias res*. The temporal experience that occurs in the (non-)present moment of the "now" is, however, complicated by the fact that stories are told, and lives are narrated, not only from singular, individual perspectives, but also when a collective of people enact and tell their own stories. But how do we distinguish between the individual and the collective in political terms?

In the final section of the second part of *The Life of the Mind*, Arendt shifts away from her musings on the *vita contemplativa* and fastens her attention on the *vita activa*, discussing the important but oft overlooked distinction between philosophic freedom and political liberty.[93] For Arendt, "philosophic freedom" is "relevant only to people who live outside political communities" as "solitary individuals," while "political freedom" is that which can be made manifest "in communities where the many who live together have their intercourse both in word and deed"; this is only "possible in the sphere of human plurality."[94] The conceptual change from an "I," or a "he," to a "we" transforms the *nunc stans* from a lonely moment in time, occupied by a single human being, to that of the "abyss of freedom," where the forces of past and future antagonize a plurality of people who appear to speak and act together: a "faceless 'they'" of a "community ready for action."[95] And so we go from state to *polis*, from *polis* to person: the individual representing the multitude of humanity. While it is Derridean thought which allows us to move conceptually from a Kantian notion of the state to a city-centric "cosmopolitics," what Damai describes as a "messianic-*city*" capable of welcoming the (unknown) Other, we can "dilate" (Hugo) our thinking once again, transforming the "now" as that which is experienced by a single person, to a moment of *public* narration that a plural "they" comes to (re)make and/or care for its "common home."

It is useful to think about the city and such dynamics of care—or what I have called "homemaking"—associated with how a public can be said to act freely in the "darkness" of the "now," founding new storylines in this (n)ever fully present moment in time. These are moments of new beginnings and new courses of action, or of creating new temporal-spatial imaginaries. This allows us to transform the "now" into a moment of founding. In fact, we often speak of founding myths, or the *story* of the founding of a city—for example, Romulus and Remus in the Roman tradition, and Cain and Abel in the biblical tradition. When thinking politically about the "world," this notion of "founding" ceases to be played out in purely mythological or theological terms, instead becoming—as Ricardo Quinones writes about Cain and Abel—a "theme of civilization, where its historicized context extends to broader issues of social injustice."[96] These are cities founded upon violence and sin; Romulus kills Remus before going on to found Rome, and Cain murders Abel prior to establishing the city of Enoch. But what new city, as *polis*, can be established when we forgive and when we act hospitably to the narrative voice of the (unknown) Other? As Quinones observes, in the instance of Cain and Abel, "Civilization is undone, not by radical evil, but rather by the *inégalité qui est parmi nous* (the inequality which is between or among us)."[97] The brothers begin their lives equal in all regards, born to the same parents, but when an inequality is introduced between them—with God favoring Abel's sacrifice over Cain's—their relationship deteriorates and ends in fratricide. This is an act that begins Cain's new story as a displaced person, who is thereafter "under a curse and driven from the ground," left to be a "restless wanderer on the Earth."[98] Not only is it worthwhile to consider what type of city may have been founded if such violence had not taken place—or to think about what could have transpired between these two brothers if their relationship had been more carefully maintained, preserved, and enhanced—but it also worth wondering how political communities might go about caring for worldly public spaces, where the *inégalité qui est parmi nous* can be overcome when a plurality of people act politically together. It is in such spaces that a collection of distinct but equal people can enact their freedom, beginning a new course of political action in a temporal moment of sheer "madness": the abyssal moment of the "now."

This temporally-situated rift corresponds with the "abyss of freedom," which can be understood as a "hiatus" in time,[99] or the moment of political action that is shrouded by the uncertainty of not knowing what to do, where to go, or how to get there. In the darkness of the unknown, the "abyss of nothingness," freedom necessitates a negotiation between the indissociable, incommensurable forces of past and future. As Arendt writes, "The *abyss* of nothingness that opens up before any deed that cannot be accounted for by a reliable chain of cause and effect," leaving "nothing" for the "'beginner' to hold on to."[100] This experience of an "absolute beginning—*creation ex nihilio*—abolishes the sequence of temporality no less than does the thought of an absolute end, now rightly referred to as 'thinking the unthinkable.'"[101] The darkness of the "standing now" can therefore be understood as a moment in time when a public body—a communal "they" composed of a plurality of persons—must confront the "unthinkable," thinking into and between the dark abysses of both past and future. Although the unthinkability of this state of "nothingness" demands that "they" do the impossible—which I have conceptualized in terms of Derrida's notion of "negotiation" and Arendt's understanding of the imagination—it is precisely this temporal state of uncertainty and "darkness" that must exist within the flow of time if freedom is to be experienced in the world.

The "standing now," a perpetually fleeting temporal abyss, is a "hiatus" in time where the miraculous experience of freedom takes place. The temporal abyss of the *nunc stans* is thus an essential space in time for the doing of politics, for the "abyss of nothingness" that corresponds to the experience of acting politically in the world requires such a gap to exist if action is to occur at all. It is at this point that I believe one can begin to see more fully the role that "care" plays in the public doing of politics, since freedom hinges upon the continued existence of abyssal moments in time where nothingness can be experienced, which indicates the need to "care for the world." This is not a Heideggerian conceptualization of care as *Sorge* but, rather, one understood in terms of what Bowen-Moore describes as Arendt's "philosophy of natality," which is a theory of and for new beginnings. In terms of public practices of "caring for the world" more broadly, then, my point is that the temporal "hiatus" of freedom must be cultivated and protected. Efforts must be made to ensure that the "small non-time space in the very heart of time" is maintained, continued, and repaired so that it can remain a temporal "abode" for natality and the birthplace of new courses of action.

Unlike private practices of care that relate to the cyclical temporality of the activity of "labor," public acts of caring for the world correspond with a linear temporality, and they "produce"—if we can be so bold as to use a term typically assigned to the private efforts of *homo faber*—new gaps in time where action can occur. Temporally speaking, practices of caring for the world are forms of public *praxis* which effectively open, or reopen, abysses in time where political actors can experience the "nothingness" that characterizes freedom. Because worldly interactions between a plurality of distinct but equal people occur in the abyssal moment of the "now," acts of caring for the world are public forms of *praxis* that paradoxically induce a state of darkness, figuratively engulfing political actors in the moment of the "now." It is the voided, abyssal moments of darkness that bring new light into the public realm of "the political," which—for Arendt—is the space of appearance where the light should shine the brightest. Practices of caring for the world illuminate spaces of action by opening abysses in time: voids of darkness that can become the temporal "abode" of freedom. These abyssal moments in time can come to exist only in terms of a rectilinear, narratable temporality and only insofar as persons and people recognize the new beginning inherent to the "second birth" experienced when people both end and originate courses of action. From this perspective, practices of caring for the world are acts that effectively serve to (re-)illuminate the public realm that forms when a plurality of people speak and act together, by inserting abyssal breaks in time, where the darkness can wake and stir the collective imagination of those who—out of *amor mundi*—freely and spontaneously co-narrate the "storybook of mankind."

A caring forgiveness and a caring cosmopolitanism are two different, but closely related, forms of public care that engender or re-engender the "abyss of freedom." They each care for the worldly experience of action. As argued in chapter 2, forgiveness cares for the world and the experience of freedom by tending to or preserving the civic bonds between people, when a wrongdoing has occurred and/or people have become alienated following sociopolitical breakdown. A caring forgiveness is a world-centric, political practice devoted to natality and is one that maintains and preserves the "world," so that the free doing of action may begin (anew). A caring cosmopolitanism is a type of radical welcoming of the narrative voice of the (unknown) Other, an act that encourages the inclusion of new people in the public, political realm. In other words, cosmopolitanism is a matter of acting hospitably to the narrative voice of the (unknown) Other, welcoming them as equal co-storytellers capable of partaking in the narration of a more plural, democratic story. Acts of caring forgiveness consequently release people from the "spell"[102] of reactionary courses of vicious, automatic vengeance. This puts an end to an unfree, cyclical temporality. Practices of a caring cosmopolitanism effectively foster freedom by cultivating the formation of worldly interactions between a plurality of people, giving rise to a group of civic friends—a "we," "us," "they," and so on—who co-narrate new courses of political action. Both a caring forgiveness and caring cosmopolitanism insert into the flow of time an "abyss of nothingness," a point at which, or when, new storylines can begin. In this sense, the two primary examples of caring for the world that I have theorized throughout this book, publicly practice care in each their own way, yet they share a common temporal function: the establishment of abyssal spaces in the flow of time, so that old plotlines of human history can come to an end and new ones can begin. It is in such gaps, which are the "small non-time space[s] at the very heart of time," that freedom is experienced and that actors can meaningfully imagine and/or reimagine—or (re)negotiate, as Derrida might say—their worldly existence in time. In sum, "they" can "mind the gap" in time anew, taking care of the world by fostering or re-fostering freedom within the ever-fleeing moment of the *nunc stans*.

3. MEGAN PHELPS-ROPER: BEGINNING ANEW IN THE ABYSS BEYOND THE WBC

While Rebecca Barrett-Fox's work[103] investigates life in the radically fundamental Westboro Baptist Church, and Amanda van Eck Duymaer van Twist's research[104] explores the effects of growing up in communities on the religious fringe (such as the WBC), I examine here a transitional period of time within the life-story of a single WBC parishioner: Megan Phelps-Roper. I do so in order to illustrate my arguments about the temporal dynamic associated with public acts of caring for the world, and as a means of demonstrating how people—in terms of a "he"/"she" and/or an "us"/"we"/"they"—can negotiate their movement through time. To understand Phelps-Roper's disassociation from the WBC, it is important to highlight that her choice to leave her church/ family corresponds directly to the period of time during which she renewed her relationship with the world, a relationship that had once been defined by a distinctive sense of loathing for all worldly affairs and an enmity for all persons and peoples who exist outwith the WBC.

Building upon the theoretical framework that I have laid down throughout the first two sections of this chapter, I now turn to a discussion of Phelps-Roper's story as a means of demonstrating how "mind[ing] the gap" in time is an imaginative process of negotiating between the forces of both past and future. It is a temporal negotiation closely related to public acts of caring for the world—namely, a caring cosmopolitanism and a caring forgiveness. Because she acknowledges the powerful potential of beginning a new course of action within the narrative flow of time, Phelps-Roper is an example of an individual who has chosen to re-reconcile herself to the world by embracing a forward-looking, backward-focused temporal orientation: a reflective, reflexive perspective resultant of an expanded, imaginative understanding. A "she," not unlike Kafka's "he," Phelps-Roper negotiates the "abyss of nothingness."

As an intense period of change within her life-story, this transitional moment exemplifies the temporal conflict "she" was forced to face as she renegotiated her place in time and space. Phelps-Roper was forced to "fight" in the way Kafka suggests—as all people must soldier on through time, and confront ceaselessly their "two antagonists": a "she" who begins anew in the "standing now" between past and future. She has had to "fight" a battle in the "small non-time space in the very heart of time," doing so as a means of beginning a new course of action in the wake of her departure from the WBC. It became clear to her that she had "no idea how to navigate relationships outside the church's black-and-white, all-or-nothing paradigm."[105] She was stuck, unable to compromise, and unable to "move forward."[106] Indeed, "without an absolute authority who could resolve the problem and declare one side as just and righteous," she "floundered."[107] Where she contemplates the biblical question of whether it is possible for two people to walk together if they are not in agreement, if light can be in communion with darkness (2 Corinthians 6:14),[108] it is, perhaps, in the dark that we find the light. This darkness, this abyssal moment engulfing us, *is* the moment in time when revelation is possible. The all-encompassing character of "nothingness" is what must stir and wake the imagination if one is ever to be at "home" in the *nunc stans*.

In considering Phelps-Roper's story from a theoretical vantage point, constructed from an Arendtian conception of cyclical and rectilinear temporality, it is important to note two things: first, that her life within the WBC—one guided entirely by a rigid ideology—corresponds to a certain existential circularity, and, second, that I have approached her narrative in an abstract manner (as a historian might do) in order to view a period of time—the days, weeks, months, and so on—following her departure from the WBC as a protracted "now." In terms of the former point, life within the WBC is defined by a cyclicality inherent to this church's worldview and its strict, unreflective doctrinal guidelines. This is a point which Phelps-Roper touches upon in an interview with Sam Harris, when she comments:

> [W]e were [. . .] taught how to interpret evidence, how to see everything in the world and to have every objection that might ever arise and have the answer to that objection already—having repeated it over and over again. [. . .] once you accept the premise, it's almost impossible to argue yourself out of that paradigm.[109]

While this statement does not make an explicit point about temporality, such a closed "paradigm" based upon preconceived understandings and ideas perpetuated through repetition impedes the development of new trains of thought, as well as new courses of action. Writing about this "paradigm" of thought in *Unfollow*, Phelps-Roper underscores that "for many of our beliefs, there was absolutely no evidence that could be introduced to us that would cause us to change our minds," with the WBC's views and message presented in an "unfalsifiable" manner.[110] She continues, "We *never* appealed to our own thoughts or feelings as reliable evidence of truth, and we routinely disparaged others for doing so."[111] There is a closed, circular logic ever present in the WBC's doctrine, which made Phelps-Roper's departure more difficult because she was forced to break away from this logical framework.[112]

I examine Phelps-Roper's break from the WBC not as the instantaneous "now" experienced by the "thinking ego," but as a protracted period of time within the broader context of her life: a biography *in medias res*. In metaphorical terms, the transitional moment in Phelps-Roper's story is a distinct chapter—one which is comprised of a variety of events and moments across a period of time—that sits between the much larger WBC chapter(s) and the post-WBC chapter(s) of her narrative, one which is still unfolding. Accordingly, I consider the "abyss of nothingness" Phelps-Roper experiences between past and future in protracted terms, so that the "now" is the moment in-between her former life, as a member of the WBC, and her new one, as an ex-member of this organization.

The building of a new temporal-spatial imaginary occurs in this new chapter of Phelps-Roper's life. In order for her to "grow out of the mental and emotional boundaries that had so long characterized [her] existence—*the bounds of [her] habitation*—[she] would need to forge [her] own path."[113] The decision to leave the church led to, as she states in her TED Talk, "a period [. . .] full of turmoil."[114] She and her sister, Grace, "spent [their] first year away from home adrift," having "walked into an *abyss*."[115] Phelps-Roper's explanation echoes Arendt's understanding of the "abyss of nothingness," as well as her understanding of (not) being at home in the world. This is understood on a dual level, both a matter of having a physical home in the world and of being reconciled to the fact of one's throwness in time and space. Phelps-Roper's homelessness can also be understood on this dual level, as she and her sister were both figuratively and literally homeless. But in the interest of theorizing the experience of being in the "now," and thinking about the process of making a home in the *nunc stans*, it is the figurative homelessness that is of significance here, and is considered in Arendtian terms.

In 1943, Arendt published a short article entitled "We Refugees," where she writes about the state of homelessness experienced by Jewish newcomers to America: "We [refugees] lost our homes, which means the familiarity of daily life."[116] The loss of their homes was—for the Jewish people forced to flee Nazi Germany—compounded by the horrors of trying to escape a system intent on exterminating their entire race. The ensuing loss of a sense of the "familiarity of daily life," which Arendt describes, is akin to—though far from being equivalent to—the homelessness experienced by Phelps-Roper when she and her sister left the WBC. These two women lost their "home," and as Phelps-Roper states, "suddenly my entire worldview was completely up in the air—I wasn't sure about anything and suddenly we had no idea [what to do]."[117] In the transitory moment of the *nunc stans*, Phelps-Roper was homeless in time, as she lacked, to a large extent, "familiarity" with the world, having never been freely "adrift" in the world beyond the ideological walls and cyclical reasoning of her former community. Groomed within the thoroughly ideological "framework," violent processes of indoctrination perverted her understanding.[118] This kept her ensnared in an unfree logic of circular arguments/evidence, and life was consequently characterized by an abyssal darkness engendered by the fact that her "entire worldview" had fallen away, voiding the past as a source of support in her confrontation with the future ahead. The certainty of her faith in God's ultimate judgment had been eroded to such an extent that the very foundations of her existence in the world had been destabilized: requiring her to "mind the gap" in time, reimagining—or renegotiating—her movement through time.

During the transitory period of time between her time at the WBC and her post-WBC life, Phelps-Roper and her sister "were shocked to find the light and a way forward in the same communities [they'd] targeted for so long."[119] The figurative sense of homelessness experienced by her thinking ego in the abyssal darkness of the "standing now," however, corresponded to her need to think through everything, which means—from an Arendtian perspective—to (re-)reconcile herself or to try to understand anew the realities of the world as well as her place in the world. Recognizing this need, and demonstrating her self-awareness of having a more developed, critical understanding of herself and the world, Phelps-Roper writes:

> I wouldn't have had the vocabulary or self-awareness to convey it at the time, but at the root of all my words was a pathological imperative that has never left me, one that continues to override the usual etiquette of distant, restrained discourse with strangers. I was animated by a set of twin desires that I now understand will never be satisfied: the need to understand, and to be understood.[120]

For Arendt, as one will recall, understanding "is an unending [mental] activity" by which we "come to terms with, and reconcile ourselves to reality, that is, to try to be at home in the world."[121] We can identify in Phelps-Roper's words a similar strain of thought, recognition of the significance of making a "home," or of "understanding" her place in both time and space. This cognitive process lays the foundations for the creation of new temporal-spatial imaginaries. Actively attempting to be at "home" in the world, which required Phelps-Roper to renew her understanding of "everything," was/is a most difficult mental process. She states, in an April 2016 interview with *The Guardian*: "It's an ongoing process of deep deprogramming."[122] The need for this process of "deep deprogramming" emerges as a result of her coming to dwell in "abyss of nothingness," where her very presence in the gap between past and future requires her to (re)imagine her very beingness in space and time. This is a mental practice that she now has to undertake without the prejudices, principles, and people of the WBC to frame her thinking.

Alone in her "fight" in time, with only her imagination to dispel the darkness of the abyssal gap of the *nunc stans*, Phelps-Roper must make herself at "home" in the "abyss of nothingness," within the "small non-time space at the very heart of time," beginning anew is to reflectively and reflexively (re)negotiate her own understanding. Like Kafka's "he," "she" must do her best to "give battle" to the forces that press upon her from behind and that block the road ahead; this is a temporal conflict that Phelps-Roper cannot escape, though it is one that can be endured with the "gift" of the imagination. Furthermore, it is the imagination, which "actually is understanding," that will allow her to be at "home" in the ever-fleeting moment of the "standing now": the point in time which is necessarily voided by the freedom inherent to beginning anew in the world.

To act anew from within this perpetually shifting moment is to stand bravely resolute on the temporal "fighting line" and to "think the unthinkable," that is, to assume a forward-looking, backward-focused temporal orientation in order to face her "two antagonists." In other words, "she" can be lauded for her courage as well as her efforts to "mind the gap" in time and to "give battle" to the forces of both past and future, a "fight" that occurs in an "abyss" in time that is voided of any and all certainty; such uncertainty is the very factor that induces a figurative sense of homelessness which causes a sort of unfamiliarity that "she" had to come to understand. Phelps-Roper's departure from the WBC, then, was not easy, for the darkness of this voided moment of nothingness was especially dense as a result of her lifetime of indoctrination, yet it is she who acknowledges that such abysses are the very place in time to begin anew in the world and to put an end to the unending "spiral of rage and blame [. . .] we just have to decide that it's going to start with us."[123] Beginnings can be founded by public acts of care (such as a caring forgiveness and a caring cosmopolitanism), as illustrated by the actions of Phelps-Roper's Twitter friends, since such acts open "abysses of nothingness" in time where people can act and begin anew: such beginnings are possible even if narratives that have previously been unfolding appear to be dark and deplorable.

While Phelps-Roper is but a single "she" who has determined how to "mind the gap" in time and renew her relationship to the world, her story can nevertheless serve as an example when reflecting upon political bodies of people since both an individual "she" and a collective "we" must constantly (re)negotiate the rift in time between past and future if freedom is to be (continuously) experienced in worldly, public spaces. For both a "she" and a "we," it is necessary to open abysses of "nothingness" in time, for such abyssal gaps are where freedom can be experienced and in which a sense of worldly homeliness can be established in between the indissociable, incommensurable temporal tenses of past and future. If life is to be more than a mere matter of caring for one's eternally recurring private needs, which are and will forever be the existential foundation for all (non-)human life, it is necessary to publicly take care of such abysses in time, that is, to care for the world by facilitating the (re)opening of rifts in time where "nothingness" can become the point of origination of new, free courses of political action. Moreover, it is critically important to attempt ceaselessly to be more and more at "home" in such abysses, which is to say become "familiar" with the darkness of this temporal in-between space. To come to dwell in this moment between past and future is difficult, but, as Phelps-Roper states, "I sincerely believe we can do hard things, not just for the [Other with whom we share the world] but for us and our future."[124] In short, negotiating a "she" or a "we" through the dark temporal space of the "now" is no easy feat, but it must be done for the sake of the world, freedom, and the future.

NOTES

1. *"Tutte le volpi si trovano in pellicaria."*—Italian proverb.
2. Hannah Arendt, "Heidegger the Fox," in *Essays in Understanding, 1930–1954: Formation, Exile, and Totalitarianism*, ed. Jerome Kohn (New York: Schocken Books, 1994), 361.
3. Hannah Arendt, *Denktagebuch, 1950 bis 1973*, hrsg. Ursula Ludz und Ingeborg Nordmann, Erster Band 1 (München: Piper Verlag, 2002), 403–4. Throughout this chapter, I have relied on the Robert and Rita Kimber translation of this allegory: Arendt, "Heidegger the Fox."
4. Jacques Derrida, *The Beast and the Sovereign: Volume I*, eds. Michel Lisse, Marie-Louise Mallet, and Ginette Michaud, trans. Geoffrey Bennington (London: The University of Chicago Press, 2009), 80.
5. Ibid., 89.
6. Arendt, "Heidegger the Fox," 361.
7. Ibid.
8. Leland de la Durantaye, *Giorgio Agamben: A Critical Introduction* (Stanford, CA: Stanford University Press, 2009), 307.

9. Arendt, "Heidegger the Fox," 362.
10. Heidegger, *Being and Time*, 44.
11. Jacques Derrida, *Positions*, trans. Alan Bass (Chicago: The University of Chicago Press, 1972), 10.
12. Heidegger, *Being and Time*, 473.
13. Gayatri Chakravorty Spivak, "Translator's Press," in *Of Grammatology*, trans. Gayatri Chakravorty Spivak (London: The Johns Hopkins University Press, 1997), xlix–l.
14. Charles A. Pressler, "Redoubled: The Bridging of Derrida and Heidegger," *Human Studies* 7 (1984): 329.
15. Ibid.
16. Derrida, *Speech and Phenomena*, 154.
17. Pressler, "Redoubled," 329.
18. Derrida, *Speech and Phenomena*, 131.
19. Richard Beardsworth, *Derrida & the Political* (London: Routledge, 1996), 106.
20. Ibid., 33.
21. I use the phrase "private care" in reference to the activity of labor and "public care" to refer to practices of caring for the world; additionally, it is worth noting here that work is an activity closely related to both private and public care as well as the two forms of temporality associated with each of these two spatially determined types of care.
22. Jacques Derrida, "Ousia and Grammē: Note on a Note from Being and Time," in *Margins of Philosophy*, trans. Alan Bass (Brighton, UK: The Harverster Press, 1982), 31–67. In this essay, Derrida suggests that "there is no chance that within the thematic of metaphysics anything might have budged, as concerns the concept of time, from Aristotle to Hegel." [1968: 39] That is, Derrida asserts that the Western philosophic tradition began with, and stayed true to, Aristotle's formulation of time as an aporetic notion that is expounded upon in *Physics* (IV, chapters 10–14). [See Aristotle, *Physics*, trans. Robin Waterfield (Oxford: Oxford University Press, 1996), 102–17.]
23. Arendt, *The Life of Mind*, pt. II, pg. 207.
24. Ibid., pt. I, pgs. 202–16. In terms of the *nunc stans*, see Arendt's discussion of "Willing" in Part II of *The Life of the Mind*. See also Arendt's discussion of the *nunc stans* in her doctoral thesis: Arendt, *Love and Saint Augustine*.
25. In the second section of this chapter, I use the phrase "temporal orientation" to describe the perspectival direction of one's glance as one moves through time. I use this term to consider the direction political actors need to face—in an abstract sense—as they negotiate the "standing now," which permits me to challenge perspectives which are entirely past-centric, present-centric, or future-centric.
26. Arendt, *The Life of Mind*, pt. I, pg. 210.
27. Arendt, *The Human Condition*, 88 and 83–84.
28. Ibid., 96. Emphasis added.
29. Ibid., 144.
30. Taminiaux, *The Thracian Maid and the Professional Thinker*, 200.

31. Arendt, *The Human Condition*, 143–44.
32. Ibid., 136–37.
33. Ibid., 97.
34. It is useful to recall the central thesis of Paul Ricœur's magnum opus, *Time and Narrative*: "time becomes human time to the extent that it is organized after the manner of a narrative; narrative, in turn, is meaningful to the extent that it portrays the features of temporal experience." [Paul Ricœur, *Time and Narrative*, trans. Kathleen McLaughlin and David Pellauer, vol. 1 (London: University of Chicago Press, 1984), 3.] For Ricœur, like Arendt, human time is narratable time, and stories told of such time are significant because they are thoroughly human. It also worth noting here that Ricœur was sympathetic to Arendt's work, and that it was he who penned the preface to French edition of *The Human Condition*; see Hannah Arendt, *Condition de l'homme Moderne*, trans. Georges Fradier (Paris: Calmann-Lévy, 1961).
35. Kristeva, *Hannah Arendt: Life Is a Narrative*, 8. Original emphasis.
36. In reference to Augustine's *City of God*, Arendt highlights the important role of memory in differentiating human beings from non-human beings when she asserts that "the difference between 'the species of rational mortals' and other created things, such as 'beasts, trees, stones,' is that the former possess consciousness, hence memory, and therefore can relate back to its own origin." [Arendt, *Love and Saint Augustine*, 51.]
37. Scott and Stark, "Rediscovering Hannah Arendt," 144.
38. Ibid., 145.
39. Arendt, *The Human Condition*, 9.
40. Ibid., 176–77. The stability of the public, political realm also requires various forms of work to take place in order to (re-)build a society's sociopolitical institutions and public spaces within which freedom can be housed.
41. Ibid., 177.
42. Arendt, *Between Past and Future*, 164–66. Original emphasis.
43. Genesis 3:17-19.
44. For Arendt, "power and freedom in the sphere of human plurality are in fact synonyms." [Arendt, *The Life of Mind*, pt. II, pg. 201.]
45. A discussion of themes similar to her reflections on Kafka's "He" can be found in: Hannah Arendt, "No Longer and Not Yet," in *Essays in Understanding, 1930–1954: Formation, Exile, and Totalitarianism*, ed. Jerome Kohn (New York: Schocken Books, 1994), 158–62.
46. Arendt, *Between Past and Future*, 12.
47. Arendt, *The Life of Mind*, pt. I, pg. 202.
48. Elisabeth Young-Bruehl, "Reflections on Hannah Arendt's the Life of the Mind," *Political Theory* 10, no. 2 (1982): 277.
49. On this point about humankind's conditioned existence in time and space, it is worth noting that Arendt outlines a non-deterministic theory of history in various places throughout her corpus, doing so most notably as a part of her efforts to understand totalitarianism. More specifically, her critique of historical determinism can be felt when she calls into question how totalitarian regimes—whether they be theoretically rooted in Marxism or the racist scientism of National Socialism—purport to be

supported by the "eternal laws of nature and life," which are—if one takes to heart the fallacies of materially deterministic approaches to the study of history—the "hidden forces" powering the unstoppable "train of history" that is progressing toward a predetermined final destination along a track of "fatality." [Arendt, *The Origins of Totalitarianism*, 345–46. See also: Margaret Canovan, "The Contradictions of Hannah Arendt's Political Thought," *Political Theory* 6, no. 1 (1978): 11.]

    50. Arendt, *The Life of Mind*, pt. I, pgs. 197 and 202.
    51. Ibid., pt. I, pg. 203.
    52. Ibid., pt. I, pgs. 202–3.
    53. Ibid., pt. I, pg. 203. Original emphasis.
    54. Arendt, *Between Past and Future*, 7; Arendt, *The Life of Mind*, pt. I, pg. 202; Franz Kafka, *The Great Wall of China*, trans. Willa Muir and Edwin Muir (New York: Schocken Books, 1946), 276–77. The currently available English version of this short parable differs from that which Arendt provides and that which she references, a matter of translation undoubtedly resultant of her taking liberties when "in a few places [. . .] a more literal translation was needed for [her] purposes" [Arendt, *Between Past and Future*, n. 3, p. 276]. Today, one can find this parable in: Franz Kafka, *Aphorisms*, trans. Willa Muir, Edwin Muir, and Michael Hofmann (New York: Schocken Books, 2015), 146.
    55. Arendt, *Between Past and Future*, 10.
    56. Arendt, *The Life of Mind*, pt. 1, pg. 207.
    57. Taminiaux, *The Thracian Maid and the Professional Thinker*, 207.
    58. Arendt, *The Life of Mind*, pt. I, pg. 205.
    59. Arendt, *Between Past and Future*, 10.
    60. Arendt, *The Life of Mind*, pt. I, pg. 207.
    61. In her reflections on Kafka's "He," in *The Life of the Mind*, Arendt refers to a diagram of temporal vectors that creates what physicists might call a "parallelogram of forces." By providing an illustration of the thinking ego's temporal experience, it depicts how the collision of two infinite forces, at the point where "he" stands in time, generates a new timeline, as "he" is a being whose very presence in the present moment begins a novel course of action. The diagonal line which originates at the terminal point of both past and future is a line which extends outward, "toward an undetermined end," as though "it could reach out into infinity." [Arendt, pt. I, pgs. 207–211.]
    62. Taminiaux, *The Thracian Maid and the Professional Thinker*, 211.
    63. Arendt, *The Life of Mind*, pt. I, pg. 78.
    64. Taminiaux, *The Thracian Maid and the Professional Thinker*, 211.
    65. Arendt, *The Life of Mind*, pt. I, pg. 205.
    66. Scott and Stark, "Rediscovering Hannah Arendt," 124.
    67. Heidegger, *Being and Time*, 289.
    68. Arendt, *Love and Saint Augustine*, 51.
    69. Patricia Bowen-Moore, *Hannah Arendt's Philosophy of Natality* (London: Macmillan Press, 1989), 1.
    70. Arendt, *Love and Saint Augustine*, 56.
    71. Arendt, *The Life of Mind*, pt. I, pg. 85.

72. Arendt, "Understanding and Politics," 309.
73. Derrida, *Negotiations*, 12.
74. Ibid.
75. Ibid., 13.
76. Marko Zlomislic, *Jacques Derrida's Aporetic Ethics* (New York: Lexington Books, 2007), 103.
77. Arendt, *The Life of Mind*, pt. I, pg. 72.
78. Ibid., pt. I, pg. 175.
79. Blunt and Dowling, *Home*, 2.
80. Ibid.
81. Arendt, *The Life of Mind*, pt. I, pg. 76.
82. Arendt, "Understanding and Politics," 323.
83. Ibid., 308. Emphasis added.
84. See in particular: Ronald Beiner, "Hannah Arendt on Judging," in *Lectures on Kant's Political Philosophy*, ed. Ronald Beiner (Chicago: The University of Chicago Press, 1992), 89–156; Ronald Beiner and Jennifer Nedelsky, eds., *Judgment, Imagination, and Politics: Themes from Kant and Arendt* (Oxford: Rowman & Littlefield Publishers, Inc., 2001); Seyla Benhabib, "Judgment and the Moral Foundations of Politics in Arendt's Thought," *Political Theory* 16, no. 1 (1988): 29–51; Patrick Hayden, "Arendt and the Political Power of Judgement," in *Hannah Arendt: Key Concepts*, ed. Patrick Hayden (Durham, UK: Acumen Publishing, 2014), 167–84; Naomi Head, "Bringing Reflective Judgement into International Relations: Exploring the Rwandan Genocide," *Journal of Global Ethics* 6, no. 2 (2010): 191–204; Bronwyn Leebaw, *Judging State-Sponsored Violence, Imagining Political Change* (Cambridge: Cambridge University Press, 2011); Mathias Thaler, "Political Judgment beyond Paralysis and Heroism," *European Journal of Political Theory* 10, no. 2 (2011): 225–53; Albrecht Wellmer, "Hannah Arendt on Judgment: The Unwritten Doctrine of Reason," in *Hannah Arendt: Twenty Years Later*, eds. Larry May and Jerome Kohn (Cambridge, MA: The MIT Press, 1997), 33–52; Linda M. G. Zerilli, "'We Feel Our Freedom': Imagination and Judgment in the Thought of Hannah Arendt," *Political Theory* 33, no. 2 (2005): 158–88.
85. Arendt, *Lectures on Kant's Political Philosophy*, 80.
86. Arendt, "Understanding and Politics," 323.
87. Arendt, *Lectures on Kant's Political Philosophy*, 43.
88. I am referring here to Arendt's reference to the "darkness of the human heart," as can be found in her discussion of the practice of making/keeping promises in *The Human Condition* and her reflections in "Understanding and Politics" (1954).
89. Arendt, *The Human Condition*, 244.
90. Arendt, *Love and Saint Augustine*, 26.
91. Respectively: Arendt, *The Human Condition*, 244; Arendt, "Understanding and Politics," 322.
92. Arendt, *The Origins of Totalitarianism*, 478–79.
93. Arendt, *The Life of Mind*, pt. II, pg. 198. A parallel discussion of this aspect of her understanding can also be found in Arendt, *On Revolution*, 171–206.
94. Arendt, *The Life of Mind*, pt. II, pgs. 198–200.
95. Ibid., pt. II, pg. 201.

96. Ricardo J. Quinones, "Byron's Cain: Between History and Theology," in *Byron, the Bible, and Religion: Essays from the Twelfth International Byron Seminar*, ed. Wolf Z. Hirst (Newark: University of Delaware Press, 1991), 48.

97. Ibid.

98. Genesis 4:11-12. NIV.

99. Arendt, *On Revolution*, 132; Arendt, *The Life of Mind*, pt. II, pg. 204.

100. Arendt, *The Life of Mind*, pt. II, pgs. 207–8. Original emphasis.

101. Ibid.

102. Arendt, *The Human Condition*, 237.

103. Barrett-Fox, *God Hates*.

104. Amanda van Eck Duymaer van Twist, *Perfect Children: Growing Up on the Religious Fringe* (Oxford: Oxford University Press, 2015).

105. Phelps-Roper, *Unfollow*, 227.

106. Ibid.

107. Ibid.

108. Ibid.

109. Harris, "Leaving the Church: A Conversation with Megan Phelps-Roper."

110. Phelps-Roper, *Unfollow*, 168–69.

111. Ibid., 169–70.

112. Here, Arendt's discussion of thoughtlessness is most useful in understanding how rule-based ethico-political systems can easily give way to a dogmatic subservience that props up paradigms of cruelty and inhumanity. It is also interesting to note how the WBC has been able to cultivate and perpetuate a form of what Arendt describes as an "ideological supersense," whereby this group has managed to "establish a functioning world of no-sense." [Arendt, *The Origins of Totalitarianism*, 457–58.]

113. Phelps-Roper, *Unfollow*, 238–39.

114. Phelps-Roper, "I Grew up in the Westboro Baptist Church. Here's Why I Left." Emphasis added.

115. Ibid. Emphasis added.

116. Arendt, *The Jewish Writings*, 264.

117. Harris, "Leaving the Church: A Conversation with Megan Phelps-Roper."

118. In her reflections on "understanding," Arendt highlights how indoctrination, which is a type of weapon when in the hands of totalitarian governments, "is dangerous because it springs primarily from a perversion, not of knowledge, but of understanding." [Arendt, "Understanding and Politics," 308–9.]

119. Phelps-Roper, "I Grew up in the Westboro Baptist Church. Here's Why I Left."

120. Phelps-Roper, *Unfollow*, 66.

121. Arendt, "Understanding and Politics," 307–8.

122. Shahesta Shaitly, "Losing My Religion: Life after Extreme Belief," *The Guardian*, April 10, 2016, https://www.theguardian.com/world/2016/apr/10/losing-my-religion-life-after-extreme-belief-faith.

123. Phelps-Roper, "I Grew up in the Westboro Baptist Church. Here's Why I Left."

124. Ibid.

Conclusion

In concluding this book, it is significant that I should return once again to the subject of beginning anew. After all, Arendt is foremost a theorist of new beginnings: the promise that is identical with human freedom and which is guaranteed by each new birth. This new beginning, this potentiality, or this power of "freedom"—which "is indeed every man"—*is* the "miracle" of life,[1] where the "is" that I have emphasized here corresponds with the "is"-ness of how people are themselves new beginnings and how this capacity takes place right "now," in the "gap" between past and future. This temporal "in-between" is "where" miracles happen, which is to say, "when" the miraculous transpires and a new beginning takes place. Though Derrida is perhaps right to suggest that the "now" is never fully now, as it is always a past present and a present future, we can nevertheless be said to perform, or enact, this miracle from within the ever-fleeting moment of the *nunc stans*. This is the "standing now" where we presently exist in time, a "place" where we are perfectly positioned to begin—spontaneously and freely—new courses of action as we transition from what has been to what is yet to come.

The "now" *is* the time of and for new beginnings, when—so to speak—we might keep the "promise" of our humanity and embody this miraculous "capacity," one which "bestow[s] upon human affairs faith and hope, those two essential characteristics of human existence" that accompany the "miracle that saves the world [. . .] from its normal, 'natural' ruin [. . .] the fact of natality."[2] About these "two essential characteristics" of human life, Arendt writes:

> It is this faith in and hope for the world that found perhaps its most glorious and most succinct expression in the few words with which the Gospels announced their "glad tidings": "A child has been born unto us."[3]

The birth of this "child," the arrival of the "messiah" (or "savior"), who marks the presence of God on Earth, is precisely that which is promised, nay—as Arendt suggests—"it *is* indeed every man."[4] When thinking about the miracle of human *beginning*-ness, or of *being* a new beginning, it is consequently amazing and invigorating to know that we—as mere mortals—can tap into the very power of God (as Creator and the "I AM" present equally in the human "was," "is," and "is to come"), which is to say, make real—in the mode of human togetherness—the power of freedom. In recognition of this aspect of our humanity, I have—throughout this book—considered how we might go about better facilitating and caring for worldly spaces, within which the "promise" of freedom that *is* us can be renewed and made flesh *with* a plurality of other people in the public realm of the political. It is in "action"—the "one miracle-working faculty of man"[5]—that we realize, literally bring into the "real world," as if a "child" was "born unto us," the most human of human capacities: the ability to begin.

In reconsidering the notions of cosmopolitanism and forgiveness in terms of "care," my intent has been to understand how we might ensure that the "promise of politics" (to borrow the title of Arendt's book of the same name)—a new beginning—can be made manifest in the "world." In a period of human history when "nobody cares any longer what the world looks like" (Arendt), and when we must manage to "scratch out a pleasant, simple tune" without any "roof" to stand on, my goal has been to illustrate several of the ways in which we might care for our "world." In particular, I have—through an investigation of the notions of cosmopolitanism and forgiveness, two "pearls" that I have pulled from the "depths" of *le héritage*—sought to understand how we can facilitate the opening of abysses in time, when and where we can embody the power of God himself: "I AM!" This is the power of freedom: the "promise" of a new beginning—of salvation from that which has already been—that both a caring cosmopolitanism and forgiveness hope to (re-)engender in the realm of human affairs. This is why each of these two notions is powerful: they are acts of and for the power of human freedom.

Where a caring forgiveness is devoted to freeing people from endless cycles of violence and counterviolence, and thus of "undo[ing] the deeds of the past, whose 'sins' hang like Damocles' sword over every new generation,"[6] a caring cosmopolitanism is dedicated to welcoming the narrative voice of the (unknown) Other, thereby acting hospitably to them as equal co-storytellers in the ever-unfolding "storybook of mankind": history. Both in forgiving and acting hospitably to the voice of the (unknown) Other, we practice what I have presented throughout this book in terms of the notion of "dilatation" that Victor Hugo describes when he writes: "*La réduction de l'univers à un seul être, la dilatation d'un seul être jusqu'à Dieu, voilà l'amour.*"[7] To forgive and to welcome the Other as a co-storyteller in the "world" is, effectively, to "dilate"—to open in a radical manner—the public realm of "the political," or to widen in a hyperbolic way the "space for politics." It is in terms of a caring cosmopolitanism and forgiveness that I have pursued the aim of theorizing what Derrida describes as a "democracy to come": the so-called *khôra* of the political.[8] Thus, when we deconstruct the ideas of forgiveness and cosmopolitanism, and subsequently *re*-construct them in terms of "care" and "caring for the world," it is my belief that we might be able *to do* justice, putting "thinking into action" in the mode of a "ruthless criticism of everything existing" (Marx). This is to make, as Critchley and Kearney suggest, a "concrete intervention in contexts that is governed by an undeconstructable concern for justice."[9] This being said, and to distinguish a more thoroughly Derridean approach from the more Arendtian theory that I have developed throughout this book, this is a sense of justice that we must seek not in terms of the Other *as* Other, but in terms of the "world" shared with them. That is, when practicing a caring cosmopolitanism and caring forgiveness, we are thinking not only about the "face" of the (unknown) Other but, rather, the "in-between" that both binds and separates those persons and peoples who appear to speak and act together in the "world." This is not to say that we do not care about the "stranger," "widow," and "orphan" but, instead, that we recognize the political significance of caring for the "space for politics," which is where the power of freedom can be enacted, and thus miracles can be performed *with* these people. It is by thinking and acting in terms of the "world," and out of a sense of *amor mundi*, that we might—for instance—avoid becoming ensnared in any "fox traps," and that we might be able to begin re-illuminating the public, realm of "the political" when darkness has descended.

Whether it be the "dark times" about which Arendt writes in her work on totalitarianism or those of today, a period in history when we have seen a rise in extreme sociopolitical polarization and a troubling resurgence of populist politics around the globe, there is—paradoxically—a need to embrace moments of darkness for what they might be: abyssal spaces in time where freedom can be experienced. Borrowed from Bertolt Brecht's 1939 poem "To Posterity" (which is sometimes alternatively translated from the original German as "To Those Who Follow in Our Wake"),[10] the phrase "dark times" is used by Arendt to encapsulate her understanding of the darkness associated with the storm clouds of violence and terror that enshrouded her "world." Brecht writes in his poem: "The old books teach us what wisdom is/ To retreat from the strife of the world [. . .] But I cannot heed this:/ Truly I live in dark times!"[11] Each recognizing the impossibility of retreating from the world or seeking shelter within their individual private spheres, both Arendt and Brecht assert that people must continue to live and act in public spaces regardless of the "sandstorms" which may "whip up" a violent, terrifying movement around them.[12] The message of Brecht's poem and

Arendt's work is intended for "those who follow in [their] wake"; people who are bequeathed the burdensome task of conserving and (re)constructing the "in-between" spaces and the common realms of human existence, that is, the "world." Here, the words of philosopher and ecocritical scholar Charles Eisenstein spring to mind. In a passage that captures well the inherently paradoxical, beautiful difficulty of being situated in time and experiencing the abyssal in-between space where freedom is possible and new narrative beginnings can emerge, he writes:

> If we are stuck and do not choose to visit the empty place, eventually we will end up there anyway. [. . .] The old world falls apart, but the new has not emerged. [. . .] You don't know what to think, what to do; you don't know what anything means anymore. The life trajectory you had plotted out seems absurd, and you can't imagine another one. Everything is uncertain. [. . .] Without the mirages of order that once seemed to protect you and filter reality, you feel naked and vulnerable, but also a kind of freedom. Possibilities that didn't even exist in the old story lie before you, even if you have no idea how to get there. The challenge in our culture is to allow yourself to be in that space, to trust that the next story will emerge when the time in between has ended, and that you will recognize it. [. . .] The old story we leave behind, which is usually part of the consensus Story of the People, releases us with great reluctance. [. . .] If you are in the sacred spaces between stories, allow yourself to be there. [. . .] You will find yourself in closer contact to something much more precious, something that fires cannot burn, and thieves cannot steal, something that no one can take and cannot be lost. We might lose sight of it sometimes, but it is always there waiting for us. This is the resting place we return to when the old story falls apart. Clear of its fog, we can now receive a true vision of the next world, the next story, the next phase of life. From the marriage of this vision and this emptiness, a great power is born.[13]

As Eisenstein suggests, it is in these empty moments, these "in-betweens," that people can be free, can experience power, and can begin anew. This book has demonstrated how forgiveness and cosmopolitanism "care for the world" by ensuring that political actors can continue to possess the ability to initiate new action(s) and to develop freely new plot lines in the ever-unfolding metanarrative of human history: this capacity is the power to perform miracles.

NOTES

1. Arendt, *The Origins of Totalitarianism*, 479.
2. Arendt, *The Human Condition*, 247.
3. Ibid.
4. Arendt, *The Origins of Totalitarianism*, 479.

5. Arendt, *The Human Condition*, 246.
6. Ibid., 237.
7. Hugo, *Les Misérables*, 194.
8. Derrida, *Rogues: Two Essays on Reason*, 82.
9. Derrida, *On Cosmopolitanism and Forgiveness*, viii.
10. Brecht, *Bertolt Brecht: Plays, Poetry and Prose*.
11. Ibid., 318.
12. Arendt, *The Promise of Politics*, 201–2.
13. Charles Eisenstein, *The More Beautiful World Our Hearts Know Is Possible* (Berkeley, CA: North Atlantic Books, 2013), 122.

Bibliography

Arendt, Hannah. *Men in Dark Times*. New York: Harcourt, Brace & World, Inc., 1951.
———. *The Human Condition*. Chicago: The University of Chicago Press, 1958.
———. "Action and the 'Pursuit of Happiness': A Lecture." In *Annual Meeting of the American Political Science Association*. New York, 1960.
———. "Introduction: Walter Benjamin, 1892–1940." In *Illuminations: Essays and Reflections*, edited by Hannah Arendt, translated by Harry Zorn, 1–55. New York: Schocken Books, 1968.
———. *The Origins of Totalitarianism*. London: Harvest Book, 1968.
———. *On Violence*. New York: Harcourt Publishing Company, 1969.
———. *The Life of Mind*. London: Harvest Book, 1978.
———. "On Hannah Arendt." In *Hannah Arendt: The Recovery of the Public World*, edited by Melvyn Hill, 301–39. New York: St. Martin's Press, 1979.
———. *Lectures on Kant's Political Philosophy*. Edited by Ronald Beiner. Chicago: University of Chicago Press, 1992.
———. *Love and Saint Augustine*. Edited by Joanna Vecchiarelli Scott and Judith Chelius Stark. London: The University of Chicago Press, 1996.
———. *Denktagebuch, 1950 Bis 1973*. Edited by Ursula Ludz and Ingeborg Nordmann. Vol. 1. München: Piper Verlag, 2002.
———. *Responsibility and Judgment*. Edited by Jerome Kohn. New York: Schocken Books, 2003.
———. *The Promise of Politics*. New York: Schocken Books, 2005.
———. *Between Past and Future*. New York: Penguin Books, 2006.
———. *Eichmann in Jerusalem: A Report on the Banality of Evil*. London: Penguin Books, 2006.
———. *On Revolution*. London: Penguin Books, 2006.
———. "The Great Tradition: II. Ruling and Being Ruled." *Social Research* 74, no. 4 (2007): 941–54.

———. *The Jewish Writings*. Edited by Jerome Kohn and Ron H. Feldman. New York: Schocken Books, 2007.
Arendt, Hannah, and Karl Jaspers. *Hannah Arendt Karl Jaspers Correspondence: 1926–1969*. Edited by Lotte Kohler and Hans Saner. Translated by Robert and Rita Kimber. London: Harvest Book, 1985.
Aristotle. *The Complete Works of Aristotle: Volume II*. Edited by Jonathan Barnes. Princeton: Princeton University Press, 1984.
———. *Physics*. Translated by Robin Waterfield. Oxford: Oxford University Press, 1996.
Bacon, Francis. *The Essays of Francis Bacon*. Edited by Mary Augusta Scott. New York: Charles Scribner's Sons, 1908.
Baehr, Peter. *Hannah Arendt, Totalitarianism, and the Social Sciences*. Stanford: Stanford University Press, 2010.
Barrett-Fox, Rebecca. *God Hates: Westboro Baptist Church, American Nationalism, and the Religious Right*. Lawrence, KS: University Press of Kansas, 2016.
Barthes, Roland. *Image-Music-Text*. Translated by Stephen Heath. New York: Fontana Press, 1977.
Beardsworth, Richard. *Derrida & the Political*. London: Routledge, 1996.
Beck, Ulrich. *Cosmopolitan Vision*. Oxford: Polity Press, 2006.
Beiner, Ronald. "Hannah Arendt on Judging." In *Lectures On Kant's Political Philosophy*, edited by Ronald Beiner, 89–156. Chicago: The University of Chicago Press, 1992.
Beiner, Ronald, and Jennifer Nedelsky, eds. *Judgment, Imagination, and Politics: Themes from Kant and Arendt*. Oxford: Rowman & Littlefield Publishers, Inc., 2001.
Benhabib, Seyla. "Judgment and the Moral Foundations of Politics in Arendt's Thought." *Political Theory* 16, no. 1 (1988): 29–51.
———. "Hannah Arendt and the Redemptive Power of Narrative." *Social Research* 57, no. 1 (1990): 167–96.
———. *The Reluctant Modernism of Hannah Arendt*. London: Sage Publications, 1996.
Berkowitz, Roger. "Bearing Logs on Our Shoulders: Reconciliation, Non-Reconciliation, and the Building of a Common World." *Theory & Event* 14, no. 1 (2011a). doi:10.1353/tae.2011.0001.
———. "'The Angry Jew Has Gotten His Revenge': Hannah Arendt on Revenge and Reconciliation." *Philosophical Topics* 39, no. 2 (2011b): 1–20.
———. "Reconciling Oneself to the Impossibility of Reconciliation: Judgment and Worldliness in Hannah Arendt's Politics." In *Artifacts of Thinking: Reading Hannah Arendt's Denktagebuch*, edited by Roger Berkowitz and Ian Storey, 9–36. New York: Fordham University Press, 2017.
Berlin, Isaiah. "Two Concepts of Liberty." In *Liberty*, edited by Henry Hardy, 166–217. Oxford: Oxford University Press, 2002.
Blunt, Alison, and Robyn Dowling. *Home*. London: Routledge, 2006.
Borradori, Giovanna. *Philosophy in a Time of Terror: Dialogues with Jürgen Habermas and Jacques Derrida*. Chicago: The University of Chicago Press, 2003.
Bowen-Moore, Patricia. *Hannah Arendt's Philosophy of Natality*. London: Macmillan Press, 1989.

Brecht, Bertolt. "To Those Born Later." In *Bertolt Brecht: Plays, Poetry and Prose*, edited by John Willett and Ralph Manheim, 318–20. London: Eyre Methuen, 1976.

Broggi, Joshua D. *Sacred Language, Sacred World: The Unity of Scriptural and Philosophical Hermeneutics*. London: Bloomsbury, 2016.

Buckler, Steve. *Hannah Arendt and Political Theory: Challenging the Tradition*. Edinburgh: Edinburgh University Press, 2011.

Canovan, Margaret. "The Contradictions of Hannah Arendt's Political Thought." *Political Theory* 6, no. 1 (1978): 5–26.

Caze, Marguerite La. *Wonder and Generosity: Their Role in Ethics and Politics*. Albany, NY: State University of New York Press, 2013.

———. "It's Easier to Lie If You Believe It Yourself: Derrida, Arendt, and the Modern Lie." *Law, Culture and the Humanities* 13, no. 2 (2017): 193–210.

———. "Introduction: Situating Forgiveness within Phenomenology." In *Phenomenology and Forgiveness*, edited by Marguerite La Caze, vii–xxii. London: Rowman & Littlefield International, 2018.

Chen, Adrian. "Unfollow: How a Prized Daughter of the Westboro Baptist Church Came to Question Its Beliefs." *The New Yorker*, November 16, 2015. https://www.newyorker.com/magazine/2015/11/23/conversion-via-twitter-westboro-baptist-church-megan-phelps-roper.

Critchley, Simon. *Ethics-Politics-Subjectivity: Essays on Derrida, Levinas and Contemporary French Thought*. London: Verso, 1999.

Critchley, Simon, and Richard Kearney. "Preface." In *On Cosmopolitanism and Forgiveness*, edited by Simon Critchley and Richard Kearney, translated by Mark Dooley and Michael Hughes, vii–xii. London: Routledge, 2001.

Damai, Puspa. "Messianic-City: Ruins, Refuge and Hospitality in Derrida." *Discourse* 27 (2005): 68–94.

Derrida, Jacques. *De La Grammatologie*. Paris: Les Éditions de Minuit, 1967.

———. *Positions*. Translated by Alan Bass. Chicago: The University of Chicago Press, 1972.

———. *Speech and Phenomena: And Other Essays on Husserl's Theory of Signs*. Translated by David B. Allison and Newton Garver. Evanston, IL: Northwestern University Press, 1973.

———. *Dissemination*. Translated by Barbara Johnson. London: The Athlone Press, 1981.

———. *Margins of Philosophy*. Translated by Alan Bass. Brighton, UK: The Harverster Press, 1982.

———. "Letter to a Japanese Friend." In *Derrida and Différance*, edited by David Wood and Robert Bernasconi, translated by Andrew Benjamin, 1–5. Evanston, IL: Northwestern University Press, 1988.

———. *Limited Inc*. Edited by Gerald Graff. Evanston, IL: Northwestern University Press, 1988.

———. "Force of Law: The 'Mystical Foundation of Authority.'" In *Deconstruction and the Possibility of Justice*, edited by Drucilla Cornell, Michel Rosenfeld, and David Gray Carlson, 3–67. London: Routledge, 1992.

———. *Given Time: I. Counterfeit Money*. Edited by Peggy Kamuf. Chicago: The University of Chicago Press, 1992.

———. *Aporias*. Stanford: Stanford University Press, 1993.
———. *Khôra*. Paris: Galilée, 1993.
———. *On the Name*. Stanford, CA: Stanford University Press, 1995.
———. *The Gift of Death*. Chicago: University of Chicago Press, 1995.
———. *Of Grammatology*. Translated by Gayatri Chakravorty Spivak. London: The Johns Hopkins University Press, 1997.
———. "Hostipitality." Translated by Barry Stocker and Forbes Morlock. *Angelaki: Journal of the Theoretical Humanities* 5, no. 3 (2000): 3–18.
———. *Of Hospitality: Anne Dufourmantelle Invites Jacques Derrida to Respond*. Stanford: Stanford University Press, 2000.
———. *On Cosmopolitanism and Forgiveness*. Translated by Mark Dooley and Michael Hughes. London: Routledge, 2001.
———. "The Future of the Profession or the University without Condition (Thanks to the 'Humanities', What Could Take Place Tomorrow)." In *Jacques Derrida and the Humanities: A Critical Reader*, edited by Tom Cohen, 24–57. Cambridge: Cambridge University Press, 2001.
———. "To Forgive: The Unforgivable and the Imprescriptable." In *Questioning God*, edited by John D. Caputo, Mark Dooley, and Michael J. Scanlon, 21–51. Bloomington, IN: Indiana University Press, 2001.
———. *Writing and Difference*. Translated by Alan Bass. London: Routledge, 2001.
———. *Acts of Religion*. Edited by Gil Anidjar. London: Routledge, 2002.
———. *Negotiations: Interventions and Interviews, 1971–2001*. Edited by Elizabeth Rottenberg. Stanford, CA: Stanford University Press, 2002.
———. *Without Alibi*. Edited and translated by Peggy Kamuf. Stanford, CA: Stanford University Press, 2002.
———. *Rogues: Two Essays on Reason*. Translated by Pascale-Anne Brault and Michael Naas. Stanford, CA: Stanford University Press, 2005.
———. *Specters of Marx: The State of the Debt, the Work of Mourning and the New International*. Edited by Bernd Magnus and Stephen Cullenberg. Translated by Peggy Kamuf. London: Routledge, 2006.
———. *The Beast and the Sovereign: Volume I*. Edited by Michel Lisse, Marie-Louise Mallet, and Ginette Michaud. Translated by Geoffrey Bennington. London: The University of Chicago Press, 2009.
———. *Theory and Practice*. Edited by Geoffrey Bennington and Peggy Kamuf. Translated by David Wills. London: The University of Chicago Press, 2019.
Derrida, Jacques, and Elizabeth Roudinesco. *For What Tomorrow... (A Dialogue)*. Translated by Jeff Fort. Stanford, CA: Stanford University Press, 2004.
Digeser, P.E. *Political Forgiveness*. Ithaca: Cornell University Press, 2001.
Disch, Lisa J. "More Truth Than Fact: Storytelling as Critical Understanding in the Writings of Hannah Arendt." *Political Theory* 21, no. 4 (1993): 665–94.
Eck Duymaer van Twist, Amanda van. *Perfect Children: Growing Up on the Religious Fringe*. Oxford: Oxford University Press, 2015.
Eisenstein, Charles. *The More Beautiful World Our Hearts Know Is Possible*. Berkeley, CA: North Atlantic Books, 2013.
Emmons, Shelese. "The Debre Bill: Immigration Legislation or a National 'Front'?" *Indiana Journal of Global Legal Studies* 5, no. 1 (1997): 357–66.

Ettinger, Elżbieta. *Hannah Arendt/Martin Heidegger*. New Haven, CT: Yale University Press, 1995.

Fischer, Gerhard, ed. *With The Sharpened Axe of Reason: Approaches to Walter Benjamin*. Oxford: Berg Publishers, 1996.

Fisher, Berenice, and Joan Tronto. "Toward a Feminist Theory of Caring." In *Circles of Care: Work and Identity in Women's Lives*, edited by Emily K. Abel and Margaret K. Nelson, 35–62. New York: State University of New York Press, 1990.

Foucault, Michel. *The Care of the Self*. New York: Pantheon Books, 1986.

Granovetter, Mark S. "The Strength of Weak Ties." *American Journal of Sociology* 78, no. 6 (1973): 1360–80.

Haddad, Samir. "Arendt, Derrida, and the Inheritance of Forgiveness." *Philosophy Today* 51, no. 4 (2007): 416–26.

Harris, Sam. "Leaving the Church: A Conversation with Megan Phelps-Roper." *Making Sense*, July 3, 2015. https://samharris.org/podcasts/leaving-the-church/.

Hayden, Patrick. "Arendt and the Political Power of Judgement." In *Hannah Arendt: Key Concepts*, edited by Patrick Hayden, 167–84. Durham, UK: Acumen Publishing, 2014.

———. "From Political Friendship to Befriending the World." *The European Legacy* 20, no. 7 (2015): 745–64.

Head, Naomi. "Bringing Reflective Judgement into International Relations: Exploring the Rwandan Genocide." *Journal of Global Ethics* 6, no. 2 (2010): 191–204.

Heater, Derek. *World Citizenship and Government: Cosmopolitan Ideas and the History of Western Political Thought*. London: Palgrave Macmillan, 1996.

Heidegger, Martin. *Being and Time*. Translated by John Macquarrie and Edward Robinson. Oxford: Blackwell Publishing, 1962.

———. *Heidegger: Basic Writings*. Edited by David Farrell Krell. London: Routledge, 2011.

———. *The Concept of Time*. Translated by William McNeill. Oxford: Blackwell Publishing, 1992.

Herodotus. *Herodotus*. Translated by A.D. Godley. Vol. II. London: William Heinemann, 1928.

Hinchman, Lewis P., and Sandra K. Hinchman. "In Heidegger's Shadow: Hannah Arendt's Phenomenological Humanism." *The Review of Politics* 46, no. 2 (1984): 183–211.

Honig, Bonnie. "Declarations of Independence: Arendt and Derrida on the Problem of Founding a Republic." *The American Political Science Review* 85, no. 1 (1991): 97–113.

Hugo, Victor. *Les Misérables*. Edited by Émile Testard. Vol. IV. Paris: Edition Nationale, 1890.

Ignatieff, Michael. *The Ordinary Virtues: Moral Order in a Divided World*. Cambridge, MA: Harvard University Press, 2017.

Jacobitti, Suzanne D. "Thinking about the Self." In *Hannah Arendt: Twenty Years Later*, edited by Larry May and Jerome Kohn, 199–220. Cambridge, MA: The MIT Press, 1997.

Jankélévitch, Vladimir. "Should We Pardon Them?" *Critical Inquiry* 22, no. 3 (1996): 552–72.

Janover, Michael. "The Limits of Forgiveness and the Ends of Politics." *Journal of Intercultural Studies* 26, no. 3 (2005): 221–35.

Jennings, Theodore W. *Reading Derrida/Thinking Paul: On Justice*. Stanford, CA: Stanford University Press, 2006.

Jewison, Norman. *Fiddler on the Roof*. Los Angeles: United Artists, 1971.

Kafka, Franz. *The Great Wall of China*. Translated by Willa Muir and Edwin Muir. New York: Schocken Books, 1946.

———. *Aphorisms*. Translated by Willa Muir, Edwin Muir, and Michael Hofmann. New York: Schocken Books, 2015.

Kant, Immanuel. *Perpetual Peace*. Edited by Lewis White Beck. New York: The Library of Liberal Arts, 1957.

Kateb, George. "Freedom and Worldliness in the Thought of Hannah Arendt." *Political Theory* 5, no. 2 (1977): 141–82.

Kattago, Siobhan. "Hannah Arendt on the World." In *Hannah Arendt: Key Concepts*, edited by Patrick Hayden, 52–65. Durham: Acumen Publishing, 2014.

———. "Why the World Matters: Hannah Arendt's Philosophy of New Beginnings." *The European Legacy* 18, no. 2 (2013): 170–84.

Kearney, Richard. "On Forgiveness: A Roundtable Discussion with Jacques Derrida." In *Questioning God*, edited by John D. Caputo, Mark Dooley, and Michael J. Scanlon, 52–72. Bloomington, IN: Indiana University Press, 2001.

———. "Derrida and Messianic Atheism." In *The Trace of God: Derrida and Religion*, edited by Edward Baring and Peter E. Gordon, 199–261. New York: Fordham University Press, 2015.

Klusmeyer, Douglas B. "Hannah Arendt on Authority and Tradition." In *Hannah Arendt: Key Concepts*, edited by Patrick Hayden, 138–52. Durham, UK: Acumen Publishing, 2014.

Kristeva, Julia. *Hannah Arendt: Life Is a Narrative*. London: University of Toronto Press, 2001.

La Durantaye, Leland de. *Giorgio Agamben: A Critical Introduction*. Stanford, CA: Stanford University Press, 2009.

Leebaw, Bronwyn. *Judging State-Sponsored Violence, Imagining Political Change*. Cambridge: Cambridge University Press, 2011.

Levinas, Emmanuel. *Totalité et Infini: Essai Sur l'extériorité*. Dordrecht: Martinus Nijhoff Publishers, 1987.

———. *Totality and Infinity: An Essay on Exteriority*. Translated by Alphonso Lingis. London: Martinus Nijhoff Publishers, 1979.

Martel, James R. "Can There Be Politics Without Sovereignty? Arendt, Derrida and the Question of Sovereign Inevitability." *Law, Culture and the Humanities* 6, no. 2 (2010): 153–66.

Marx, Karl. "For a Ruthless Criticism of Everything Existing." In *The Marx-Engels Reader*, edited by Robert C. Tucker, 12–15. London: W.W. Norton & Company, Inc., 1978.

———. "Theses on Feuerbach." In *The Marx-Engels Reader*, edited by Robert C. Tucker, 143–45. London: W.W. Norton & Company, Inc., 1978.

Morriss, Peter. *Power: A Philosophical Analysis*. Manchester: Manchester University Press, 1987.

Mrovlje, Maša. "Narrating and Understanding." In *Hannah Arendt: Key Concepts*, edited by Patrick Hayden, 66–84. Durham, UK: Acumen Publishing, 2014.
Murphy, Jeffrie G. *Getting Even: Forgiveness and Its Limits*. Oxford: Oxford University Press, 2003.
Murphy, Jeffrie G., and Jean Hampton. *Forgiveness and Mercy*. Cambridge: Cambridge University Press, 1988.
Myers, Ella. *Worldly Ethics: Democratic Politics and Care for the World*. London: Duke University Press, 2013.
Nussbaum, Martha C. *Anger and Forgiveness: Resentment, Generosity, Justice*. Oxford: Oxford University Press, 2016.
Pangle, Thomas L. "Socratic Cosmopolitanism: Cicero's Critique and Transformation of the Stoic Ideal." *Canadian Journal of Political Science* 31, no. 2 (1998): 235–62.
Pansardi, Pamela. "Power to and Power Over." In *Encyclopedia of Power*, edited by Keith Dowding, 522–25. Thousand Oaks, CA: Sage Publications, 2011.
Perrone-Moisés, Cláudia. "Forgiveness and Crimes against Humanity: A Dialogue between Hannah Arendt and Jacques Derrida." *HannahArendt.Net: Journal for Political Thinking* 2, no. 1 (2006).http://www.hannaharendt.net/index.php/han/article/view/90/146.
Phelps-Roper, Megan. "Head Full of Doubt/Road Full of Promise." Medium, 2013. https://medium.com/@meganphelps/head-full-of-doubt-road-full-of-promise-83d2ef8ba4f5.
———. "I Grew up in the Westboro Baptist Church. Here's Why I Left." TED Talks, 2017. https://www.ted.com.
———. *Unfollow: A Journey from Hatred to Hope, Leaving the Westboro Baptist Church*. London: Riverrun, 2019.
Pressler, Charles A. "Redoubled: The Bridging of Derrida and Heidegger." *Human Studies* 7 (1984): 325–42.
Quinones, Ricardo J. "Byron's Cain: Between History and Theology." In *Byron, the Bible, and Religion: Essays from the Twelfth International Byron Seminar*, edited by Wolf Z. Hirst, 39–57. Newark: University of Delaware Press, 1991.
Rancière, Jacques. *Dissensus: On Politics and Aesthetics*. Translated by Steven Cocroran. London: Continuum, 2010.
Ricœur, Paul. *Time and Narrative*. Translated by Kathleen McLaughlin and David Pellauer. Vol. 1. London: University of Chicago Press, 1984.
Robbins, Jill, ed. *Is It Righteous to Be?: Interviews with Emmanuel Levinas*. Stanford, CA: Stanford University Press, 2001.
Roberts, Roberts C. *Emotions: An Essay in Aid of Moral Psychology*. Cambridge: Cambridge University Press, 2003.
Rogat, Yosal. *The Eichmann Trial and the Rule of Law*. Santa Barbara, CA: Center for the Study of Democratic Institutions, 1961.
Royle, Nicholas. "What Is Deconstruction?" In *Deconstructions: A User's Guide*, edited by Nicholas Royle, 1–13. London: Palgrave, 2000.
Rūmī, Jalāl ad-Dīn Muhammad. *Mystical Poems of Rūmī: Second Selection, Poems 201–400*. Translated by A.J. Arberry. London: The University of Chicago Press, 1979.

Schaap, Andrew. "The Proto-Politics of Reconciliation: Lefort and the Aporia of Forgiveness in Arendt and Derrida." *Australian Journal of Political Science* 41, no. 4 (2006): 615–30.

Schell, Jonathan. "Introduction." In *On Revolution*, xi–xxix. London: Penguin Books, 2006.

Schmitt, Carl. *The Concept of the Political*. Translated by George Schwab. London: The University of Chicago Press, 2007.

Scott, Joanna Vecchiarelli, and Judith Chelius Stark. "Rediscovering Hannah Arendt." In *Love and Saint Augustine*, edited by Joanna Vecchiarelli Scott and Judith Chelius Stark, 113–211. Chicago: University of Chicago Press, 1996.

Shaitly, Shahesta. "Losing My Religion: Life after Extreme Belief." *The Guardian*, April 10, 2016. https://www.theguardian.com/world/2016/apr/10/losing-my-religion-life-after-extreme-belief-faith.

Shakespeare, William. "The Tragedy of Hamlet, Prince of Denmark." In *The New Oxford Shakespeare: The Complete Works, Modern Critical Edition*, edited by Gary Taylor, John Jowett, Terri Bourus, and Gabriel Egan, 1993–2099. Oxford: Oxford University Press, 2016.

Smith, Graham M. *Friendship and the Political: Kierkegaard, Nietzsche, Schmitt*. Exeter, UK: Imprint Academic, 2011.

Smith, Trevor G. *Politicizing Digital Space: Theory, the Internet and Renewing Democracy*. London: University of Westminster Press, 2017.

Solomon, Robert C. "Justice and the Passion for Vengeance." In *What Is Justice?: Classic and Contemporary Readings*, edited by Robert C. Solomon and Mark C. Murphy, 292–302. Oxford: Oxford University Press, 1990.

Speight, Allen. "Arendt on Narrative Theory and Practice." *College Literature* 38, no. 1 (2011): 115–30.

Spivak, Gayatri Chakravorty. "Translator's Press." In *Of Grammatology*, translated by Gayatri Chakravorty Spivak, ix–lxxxvii. London: The Johns Hopkins University Press, 1997.

Stone-Mediatore, Shari. *Reading Across Borders: Storytelling and Knowledges of Resistance*. New York: Palgrave Macmillan, 2003.

Taminiaux, Jacques. *The Thracian Maid and the Professional Thinker: Arendt and Heidegger*. Translated by Michael Gendre. Albany, NY: State University of New York Press, 1992.

Thaler, Mathias. "Political Judgment beyond Paralysis and Heroism." *European Journal of Political Theory* 10, no. 2 (2011): 225–53.

Thomassen, Lasse, ed. *The Derrida-Habermas Reader*. Chicago: University of Chicago Press, 2006.

Tronto, Joan. *Moral Boundaries: A Political Argument for an Ethic of Care*. London: Routledge, 1993.

Verdeja, Ernesto. "Derrida and the Impossibility of Forgiveness." *Contemporary Political Theory* 3 (2004): 23–47.

———. *Unchopping a Tree: Reconciliation in the Aftermath of Political Violence*. Philadelphia: Temple University Press, 2009.

Villa, Dana R. *Arendt and Heidegger: The Fate of the Political*. Princeton: Princeton University Press, 1996.

———. *Politics, Philosophy, Terror: Essays on the Thought of Hannah Arendt*. Princeton: Princeton University Press, 1999.

———. "Arendt, Heidegger, and the Tradition." *Social Research* 74, no. 4 (2007): 983–1002.

Voice, Paul. "Labour, Work and Action." In *Hannah Arendt: Key Concepts*, edited by Patrick Hayden, 36–51. Durham, UK: Acumen Publishing, 2014.

Vries, Hent De. *Religion and Violence: Philosophical Perspectives from Kant to Derrida*. London: The Johns Hopkins University Press, 2002.

Warren, Nicolas De. "For the Love of the World: Redemption and Forgiveness in Arendt." In *Phenomenology and Forgiveness*, edited by Marguerite La Caze, 25–41. London: Rowman & Littlefield International, 2018.

Weber, Samuel. *Benjamin's -Abilities*. London: Harvard University Press, 2008.

Wellmer, Albrecht. "Hannah Arendt on Judgment: The Unwritten Doctrine of Reason." In *Hannah Arendt: Twenty Years Later*, edited by Larry May and Jerome Kohn, 33–52. Cambridge, MA: The MIT Press, 1997.

"Westboro Baptist Church." *ADL Report*, https://www.adl.org/resources/profiles/westboro-baptist-church.

"Westboro Baptist Church." *Extremist Files Database*. Southern Poverty Law Center, 2018. https://www.splcenter.org/fighting-hate/extremist-files/group/westboro-baptist-church.

Wiley, James. *Politics and the Concept of the Political: The Political Imagination*. New York: Routledge, 2016.

Williams, Caroline. *Contemporary French Philosophy: Modernity and the Persistence of the Subject*. London: Continuum, 2001.

Wittgenstein, Ludwig. *Philosophical Investigations*. Edited by G.E.M. Anscombe, R. Rhees, and G.H. Von Wright. Translated by G.E.M. Anscombe. *The Philosophical Quarterly*. Oxford: Basil Blackwell, 1958.

Yeatman, Anna. "Individuality and Politics: Thinking with and beyond Hannah Arendt." In *Action and Appearance: Ethics and the Politics of Writing in Hannah Arendt*, edited by Anna Yeatman, Phillip Hansen, Magdelena Zolkos, and Charles Barbour, 69–86. London: Continuum, 2011.

Young-Bruehl, Elisabeth. "Reflections on Hannah Arendt's the Life of the Mind." *Political Theory* 10, no. 2 (1982): 277–305.

———. *Hannah Arendt: For Love of the World*. New Haven, CT: Yale University Press, 2004.

Zerilli, Linda M.G. "'We Feel Our Freedom': Imagination and Judgment in the Thought of Hannah Arendt." *Political Theory* 33, no. 2 (2005): 158–88.

Zlomislic, Marko. *Jacques Derrida's Aporetic Ethics*. New York: Lexington Books, 2007.

Index

Abitbol, David, 98
action (Arendt), x, xii, xxviin4, 38–43, 46–49, 51, 55–56, 58, 60–67, 71n79, 77–79, 82, 85–88, 92–95, 103n52, 103n57, 111–13, 115–18, 129–31, 139n61, 143–45
alienation, x–xi, 41–42, 55; world alienation, xv–xvii, xix, 27, 41, 65, 67
alterity, 6, 19
American Revolution, 57–58
amor mundi, xii, xxv, xxviiin15, 37, 57, 130, 145
animal laborans, 49–50, 55. *See* labor (Arendt)
aporias, 5–6, 15–16, 124
arche-writing ("*archi-écriture*"), 3
Aristotle, 59, 88, 103n52, 109, 111, 115–16, 137n22
Augustine, xxiv, 56, 60, 122–23, 126, 138n36
authenticity, xxii, 108
authority, xviii, 132

Baehr, Peter, 101n21
Barrett-Fox, Rebecca, xiv, xxixn50, 131
Barthes, Roland, 79, 86, 101
Beardsworth, Richard, 109
Beck, Ulrich, 28

Being. *See Dasein*
"being-in-the-world", xxii–xxiii
"being-towards-death", xxii–xxiii, 60, 93–94, 108, 123–24
Benhabib, Seyla, 78, 101n21, 102n23
Benjamin, Walter, xx, 4, 30n17
Berkowitz, Roger, 46–47, 51, 54, 69n44
Berlin, Isaiah, 58, 71n95
Blunt, Alison, 33n99, 125
Bowen-Moore, Patricia, 123, 129
Brecht, Bertolt, xxixn30, 145–46
Broggi, Joshua, xxii
Buber, Martin, 35n129
Buckler, Steve, 84

Calvinism, xiv
care (notion of), x–xiv, xx–xxi, xxiv, xvi–xvii, xix–xxvii, xxxn56, 110; private care, 137n21; public care. *See* "care for the world". *See also* Sorge ("Care")
Care Ethics (Ethics of Care), xxi, xxxn56
"care for the world", x–xiv, xvi–xvii, xix–xx, xxiv–xxv, xxviiin15, 2, 16, 27, 38–39, 41, 47, 64–67, 77, 80–81, 86, 95, 100–1, 107, 129–30, 136, 143–46; caring cosmopolitanism, xiii, xxiv, xxvi, xxvii, 17, 20, 26–27,

160 Index

29, 77–80, 92–101, 110, 118, 130–31, 135, 144–45; caring forgiveness, xiii, xxiv–xxvii, 26–27, 41, 63–67, 110, 118, 130–31, 135, 144–45
Christianity, xiv–xv, xvii, xxviiin15, 7–9, 17–19, 24, 27–28, 33n78, 84
Cicero, 17, 32n76
city, the, 18–19, 22–27, 33n83, 34n117, 128–29; "cities of refuge" (Derrida), 22–23, 26
common sense, xii, 46
consent, 63. See also freedom; legitimacy; power
context, 3–4, 7. See also "the text"
cosmopolitics, 22–23, 25–26, 83, 128
Critchley, Simon, xiii, 1, 3–7, 145
culture, xix, xxiv

daimōn, 93–94
Damai, Puspa, 23–25, 27, 128
Damocles' sword, 39, 47, 144
"dark times" (Arendt/Brecht), xvi–xvii, xix, 126, 145–46
Dasein, xxi–xxv, xxxi, 35n129, 56, 61, 88, 93–94, 123
deconstruction, x, xiii–xiv, xix, xxvi, 1–7, 15–17, 92, 108–10
"democracy to come" (Derrida), 26–29, 83, 90, 145
Denktagebuch, 107
"desert" (Arendt), xvi–xvii. See alienation
Destruktion, 2, 17, 109
determinism, 119, 138n49
différance, 3–4, 26, 109–11
Digeser, Paige, 45
disclosure, 62, 88
distinction, 52, 55–56, 61–63, 97
Dowling, Robyn, 33n99, 125

Eck Duymaer van Twist, Amanda van, 131
economic, 20, 49; aneconomic, 9–10, 32n49. See also gift
Edom, xv–xvi

Eichmann, Adolf, 45, 53, 68n17
Eisenstein, Charles, 146
equality, xxv, 15, 39, 52, 55–67, 81, 91–97, 128–30
Esau, xv–xvi, xxixn27, 37, 76, 98
ethics, 6–7, 20–21, 77, 80, 83, 86; *ethos*, 20–21, 25; "hyperbolic ethics" (Derrida), 8–9; "worldly ethics" (Myers), xiii, 80, 90
evil, 12, 44; "banality of evil" (Arendt), 68n17; "radical evil", 13, 40, 42, 44–46, 68n17, 88

facelessness, 79, 99
February Revolution, 58
"fiddler on the roof", xviii, 144
Foucault, Michel, 4, 80
fox(es), 107–9; 'Heidegger the fox', 108–10, 124, 136n3, 145
freedom, xii–xiii, xxv, 16, 38, 41, 55, 58–67, 71n95, 71n97, 107, 110–12, 117–18, 126–31, 136, 138n44, 143–46; "abyss of freedom", 111, 127–30, 132–36; negative freedom, 58–60, 71n95; philosophic freedom, 127; positive freedom, 58, 60
friendship, ix–x, xii, xv, xxiv–xxv, 44, 59–60, 63, 76, 90–91, 95–97, 99, 130–31
fundamentalism, ix, xiv–xv

Gaus, Günter, xvii, 82
gift, 10–11, 31n46, 65, 69n29; giving of, 10, 14–15, 20
"globalatinisation" (Derrida), 8, 28
globalization, 27
Granovetter, Mark, 105n105

Haddad, Samir, xii–xiii
hamartanein, 44
Hampton, Jean, 50, 53
Harris, Sam, 132
Hayden, Patrick, 76
"He" (Kafka), 111–12, 119–24, 127, 131, 135, 138n45, 139n61

Hegel, Georg Wilhelm Friedrich, 120, 137n22
Heidegger, Martin, xx–xxv, xxxn56, xxxin62, 2, 17, 35n127, 56, 60–61, 67, 72n116, 84, 88, 93, 107–10, 123; "Heidegger Affair", xxi, xxxn54; *le héritage*. *See* "the tradition"
Herodotus, 56, 71n85
history, xvi–xx, 2, 4–5, 86–87, 115–17, 119, 126–27, 131, 138n49; causality, xviii; *longue durée*, xvii; "storybook of mankind" (Arendt), 77, 87, 89, 101, 111, 117, 124, 130, 144
Hitler, Adolf, 78
Holocaust, 12–13, 133–34
home, xxiv–xxv, 18, 20–22, 25–26, 33n99, 77, 83, 89–90, 98–99, 121, 125, 128, 132–36; "common home" (Arendt), xi–xii, xix, xxv, 20–21, 26, 46, 48, 65–67, 69n44, 99, 128. *See* "world" (concept of). *See also* private realm; public realm
homeless(ness), 133–35
homo faber, 40–41, 46–49, 51–55, 85, 114–15, 126. *See also* work (Arendt)
hospitality, ix–x, xxviiin15, 17–26, 81–84, 98, 102n37; cosmopolitan hospitality, x, xii–xiii, xxvi, 22–26, 29, 90–92; discursive hospitality, ix, 97–99. *See* "care for the world", caring cosmopolitanism
Hugo, Victor, 19, 23, 80, 128, 144
Hungarian Revolution, 57–58
Husserl, Edmund, 4

"ideological supersense" (Arendt), 141n112
Ignatieff, Michael, 100
imagination, 15–16, 104n72, 125–26, 129–35, 146. *See also* meaning; understanding
immigration, 29n2
imprescriptibility, 12–13, 40, 42–45
indoctrination, 134–35, 141n118
interests, 82–83

Internet, ix, 37–38, 96, 99–100, 105n105
isonomy. *See* equality
Israel, xv

Jacob, xv, xxixn27, 37, 76, 98
Jacobitti, Suzanne, 94, 104n82
Jankélévitch, Vladimir, 12–14, 42, 44
Janus, 107, 124
Jaspers, Karl, 78, 101n21
Jesus of Nazareth, 8–9, 18–19, 42–43, 45, 71n83
judgment, 104n72, 124, 140n84
justice (Derrida), 2–3, 5–7, 15–16, 19–20, 43, 145;

Kafka, Franz. *See* "He" (Kafka)
Kant, Immanuel, xxviiin15, 17, 22–23, 26, 28–29, 40, 42, 68n17, 104n72; *Perpetual Peace* (1795), xxviiin15, 22–23; spirit of, 28–29
Kateb, George, xvii
Kattago, Siobhan, xxviiin15
Kearney, Richard, xiii, 1, 3–5, 24, 145
khôra, 26–27, 145
Kristeva, Julia, 93, 115–16

labor (Arendt), 39–41, 47–51, 55, 85, 113–15, 137n21
La Durantaye, Leland de, 108
law (as *droit*), 6, 9, 14, 44, 57
legitimacy, 54, 63
Levinas, Emmanuel, 5–7, 19–21, 23–26, 28, 31n31, 33n98, 33n100, 35n126, 35n129, 77, 80–84; 'face-to-face', 19, 24–25, 29, 81–82, 90–91, 125–26
LGBTQ community, xiv
life: βίος, 103n52, 113, 115–18, 124; ζōē, 113, 115
Lingis, Alphonso, 31n31
logos, 84, 88, 103n63, 115, 117–18
love, xv, xxv, 8–9, 19, 31n40, 37–38, 75–76, 82–83, 102n37, 103n40. *See also amor mundi*

Marxism, 3, 138n49, 145
meaning, 40–41, 88–90, 103n63, 123–31, 138n34. *See also* understanding
Medium, 67n5
memory, 116, 122–24, 138n36
messianic, 24–28, 30n17, 43, 65–66, 81, 128
"metaphysics of presence", 109, 111
mikhshol, 44–45, 50
miracle(s), xxiv, 38–41, 65, 67, 117–18, 129, 143–47. *See* natality
monde, 27, 84
mondialisation, 26–29
Morriss, Peter, 64
Mrovlje, Maša, 78
Murphy, Jeffrie, 50, 52, 70n61
Myers, Ella, xiii, 77, 80–83, 94, 102n31

narrative & narrative voice(s), xxvi, 20, 29, 77–81, 83–101, 103n52, 111, 113, 115–18, 123–24, 138n, 144; enacted stories, 86–88, 90; historical narratives/stories, 86–87, 89; storytelling, 77–79, 90–95, 97
natality, xxi, xxiii–xxv, 39, 41, 60, 62, 64, 78–79, 116–18, 123, 129–30, 143–44
National Socialism, xxi, 12, 44, 68n17, 107–8, 138n49
necessity. *See* labor (Arendt)
negotiation, xi, xxvii, 15–16, 107, 110–13, 118–19, 124–27, 129, 131–32, 134–36. *See also* aporias
nunc stans, 111–13, 118, 121–22, 124–29, 131–35, 137n24, 143
Nussbaum, Martha, 31n40

ontology, xxi–xxiii, 108–9
Other, the, x, 5–7, 19–26, 28–29, 35n126, 77, 80–84, 90, 92–97, 144–45. *See also* alterity

Pansardi, Pamela, 64
Parable of the Prodigal Son, 8, 31n40
Parmenides, 120
Paul the Apostle (Saint Paul), 17–19, 21, 27–28, 33n78, 84

"pearl diver" (Benjamin), xx, 4–5, 8
Phelps, Fred, xiv
Phelps, Shirley, xiv
Phelps-Roper, Megan, ix–x, xiv–xvi, 37–38, 65, 67, 67n5, 75–76, 79, 95–101, 112, 131–36
philia politike, xxv, 59, 76. *See also* friendship
Plato, xxi, 107–8
plurality, xxiv–xxv, 29, 41, 46–49, 55–64, 71n83, 83–86, 96–97, 116–17, 127–28, 130–31, 138n44. *See also* public realm; "world" (concept of)
political, the, x–xiii, xvii, xxviin4
populist politics (populism), ix, 145
power, xiii, xxv, xxviin4, 14–16, 21, 25, 29, 33n100, 38–41, 44, 46–47, 50–56, 58, 62–67, 90–94, 97, 111–12, 116–18, 138n44, 143–46; "power over", 14–15, 24–25, 40, 50–53, 63, 65, 67, 90–94, 97; "power to", 29, 41, 44, 55–56, 63–67, 91–92, 94, 96, 117. *See also* freedom
private realm, 47–49, 52, 84–85, 103n39, 110, 113; privacy, 48
public realm, xi–xii, xvi–xvii, xxi, 21, 29, 41, 47–49, 52, 55–57, 59, 61–62, 65–67, 84–85, 87, 95–96, 100, 103n39, 111, 113, 144–45
punishment, 12–14, 40, 42–47, 50–51. *See also* imprescriptibility

Quinones, Ricardo, 128

Rancière, Jacques, 102n31
reality. *See* public realm
reconciliation, xvi, 9–11, 39–40, 46–47, 89, 112, 124–25, 134–35
religion, xviii, 8, 17–18
remembrance, 70n67, 87–88, 122–24. *See also* memory
responsibility, 5–7, 16, 19, 23, 43, 80–81, 83
revenge, 37, 39–40, 42–47, 49–55, 61, 63, 66, 69n44
Ricœur, Paul, 138n34
Rockwell, Norman, 57

Rogat, Yosal, 45, 54
Royle, Nicholas, 4
Rūmī, Jalāl ad-Dīn Muhammad, 103n40

"sandstorms" (Arendt), xvi, xviii,145–46
Schell, Jonathan, 58
Schmitt, Carl, xv, 76, 95
Scott, Joana, xxiv, 123
Searle, John, 4
self, xxii–xxv, xxxin62,7, 23–26, 34n117, 59, 80, 98, 104n82, 119
skandalon, 44–45, 50
Smith, Graham, 59, 76, 96
Smith, Trevor, 100
social media, ix, 75, 96, 99–100
Sorge ('Care'), xx–xxiii, xxv, xxxn56, 123, 129
Southern Poverty Law Center, ix
sovereignty, 10, 14–15, 21–22, 25, 39, 58, 60, 63, 66, 83
speech. See *logos*
Speight, Allen, 77–78, 94
Stalinism, 68n17
Stark, Judith, xxiv, 123
statelessness, xi, 78–79
Stone-Mediatore, Shari, 91
story and stories. See narrative & narrative voice(s)

Taminiaux, Jacques, 121–22
TED, 37, 95–96, 133
temporality, xxii, xxvii, 108–20, 122, 125–26, 129–30, 132–33, 137n21
"the text", xix, 3–5, 7, 15, 17, 34n117, 79, 109
"things", xi–xii, xvii, 4–5, 48–49, 51–56, 77, 80–92, 114; thing theory, 101n15. See also world
time, xxii–xxiii, xxvii, 32n49, 34n117, 107–37; authentic, xxii–xxiii, 108; vulgar, 109, 119–20, 125
totalitarianism, xi, xvii–xviii, 40, 42, 44–45, 78–79, 138n49, 141n112, 145
trace, 34n117, 109–10, 121
"the tradition", xii–xiii, xvii–xx, 1, 7–8, 17, 28, 34n117, 78, 109–10,

137n22; break in, xvii–xx. See also "the text"
Tronto, Joan, xxxn56
Trump, Donald, ix
TULIP, xxixn19. See Calvinism
Twitter, ix, 37–38, 65, 76, 79, 95–101

undecidability, xxvi, 3, 5–7, 15, 43, 124–25
understanding, xviii, xix–xx, 61–62, 79, 84, 88–90, 104n72, 123–25, 131–35, 141n118
unforgivability, 12–14, 39–40, 42–45

vengeance. See revenge
Verdeja, Ernesto, 11
violence, 40–44, 46–47, 49–50, 53–55, 63–64, 66, 88, 128. See also power, "power over"
Voice, Paul, 54
Vries, Hent de, 17, 19, 24

Warren, Nicolas de, 38
Westboro Baptist Church (WBC), ix–x, xiv–xvi, xvii, xxixnn20, 25, 37–38, 67n5, 75–76, 95, 98, 100–1, 112, 131–35, 141n112
"who"-ness, 93–94, 98–99. See also *Dasein*; self
willing, 111, 122, 137n24
Wittgenstein, Ludwig, 34n117
work (Arendt), 39–41, 46–49, 51–55, 63, 66, 84–85, 94, 103n57, 113–14, 126, 137n21, 138n40
"world" (concept of), xi–xii, 15, 27, 48–49, 84–85, 96, 146; worldliness, xvi–xvii, 48, 52, 77, 85, 87–88; worldlessness. See alienation
"worldly ethics", xiii, 80, 90. See also Myers, Ella

Young-Bruehl, Elisabeth, xxv, xxxn54, 119

Zlomislic, Marko, 124
zōon politikon, 48–49, 85, 88

Author Information

Christopher Peys is a tutor in the School of International Relations at the University of St. Andrews. He is a Rotary Global Grant-winning scholar and an award-winning educator. As an international political theorist, his work revolves around questions of ethics, politics, and the possibilities of political friendship.

www.ingramcontent.com/pod-product-compliance
Lightning Source LLC
Chambersburg PA
CBHW032046300426
44117CB00009B/1207